To Philip
very best regards

Jim Brudapon
august 11, 2005
Door County
wisconsin

Very Brief Psychotherapy

Very Brief Psychotherapy

James P. Gustafson

Routledge
Taylor & Francis Group

NEW YORK AND HOVE

Published in 2005 by
Routledge
Taylor & Francis Group
270 Madison Avenue
New York, NY 10016

Published in Great Britain by
Routledge
Taylor & Francis Group
2 Park Square
Milton Park, Abingdon
Oxon OX14 4RN

Printed in the United States of America on acid-free paper
10 9 8 7 6 5 4 3 2 1

International Standard Book Number-10: 0-415-95058-9 (Hardcover)
International Standard Book Number-13: 978-0-415-95058-9 (Hardcover)
Library of Congress Card Number 2005001382

Library of Congress Cataloging-in-Publication Data

Gustafson, James Paul.
  Very brief psychotherapy / James P. Gustafson.
      p. ; cm.
  Includes bibliographical references and index.
  ISBN 0-415-95058-9 (hardback : alk. paper)
  1. Brief psychotherapy.
  [DNLM: 1. Psychotherapy, Brief. 2. Anxiety Disorders--therapy. 3. Depressive Disorder--therapy.
  4. Psychological Theory.] I. Title.

RC480.55.G874 2005
616.89'14--dc22   2005001382

Taylor & Francis Group
is the Academic Division of T&F Informa plc.

Visit the Taylor & Francis Web site at
http://www.taylorandfrancis.com

and the Routledge Web site at
http://www.routledge-ny.com

Contents

Preface

... the laws of nature appear simple when expressed in higher dimensional space (Kaku, 1994, p. 37).

In the mental health professions, we all have some kind of niche with some kind of procedure that is useful. I am thinking of psychology and psychiatric social work and nursing and mental health workers, with procedures of cognitive-behavior therapy and solution-focused therapy and psychodynamic therapy, and I am thinking of psychiatry with psychopharmacology. If we had a chance to add one step to what we already do, what would this step look like?

It has been my job to give this chance to trainees and staff in psychiatry, psychology, and social work at the University of Wisconsin, Department of Psychiatry for over 30 years. Since the mid-1990s, the medical school has required every patient seen by a trainee to be seen also by an attending, and I have had to practice giving this chance, most of the time, in 10 minutes. This is the time frame, the window of opportunity, for either the patient or the trainee to ask me one question. Additionally I can take 20 minutes if the question is about a dream, and once a week I can take an hour in my brief psychotherapy clinic to do a videotaped interview about a case of particular interest that is stuck and needs my opinion about how to get unstuck. But the usual chance is taken in 10 minutes, and that is *very* brief psychotherapy.

Many colleagues have been loud in their sympathy for me that I get so little time to be of help. Surely, I must only have time to write a little note and sign it. I tell them that this is quite enough time, and they are amazed, or disbelieve me. There is a simple reason why this is enough time: human beings are astoundingly repetitive or redundant. If they take a single step, say being subservient, they tend to repeat this step endlessly, and it will make for a trajectory, and the trajectory is circular. Thus, I say to the patient and the therapist that we can start anywhere they choose, for everything comes around a million times. Any one circle will show a microcosm of the whole picture.

Consider our most common case. This is a person being taken advantage of and getting a bad exchange with the world. This builds up rage, which erupts and frightens the patient back into compliance. I call this "the exploding doormat problem" (Gustafson, 1995a, 1995b, 1999). In the psychoanalytic literature, it is called "moral masochism" (Brenman, 1952). The masochism, or arranged suffering, is moral rather than sexual, and its shadow side is moral sadism which terrifies the patient more than the moral masochism. Thus, the patient circulates between two untenable horns of a dilemma (Gustafson, 1995a, 1995b), the step of claiming too little, and the step of claiming too much. Stevenson described it most memorably as the single case of the modern world in *The Strange Case of Dr. Jekyll and Mr. Hyde* (1886/1985). In our clinic it is more common as Mrs. Jekyll and Mrs. Hyde.

Thus, I am continually asked by patient or trainee how to get out of this perpetual bog (Gustafson, 1986/1997a, chap. 6; Reich, 1949)? For example, a young woman complained to us of being criticized unmercifully by her husband at every turn. She would take it and take it, and then lose it in rage and feel very guilty. In her guilt, she would review all of her past mistakes in suffering this same cycle with her parents and then again with her childhood boyfriend. What did I recommend? I simply asked her if she ever felt free of it with this husband? She didn't know. I asked her to consider it longer. Gazing off to her left she suddenly brightened and exclaimed, "Yesterday, I told him, 'You may not talk to me like that,' and walked out of the room." *That*, I said, is how you get out of this bog (Gustafson, 1986/1997a, chap. 6). That is the single step, if repeated, which will lead into a different world, of equality in a relationship, rather than subservience, or overpowering (Gustafson, 1992).

Of course, the working through (Freud, 1914/1975e) is a further matter, for such a start on a new trajectory will slip back into the old trajectory. Also, a new beginning (Balint, 1952, 1968; Gustafson, 1986/1997a, chap. 8) in one domain, as with the husband, will have to be transferred into the other domains of her life for a complete working through of her developmental impasse.

> The beauty of this way of looking at it is that a departure can be clearly sighted from the usual circularity, in any of its million episodes in any 10-minute window of opportunity. In chaos theory

(Gleick, 1988) this is called "sensitive dependence on initial conditions." Two steps which look about the same, but are slightly different, end up in completely different places when repeated a million times. This is the meaning of Frost's (1916/1969) poem, "The Road Not Taken," where he writes: And both that morning equally lay/In leaves no step had trodden black.

So *Very Brief Psychotherapy* is about grasping, like this, the implications of a *single different step*. It works on this infinitesimal level (i, or i′ or i″), by which I mean the smallest possible unit of difference, quite as in the calculus (Berlinski, 1995).

For example, returning to our single case in the clinic, the single step of giving and not getting leads by redundancy into the moral bog. The patient who compensates herself with a moral claim of taking or forcing her due, leads by redundancy into guilt, for which the punishment is giving up the claim. The second and compensatory step thus brings the trajectory full circle.

The most common variant of this attempt at service is the attempt at control. The controlling step becomes a program, by repetition, and forces its isolated will upon everything. Our patient's husband is forcing his ideal upon her, in continual criticism. Of course, it only gets her bowing lower and lower until she explodes. Then he compensates himself by withdrawal, feeling sorry for himself, and going away, as a ploy to arouse her fear of abandonment and her guilt. Thus, she is pulled back in and the game starts over, but, repeated a million times, gradually drives the two apart into a cold distance of "parallel lives" (Gustafson, 1992, chap. 8; Rose, 1984).

Thus, the entire pathology of the clinic is built upon wrong steps of exchange, either controlling, or being controlled (serving), or like Dr. Jekyll himself, a mixture of controlling *and* serving. Of course, there is organic medical pathology which needs to be ruled out, as discussed in the introduction to part I.

I also appreciate that there are many cases, as of gradual onset schizophrenia, or of semicriminal mania, or of elaborate obsessive compulsive disorder (OCD), which act as if they are hard-wired medical conditions, and respond only to strict medical regimens. In this sense, DSM-IV correctly distinguishes one illness from another, and builds up an evidence-based medicine to contain them (American Psychiatric Association, 1994).

I also appreciate that there is a synergy between brain and psychology and environment, as discussed in the exchange of letters between myself and Dr. Ronald Pies in *The Psychiatric Times* (Pies & Gustafson, 2004). Improvements in the containment of anxiety and depression and their compensations can build a platform from which psychological steps, as discussed in this book, can step forth from, and these together, psychotropic and psychological, can alter the course of the relatedness in love and work. After all, that is the basic premise of biopsychosocial psychiatry announced by Engel in 1980. The reverse is surely the case, when steps taken in relatedness of work and love, and psychologically, alter brain chemistry as well.

Nevertheless, almost all of our patients seem to have this simple isolated will (Tate, 1934/1999), in which control is the single idea. Listen to the exchanges in your clinic with the doctors, and I bet you will hear this word *control* handed back and forth as the main business. It is a kind of romance, namely, the romance of science, or of "technique." There is a technique for everything and it will control the outcome. This is what our trainees tell the patients who complain of lack of control, and, of course, they learned it from us!

This book proposes something other than the usual list of techniques for our 400 conditions of DSM-IV. It says that the flow of the case circularly, downhill, is very simply constructed by the repetition of the first step, and it says that the flow of the case to a different outcome is very simply constructed by the repetition of a significantly different first step. That is, for lack of control, forcing control in compensation is not a significant difference, but only comes full circle if a little more exhausted and resigned.

I propose four kinds of different first steps which make such a significant difference in outcome. I have to perform each of these within a 10-minute window, and you are free to do the same. I notice our residents and psychology fellows doing just this, as they spend more time with me. *Their* trajectories are changing hour by hour.

The first different step concerns what I call containment and is the subject of part I of this book. Because the isolated will to control (or control by serving) keeps getting pushed farther and farther, faster and faster, it eventually crosses a line after which the tension is unbearable. Essentially, the remainder of the body pushed along in this project joins in the conversation, unconsciously. It takes the form of rage, or anxiety about rage, or collapse into defeat. In other words, there is a discontinuous jump into anxiety and/or rage, or collapse and depression (Gustafson & Meyer, 2004).

If you are not going to get dropped, from your job, or school, or even by your spouse or children, in a society like ours in which functioning is imperative, you must keep up functioning. Thus, the emergence of anxiety and depression means that you become nonfunctional and can go rapidly down a steep slope into social disaster. Also, all the compensatory steps which arise in a highly anxious or depressed patient (person), such as histrionics, avoidance, alcohol dependence, and antisocial acting out, only threaten the niche further (Gustafson, 1999). Thus, the containment of anxiety and depression and compensatory acting out is our first subject for a different step. Anxiety must be reduced, and depression must be reduced, and compensatory acting out must be reduced, if the patient is not to go straight downhill. Of course, psychotropic medications are an immense help with this, but so are measures which address the psychological mechanism of anxiety, depression, and compensation. It is extremely simple and it involves an address of the isolated will which has become too one-sided in its forcing of control. If the isolated will can step back from attempting too much, the tension in the system drops back within a bearable range. Thus, the 60-hour day is brought back to 50, and the 20 projects of the weekend reduced to 10. This is the kind of difference that makes a huge difference in containing the emergency, and is part I of this book, "Containment."

The second step I propose is to help the patient sight, first in retrospect, and then prospectively, how he or she walks right into this nonlinear eruption or collapse. Almost invariably our patients have no idea how they got into the mess. It almost always seems to come "out of the blue" as they tell us. Of course, this is because isolated will is a kind of hypnotic trance (Freud, 1921/1975j) in which the patient is in a kind of sleepwalk! He is not looking ahead and that is called "selective inattention" (Sullivan, 1956; Gustafson, 1986/1997a, chap. 6). Thus, we back things up by returning to the point at which the patient was relatively fine, and then see what he did to bring these things to this pass. It is always one of these control operations, taken too far, with no eye out for where it is leading. This step toward a significant difference is simply to keep an eye out for where his steps lead and is part II of this book, "Selective Inattention Revised."

The third step I propose is to ask the patient to consider an opposing step, which leads to an opposing current to the usual one of disaster, as I got our patient with the criticizing husband to come up with on her own. Of course, opposing steps, and currents run different risks, and that is our subject at part III of this book, "The Opposing Current Navigated," namely, how to step in a different direction and be ready for *its* dangers. For example, yesterday a patient of mine after 2 years of grief from the death of her husband began to be a little bold at her dance class and invited a pleasant man out for coffee afterwards. He was glad to unburden himself, as he too had lost a spouse. However, at the next dance class he seemed very remote, and my patient was crushed. She simply wasn't ready for the ambivalence to be expected in such a prospective partner. Next week she will step into such bold forwardness with a better eye for the mixed results altogether likely in a lonely man.

Finally, the fourth step I propose is an extension of the third, for it is one thing to see that a prospective partner is not completely open to one's advances, but has an ambivalent reality of his own about engagement, while it is another to see that the world, *in general, is not one's egg!* We all like to think it is our egg and this is what Freud called the dream as "wish-fulfillment" (1900/1975a): I will have my way, and get just what I want. Now, that is a childish position which is very intransigent in the human being and is very difficult to get past. Balint (1952, 1968; Gustafson, 1986/ 1997a, chap. 8) followed Melanie Klein in calling it "the depressive position," which it truly is, because holding out for one's ideal world is always a setup to collapse, and is the very mechanism of depression (Bibring, 1953). A more primitive version he followed Klein in calling "the paranoid position," because the world is felt not only to be indifferent, and thus depressing, but downright hostile, and thus highly suspicious.

Ironically, the step out of such intransigence is to have a perspective from above or below one's field of action, to yield a "double description" (Bateson, 1972; Gustafson, 1986/1997a, chap. 15), so one can see both one's own dream of conquering the world, and the world's own game which is not so fitting after all, for one's dearest plans. Thus, the Cheshire Cat in *Alice* (Carroll, 1865/1985; Gustafson, 1986/1997a, chap. 19) continually comments to Alice from above about her fortunes in the game of Queen's Croquet, to wit, that the Queen calls "Off with her (his) head" for anything that does not suit her own winning. Such a *moment* is what I am talking about as a step out of the developmental impasse of being stuck in the contradiction between what I dream of doing, and what the world itself calls for. Every such moment is a step on the path of growing up.

It will not suffice to control oneself to suit the Queen, for the eruption and collapse will follow from this one-sidedness, nor will it suffice to hold onto one's ideal of having one's own way altogether, for an eruption and collapse will follow from this one-sidedness just as badly. Only a balanced step will read my claim and the world's reply equally. This is the subject of part IV of this book, "Impasse Surmounted," of the key first steps, whose difference makes a huge difference in the life of the patient.

In what sense then is this a book of very brief psychotherapy? In several, after all: First, it is about what can be done in very brief windows of opportunity like 5 or 10 minutes! As the English general practitioners found out (Balint & Norell, 1973), there is such a thing as *long brief therapy* (Gustafson, 1986/1997a), where the time spent is 6 minutes on the average, but the duration may be years or even a lifetime. A few days ago, I saw a woman in the clinic for another 5 or 10 minutes, 3 years down the road, who finally said no to her son in prison that she would not take up his burden of getting himself out. That key step of going out the back door of being a doormat had a long preparation of my posing the problem to her, and her gradually getting ready to revise her daily step of saying yes to everyone else's need. That is the argument of the research of Prochaska, diClemente, and Norcross (1992; Prochaska & Norcross, 2001): long preparation, and finally a decisive step, and then some work of slipping and getting back to the decisive step. This preparation to say no, instead of yes (Anthony, 1976), is probably the most common psychotherapy in our clinic. Essentially, this is what Selvini-Palazzoli, Cirillo, Selvini, and Sorrentino (1989) found to be fundamental in family therapy: that the mother and father finally got together to say no to a child or adolescent running rampant over them.

Second, very brief psychotherapy can take the form of what Talmon (1990) Hoyt, Rosenbaum and Talmon (1996) and Hoyt (2000) called single-session psychotherapy, because the patient, perhaps, with help, has already done the work of preparation (see, particularly, the Case of the Beautiful Wife in chapter 10 of this book, and the follow-up remarks by the patient in chapter 14, and also the Case of the Northwoods Girl in chapter 12, and her follow-up remarks in chapter 14). The latter case is illustrative of single-session psychotherapy, *and* the intrusion of further trauma requiring more work.

Third, very brief psychotherapy is about *the moment of change being only a single step* which is unprecedented, as in the "new beginning" of Michael Balint (1968), or a single step which has been taken before but is not allowed to slip away. I am arguing here the critical importance of "sensitive dependence on initial conditions," or, the first step, iterated for the entire trajectory. Thus, our patients overwhelmingly say yes (i) to being taken advantage of in their exchanges, and this doormat step always leads to eruption of anxiety and depression, compensations in fantasy, and eventual emptiness. The compensatory step (i') of psychic inflation in fantasy also leads to ruin, because the world always punctures psychic inflation, as it punctures every bull market.

Conversely, the step (i″) out the back door from compulsory yes (i), or compensatory inflation (i'), has huge consequences, and has huge applicability for our most demeaned patients, as I just described in regard to the mother of the convict. It may take a lot of waiting, and posing the problem, and letting the patient get it wrong, or hit bottom, as they say in AA, but the turn (i″) may be a different life altogether. Finally, the turn back (i‴) to face the impasse of work, or love or development may also have a long preparation, while the step itself is extremely simple, and takes but a split second. It means something like what Anthony (1976) called "*between* yes and no," because always yes means servility, and always no means breaking up, and the beauty of exchange is for yes and no to stay in balance between your demands and my demands.

Fourth, very brief psychotherapy means *psychotherapy in its entirety generated in infinitesimal form like the calculus* (Berlinski, 1995) from these four steps (i, i', i", and i'"). In other words, very brief psychotherapy is *all of psychotherapy presented in very brief form*, as a kind of *motion, from a single step, iterated, to a new trajectory. It is all of psychotherapy translated very briefly into chaos therapy.*

I recognize that this claim is not proven by this book, but I also believe that this book is entirely consistent with such a theory. All I can say at this point is that I operate in such a theory of single steps, *especially in the transitional space* (Winnicott, 1971; Gustafson, 1986) between *the steps that keep things on the same downhill course, i and i', or compulsory yes, and compensatory fantasy, and the steps that open up a new world, i" and i'", navigating the opposing current, or no, and surmounting the impasse, between yes and no.* I can also say that I can teach this readily to nearly every novice resident and psychology trainee, and to nearly every seasoned veteran I have met so far. Surely, it will be disputed, and that is what science is all about, and to be welcomed.

Finally, I want to thank those who have helped me in the last year with this book. I cannot possibly thank all of those who came before. Michael Moran, Jim Donovan, Ruth Gustafson, Michael Wood, and Lowell Cooper have stood by my work for 20 to 35 years, and have come through beautifully for me with this manuscript. My newer helpers include Chris Clancy, Peter Hoey, Matt Meyer, Andy Moore, Rick Schramm, and Gary Simoneau. My secretaries have been devoted, exact, and quick, namely, Dee Jones, Pam DeGolyer, and Tammy Ennis. The Door County Summer Institute in Egg Harbor, Wisconsin, has provided a beautiful place for my teaching since 1993, under the direction of Dr. Carl Chan at Medical College of Wisconsin, Department of Psychiatry, email dcsi@mcw.edu.

My tennis coach, Jim Shirley, has been a model to me of help, of complete alertness to the single step, awry or ready, a kind of Zen warrior (Suzuki, 1938/1970). Finally, I want to thank the Routledge staff, organized so ably by Dana Ward Bliss to publish this book, and my editor in particular, Prudence Taylor Board, for her great gift of seeing the architecture of the book as a whole and the beautiful line of march of every sentence.

PART I
Containment

When you meet a new patient, you are meeting someone who cannot contain his or her struggles. Almost invariably, the patient is more anxious and more depressed than can be borne, and has begun acting out compensations to make these signals more bearable. He or she is avoiding work, or drinking instead of going home, or even be making him- or herself the center of the universe in a psychosis—the god complex (Jones, 1923/1951).

All of these urgencies will spill over into other domains. The patient may become physically ill, and show up at the primary care office. He or she may drop off badly at work and get fired. The patient may drive the spouse into leaving. The individual's delusions may bring the police.

In other words, functioning may come to a standstill, and as a result the patient may be threatened with loss of place. Indeed, no one dares malfunction for long in this society. A niche may disappear overnight, and it may be quite impossible to get back into it once it has been lost.

All of this is why containment is always my first concern when I see a new patient, and it is almost always the first, and perhaps only concern of the patient. Our patients want control, and the loss of it is generally a terror and a despair.

So, the question to be assessed is always a matter of gauging how far out of control the patient has gone, and what it will take to bring him or her back within bounds. In general, this breakdown of control will occur in one of, or all three ways that constitute the subject matter of the chapters of part I, "Containment." Almost always, the patient has gone too far into

1

some kind of one-sided pushing of things, as in being of too much service (particularly those in the helping professions). It may be possible for the person to get away with this for some length of time in the prodromal or preillness phase, but suddenly, the patient will find himself very anxious, and this is the subject of chapter 1. Alternatively, the patient collapses into depression, which is the subject of chapter 2. The patient may fall into one of the compensatory forms of acting out, however, such as avoidance, drinking, or psychosis, which is the subject of chapter 3.

In other words, the familiar, secure, and normal routine that contains our citizen has come apart. The conscious focus that is his or her life cannot be maintained, and the unconscious forces flood in their strange and often alarming formlessness. The patient's dream of him- or herself is in serious jeopardy. So, what will it take for the patient to step back from having gone too far, and thus be able once more to contain him- or herself? Also, how will the patient make his or her container bigger so it can bear more anxiety and depression (Sashin & Callahan, 1990)?

The Assessment

So, how to read the situation quickly and reliably? I do it with my own new patients in the outpatient clinic in a half-hour, so I have a quarter of an hour for all the paperwork and setting up the next meeting. With the trainees, who take an hour and a half for their assessment, I often have only 10 minutes to read the most crucial questions.

Actually, it is usually very simple. The garden-variety problems come around remarkably alike, and usually announce themselves at the first look in the waiting room, walking back down the hall, or in the first question asked of me in my consulting room. For example, the patient shows himself very nervous for my approval. This is because the histories are essentially circular, and the patient has been going around the same circle his or her whole life. He or she has just gone too far again, as has happened many times before. Thus, we can start anywhere, and it is the same.

But here is how I write it out (see figure 1.1). First, I find out the identity of the referring person, because someone else may have more stake in the patient's survival than the patient himself. Thus, a wife may send her husband to be reformed, as a mother her son, or a primary care provider a nuisance. Second comes the chief complaint, and third, the history of the present illness. Here I outline the sequence: *when* the patient has been relatively okay, and *when* and *where* he ran into trouble. In other words, what has been the trajectory, and by what repeated step has the patient traveled it and gone over the line into the distressing signals of anxiety and depression, and the distressing compensations?

Medical Record Number:

Name:

Date of Birth:

Date:

Referring Person:

Chief Complaint:

History of Present Illness:

Mental Status Exam:

Medical Evaluation:

Psychiatric Differential Diagnosis:

History of Helping Relationships:

Psychotherapeutic Dilemma and DSM-IV-R Diagnosis on all 5 axes:

Plan:

Primary Care Consent, Hospital Master Problem List, Medication Consents, Other

Documentation, Appointment, and Treatment Plan signed by patient

Fig. I.1 Assessment.

All the while I am taking this down, I am also writing out a mental status exam, for the patient will enact the present illness right in front of me, if I track the sequence from being in control to being out of control. He will tremble, cry, and manifest how he tries to pull himself together. If there is any question of organic medical illness, I will do a minimental status exam.

This brings me naturally to consider the medical evaluation. Does the patient have a primary care doctor? Does the patient have any serious past and ongoing medical illnesses? What drugs is the patient taking? And, perhaps, most important, has the patient anything that feels wrong physically right now? It is remarkable to me how often the most important screening question is not asked by our trainees. It takes a use of the imagination to inquire about how the patient feels physically. The training, instead, tends to encourage the trainee to make a list of yes or no probes.

Now I take a turn to the most essential section of my assessment, the psychiatric differential diagnosis. Here, I must imagine the worst. This means that the patient's picture of himself in the room is likely to lead to an underestimation of his or her condition. After all, the patient is struggling in the course of a first visit to make as good an impression as possible in order to secure my good will and my help. The patient will leave out the dire findings so as not to scare me off, and leave him- or herself wide open to the unknown entity I am for the patient at a first meeting.

Therefore, I must couch this turn very carefully, to let the patient know what I need to know, and that it is in his or her interest to tell me. I say something like this: "If I am going to be your doctor, I need to know what your condition looks like at its worst. What would I see when you are in the most pain (or fear, or depression)? What goes through your mind when you are like that? How strange is it? What do you think of doing to get out of it? Suicide? Homicide? Drinking? Driving fast? How long is it apt to last, and what brings you out of it?"

Generally, our trainees do not even think of considering the patient's darkest hours. Rather, they have lists of yes or no probes, of things to rule out for any diagnosis; such as for depression, they ask if the patient is or has been suicidal, manic or does he or she drink too much. It is simpler to let the patient know you want to hear about his or her worst times, and begin to imagine what this desperation is actually like and where it is close to going over the edge into disaster. Having put yourself *near* this desperation, you get better answers about the condition. I call it "the worst news" (Gustafson, 1986/1997a, chap. 19).

Now, I turn to "the best news" by contrast. Who has helped the patient the most, and what did this help consist of? I am interested particularly in whether the help the patient got is something that I can trade on by continuing it? Perhaps someone else has set an example of helpfulness that is realistic, and so the patient will have realistic ideas about my help. This history of helping relationships also gets us outside of the present picture in the room, which may mislead us about the patient's tendencies when dependent. Is the individual likely to regress and make increasingly exorbitant demands, or is he or she likely to be satisfied with being understood? This distinction between malignant and benign regression is of the greatest interest to me (Balint, 1968, Gustafson, 1986/1997a, chap. 8). David Malan (1979, pp. 220–225) called it the "Law of Increased Disturbance," which he rightly said is a fundamental law of psychotherapeutic forecasting: "In intensive psychotherapy, a therapist always runs the risk of making a patient as disturbed as she (or he) has ever been in the past, or more so"

(p. 220). Of course, the disturbance of the past has something to do with the parents, and the disturbance of the present will have something to do with the envelope of support that is now available. The envelope could be even thinner or it could be more substantial. So this leads naturally into who are the key people in the patient's present life, how is the patient supported financially, and what is meaningful to the individual about his or her present existence?

In concluding this half-hour of assessment, I want to emphasize that it does *not* consist of a lot of questions. Often, we *will* the patient to be contained *without* imagining what he or she cannot bear. This is a case of will trying to do the work of the imagination (Yeats, as quoted in Tate, 1934/1999). No, it is the work of the imagination itself that is essential; that is, getting a *picture* of the patient at his worst and at his best, and of the conditions that bring about these extremes. When I can imagine this picture, I know what will contain the patient and what will overwhelm the containment.

Disposition

Now I have a quarter of an hour for the disposition. I write out the psychotherapeutic dilemma and the diagnosis in terms of the five axes, and I write out a *plan*. I have the patient sign the consents for the report to the primary care provider, and add the diagnosis to the master problem list of the hospital chart (or not, in which case I need the patient's written consent to be responsible for the information), and sign consents for medications, and get my card (with information on emergency calls), and get an appointment card. You see why a quarter of an hour is not too little for this degree of documentation! Finally, if the patient is in any jeopardy of acting out in terms of suicide or homicide, or with drugs or whatever, I have him or her sign a treatment plan. The patient agrees to be responsible for keeping me informed if he or she gets worse between sessions or keeping the call system informed if it happens at night or on weekends. I say to the patient, "*Only you* can be responsible for this, for I won't know when it is happening. *Before* you get to the extreme, you need to call or get to the emergency room, or I can't do my job as your doctor" (Kernberg, Selzer, Koenigsberg, Carr, & Appelbaum, 1988, chap. 3).

The Assessment and Disposition Process: Beginning, Middle, and End Problems

I think of the entire first interview as having three quarter-hours. The first quarter is the opening and has its own problems: for example, often the patient is late. If that is the case, I begin the assessment anyway by reading over the report from the triage nurses and reading the hospital chart. Often, I get what I need from this reading, because it is a microcosm of the whole situation.

The second quarter is for extending the presenting problem into imagining the whole situation at its worst and at its best, as I have already described. It is tempting to get off into too many details. Often, I have to remind the patient of what urgent matters I need to know. As Malan (1976, 1979) used to say about these interviews, I try to get close to the patient's desperation, and then I try to step back 10 paces and look at it as a whole pattern. A balanced interview will give about equal time to the near and far perspectives.

Finally, the third or exit quarter-hour also has its hazards. I always try to be finished with 5 or 10 minutes left over, because it is extremely likely the patient will drop some additional matter onto me and overload me with more responsibility than I have time or will to manage. For example, the patient may add that he or she is in danger of being fired. This is called projective identification, or turning passive into active, by which the patient puts his overloaded condition into you. My reply is likely to be that we will deal with this next time, and not now.

Lately, I have been scheduling a full hour for runover problems that turn up in an attempt to conclude fully in three quarters of an hour. It takes the pressure off of me. Also, I have been utilizing a longer form like the other doctors in the clinic. Your best defense is to have acted like most other doctors in the documentation.

A Final Word on Assessments with Trainees

The difference here is that the trainees have an hour and a half, and I have to verify their findings in 10 to 20 minutes. They summarize their findings in front of the patient, and then I ask a few questions. Generally, there is only one thing I *have* to know, and that is how the patient is at his worst, and if he is willing to take responsibility for getting himself to safety when this worst is impending. Everything else is academic as it were, for my main job is triage, or the prevention of disaster. If I have time to demonstrate the circularity of the history, improve the medical differential diagnosis, and identify the key step for getting out of this bad situation, I will. I may even get a dream to make the diagnosis and treatment, for it is the best X-ray we have in psychiatry (Gustafson, 1997b, 2000). But the main step is containment, and so I will confine myself to the main step, and its essentials, unless there is time left over for more ambitious interviews.

Exceptions

If there is a terse procedure for assessing the garden-variety cases, there are exceptions occasionally, which take a painstaking further hour. For example, there are patients who arrive with a chart that requires a cart to bear its volumes and gravity. There will be no way around going to my computer to the Micro-Medex search and typing in the 30 drugs the patient is on to see if any interactions are causing the problem. There will be no way around thinking about the patient's 15 illnesses and how they bear on the psychiatric complaints. There will be no way around checking the list of laboratory studies for their completeness, nor around checking the results.

There will be other exceptions to the rule of brevity as well, which we shall meet in the next three chapters, where I can point out what to watch for. As Malan (1979) astutely remarked about evaluation in psychiatry, the first session takes the most experience to do well. The reason for that is because you need to know all the possibilities and how to size them up. So, let us proceed to visit what is highly probable (Sullivan, 1954, 1956), and what is exceptional.

The Container and the Contained: Ongoing Treatment and Notes

I happened to cover for one of our psychology faculty a few days ago to supervise a new psychology trainee with a new case. The trainee explained to the patient that I would "only pop in for 5 minutes" and "only to observe the trainee and not the patient." I didn't agree with what she announced, but I sat back and listened for 5 minutes. I was horrified to hear the patient tell how she had nearly managed to kill herself with a massive overdose the previous week. She told this tale as blandly as if relating what she had eaten for lunch.

I asked if I could ask a question? The psychology trainee turned to me with a frightened look on her face, as if I were about to criticize her. I turned to the patient, instead, and asked if she were willing to take responsibility for notifying us when she was moving again down this dangerous slope? Oh, yes, she would agree to that, but she only knew of it at the last second, and then it was too late! In other words, we had a treatment going, with absolutely no floor under it. This was a setup for disaster.

I simply replied that these things do build up gradually, before they run out of control, and that she might get better at observing the buildup and calling us in time. I asked the trainee to make out a treatment plan, giving the patient this responsibility (Kernberg et al., 1988). The patient noted that signing the plan might not mean anything in practice. I agreed and left it to her to improve her self-observation, or not.

This incident explains why I address containment as the first step of evaluation and treatment. If there is no container, there is dire potential for acting out. The reverse is also urgent. If there is only containment, what is contained within it can become empty. This is evident in reviewing thousands of notes of residents (myself) and psychiatrists (Michael Moran, personal communication). What is contained in them is usually lifeless. There is a diagnosis, with a mental status to confirm it, interacting with an algorithm of treatment. End. This is static and empty. I cannot tell one from another. Reading them in review, I often cannot remember or picture the person alluded to.

Balint (cited in Gustafson, 1986/1997a) used to say that psychotherapy is about seeing what the patient is up to and facing it with him. In other words, every patient is trying to *go* somewhere and having difficulty getting there. This ought to be in the record. Often, I find that I gave just this, but the resident made no mention of it at all. It seems as if there is some dire process at work in the training which makes the record into the most impersonal thing in the world.

Why not put in the record what the patient is up to, and when and where the anxiety or depression began, and what is holding up the patient's motion? When the motion is violent and lacks a container, it is going to end up badly. When the container squeezes the life out of the subject, it is also going to end up badly.

I handle this problem in my private practice by a SOAP note, which describes S, for Subjective, the chief complaint of the day; O, for Objective, a picture of how the patient appears; A, for Assessment, the diagnosis, and any dangers at hand; and P, for Plan, my treatment, including the next psychotherapy session, medications, and dangers reckoned with, and summary of this session by "See letter to patient." Usually, I can do each (S, O, A, P) in one line, but urgencies must be documented and take up whatever space necessary.

My letters to the patient are usually one or two lines, and point out this motion he or she is attempting and what it is running into. For example, the last three I just wrote were:

Dear _____:
This teacher will teach you how to lie low under her radar. (For a social work student in a panic about being picked on by her supervisor.)

Best,

Jim G.

Dear _____:

It looks like you have chosen a more radical way, and are comfortable holding your own ground, but for the bump in my direction. (For a patient opposing his parents, successfully, but a little nervous about displaying his confidence to me, a transference emerging.)

Best,

Jim G.

Dear _____:

Lovely purchase of the new black, pink purse for $299. Looks like an investment in yourself, as a .299 hitter, and it's already too late to give it back. (A summary of a beautiful dream's motion of a patient finally taking care of herself, with this beautiful present —the .299 hitter is about being good enough, like a good major league hitter, getting about 3 hits out of 10 times at bat, instead of pleasing everyone.)

Best,

Jim G.

The letter invokes a single step that is decisive, as these three letters show in microcosm the next three parts of the book after containment ("Selective Inattention Revised," "The Opposing Current Navigated," "Impasse Surmounted").

The letter reminds us both of where we left off and what came across to me. It invokes both the patient's motion and the space (geometry) in which it occurs.

CHAPTER 1
Anxiety as a Signal of Danger

Danger. F., VL. *dominiarium,* for *domininium,* rule, lordship....
Sense development took place in OF, earliest surviving meaning, *in danger of,* originally subject to the jurisdiction of....
You stand within his danger, do you not? (Shakespeare, *Merchant of Venice,* IV, 1, 175, cited in Weekley, 1967)

Anxiety is now considered to be a disorder, and it *is* a disorder in the sense that when it is running high it curtails functioning. Our diagnostic system (American Psychiatric Association, 1994, DSM-IV) is entirely a diagnosis of functioning, and our patients are surely anxious to keep functioning, for their security depends upon being able to function. Therefore, they are in serious danger when they do not function, as, for example, when they are in danger of being fired from a job. Thus, we are most often called upon by the patients to contain the anxiety at manageable levels. This containment is the simplest procedure of Very Brief Psychotherapy.

In other words, anxiety has *consequences,* especially in terms of limiting the ability to function at work, at home as a parent, or in school in taking tests. This limitation works as an *alarm.* Some danger is coming like a fire! In general, alarms, such as fire alarms, put a stop to business as usual until they are shut off.

That is precisely what we do when we contain anxiety with antianxiety drugs. We turn down the alarm, so the patient can resume business as usual. Obviously, this could be good or bad. It could be good if the alarm were shut off, because the loss of business is itself a danger. It could be bad if the alarm were shut off when it demanded immediate action, as in the case of a fire.

Of course, it is paradoxical to call the practice of psychopharmacology a kind of psychotherapy. Yet, it truly is a ritual of security. The patient is not going to respond to the agent that is given, or even take it regularly, if he lacks trust in the doctor. What is calming is this context of trust plus the pharmacologic agent.

Engel (1980) argued in his beautiful essay, centered upon the case of a man in a coronary care unit, that containing a patient's anxiety is not simply a matter of prescribing drugs. Indeed, the drugs were insufficient to keep his patient in his bed on the coronary care unit. He was too desperate to resume his stance of control, so he rushed out of the confining place that was putting him into a panic. Also, he dreaded getting behind in his work, and was pulled by it back to his post.

In other words, his personality or psychology had to be reckoned with, along with his social context, along with his biological condition of angina. Anything less and the forces would become unmanageable, and the patient would burst out of his inadequate container! Conversely, an understanding of his desperate need for self-reliance could address this in him as an urgent matter, *before* he went into panic and fled the hospital. Similarly, an understanding of the social envelope of a coronary care unit could estimate its drastic effect upon him of making him feel helpless, and take steps to give him some control in the decision making process, *before* he felt robbed of control, and fled back to his post running his business, a place where he felt secure. Truly, containment, in its wisdom, is a biopsychosocial procedure.

Anxiety as a Nonlinear Response

Much of what is strange about anxiety, and leads to mistrust of any doctor trying to be helpful, is that anxiety is not a gradual development. It erupts suddenly, and supposedly out of the blue. This is called a nonlinear response, in contrast to a linear response in which there is a gradual curve of increased response to increased stimulation (Gustafson & Meyer, 2004). With a nonlinear response, the response to increased stimulation is rather flat or even nonexistent, and then suddenly jumps to a high level, which may even be a panic.

Some examples of nonlinear responses will remind us of how familiar we are with them after all. If we turn the heat up under a kettle it seems to do nothing much for a few minutes, and suddenly, it is boiling over. The same could be said of a man who is slow to anger. Nothing phases him, even many insults, until suddenly he too boils over in rage. This náture, and our nature, is full of these sudden and thus nonlinear changes of state, arising out of a gradual and thus linear buildup of stimulation. Rain and snow, lightening and thunder, erupt suddenly and nonlinearly out of a linear buildup of humidity and electricity, respectively. In other words, the pressure builds in a gradual line, but the eruption is not linear or not a straight line but a jump!

Why is this nonlinear pattern the rule in our clinic? Why is there a phase of negligible response, followed by a phase of sudden high anxiety? The answer is that most of our patients have a very repetitive pattern for dealing with just about anything in their lives. It works up to a certain point, and then it breaks down.

For example, many of our patients try to give whatever is asked of them. They believe in service, and service, if possible, with a smile. They believe in being positive. Thus, they are highly responsive to everyone else's needs, but they ignore their own. Therefore, they have little reaction to increasing stimulation or demands from others, whether it be at work or at home.

Suddenly, they are asked to do one more thing than they can bear and they snap. They snap in anger, or they feel overwhelmed with anxiety that they cannot keep up with the demands. All of a sudden, the tension has jumped.

Of course, they are then in danger of not being able to function in terms of meeting all these demands. So they are anxious that they are anxious. This makes the jump in tension even steeper. This is what brings these patients to us. They badly need to function, and they badly need the anxiety to be contained so they can function.

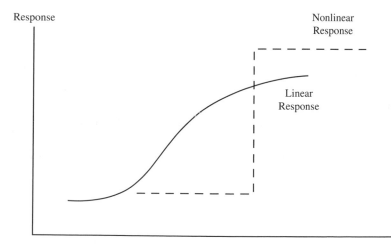

Fig. 1.1 Nonlinear response to increased stimulation.

Unequal Exchanges

Of course, there are other causes of anxiety. Anxiety will also jump in emergencies. An impending car crash or the threat of losing a child will terrify us. Also, there are medical conditions which will jump the anxiety level. There is a long list, but the common ones for us in the clinic are high blood sugars from diabetes, high thyroid hormone levels from hyperthyroidism, and occult infections or cancers (Koranyi, 1979).

These things, however, are exceptional. What mostly gets to our patients is the day in day out grind of giving too much and getting little back. In other words, they are worn down by unequal exchanges, with bosses, coworkers, spouses, children, parents, and friends. They take it and take it, showing little sign of being bothered. They are determined to be positive. Suddenly, they erupt in anxiety and can't take it any more.

A person who is agitated is soon going to be equally exhausted. This is a terrible combination, because you need to sleep to renew your energies, yet the alarm will not stop. You go to bed, but your worrying will not cease to talk to you. Continue this for a few days and nights and you are in bad shape. Continue it for weeks, months, and years and your body will break down into illness at one of its weak links. For example, you already have a tendency to pour out excessive acid in your stomach. Suddenly, it has gone over the limit of what your stomach lining can dissolve and you have a bleeding ulcer.

Once our patients become debilitated like this, the exchange tends to run in the opposite direction. They become entitled to get something for themselves, after all. It has only lagged in its expression. Now, they will avoid responsibilities, act sick, claim special privileges, get drunk, take drugs, and so forth. Now, they claim a lot, and become burdensome to everyone, including their doctors.

This dynamic of unequal exchange is so fundamental that it could be rightly said to be the basis of nearly all the psychopathology that we see in the clinic (Gustafson, 1999). Either the patient is giving too much, and being taken, or the patient is taking too much, and giving little back.

For example, a patient who has been taken advantage of in her marriage may begin to indulge herself by staying in bed. As she indulges herself, she runs the opposite risk of exhausting the patience of her husband. Thus, she will get anxious about being or acting sick and entitled to get out of work. She gets away with it for days or weeks, when suddenly her husband has had it and has a fit. Before and after this fit, she will be getting highly anxious about her special privileges. Taking too much results in high anxiety, too, because it is dangerous to try the patience of others too long!.

Personality, Character, Idiom, or Security Operations

Now, how is it that our patients can ignore the buildup of resentment that comes from giving too much and not getting back? They manage this simply by selective inattention (Gustafson, 1986/1997a; Sullivan, 1956). They attend to the positive, and ignore the negative, so the latter builds up unawares. They do this because the positive makes them feel secure. A giving person is secure that he or she is liked and valued. This is why Sullivan (1956; Gustafson, 1986/1997a) called this a security operation. At a deeper level, it may be the meaning of one's life, in a religious sense. What if this very meaning leads to disaster?

For example, a father brings home the bacon, as we say, but ignores how he is taken for granted. This is selective inattention on his part to his own feelings, driven by a security operation of being the positive, correct husband. Meanwhile, his wife manages the house, children, relatives, and social life, but ignores how she is taken for granted, driven by a security operation of being the positive correct wife.

Of course, a child learns security and its operations in a family. Out of the turmoil of childhood, she finds security in copying an adult, and repeating the gestures of her mother or an older sister or a teacher. It works well enough to get by on (Gustafson, 1986/ 1997a; Reich, 1949), and becomes highly repetitive, or rigid. In other words, it is selected, and allows a kind of survival. It is character and fate. It is personality or idiom (Coren, 2001) or style.

The term *character* has an ancient history in drama. It has the virtue as a term of tying the "character" to a dramatic outcome or "fate." Thus, the "character armor" (Reich, 1949) of self-reliance tends to ignore and neglect the buildup of needs. Then, our ignored father can be expected either to disappear into compensatory fantasy via TV or at a bar or out hunting, or to lose his temper in outbursts that baffle his family. The term *personality* suggests different styles or "idioms" for playing the part. Some of our correct husbands are passive, some are obsessional about controlling the details, and some are very narcissistic and vain about having to be listened to. In other words, they use different prevailing "defenses" to feel secure. If the defense is entirely rigid it is called a "personality disorder."

How Strange Do Things Get?

Another implication of the nonlinear jump of anxiety is that what the patient is showing in the room may not be anything like the full terror. He may simply be in the flat phase of the curve, where he is relatively secure. Little may be asked of him in the doctor's office. That is why I always ask our patients in their evaluation or first session with us to tell me how the anxiety is at its worst: as in the middle of the night, or under the gun at work, or wherever it is most disturbing.

Almost always, the patient shifts to *being* in that disturbing state, in order to tell me about it. From being relatively blank, the patient is now trembling or tearful. I ask how it feels, what is going through his mind, and how he gets through it! I am getting quite a window into a very different being than the one who sat down in the office. I get to see how shaken the patient becomes, and whether he loses his voice. I get to see if his thoughts become paranoid and scattered. I get to find out if he turns to alcohol or drugs for relief.

Naturally, I do not press the patient to answer my questions, or I'm in danger of being felt to be a persecutor. I simply say that I'd like to know what it's like at the worst, *if* he wants to tell me. I can be a better doctor if I know just how bad the condition is that I am taking care of. Generally, this sets a context in which the patient is relieved to let down a little. But there are patients who do not want to let me know things, out of shame or dread of being known.

The Case of the Potlatch Grandma

It is very important to catch on to how a patient talks herself out of feeling the anxiety that she indeed feels anyway. Otherwise, we will get nowhere in helping her see how she walks right into it, into, that is, a bad exchange for herself. Such cases become chronic, even if we can keep the patient functioning by containing the anxiety with our antianxiety agents. For the patient is simply replicating her own misery every day.

This patient was presented to me in the Brief Psychotherapy Clinic for consultation, after she had spent a year in the regular Psychiatry Clinic for insomnia. Generally, this insomnia means anxiety put off in the daytime, and coming out at night, especially in worrying that won't turn off, or in nightmares. Often, the patient will delay going to sleep, or stay awake in the middle of the night, or wake up early, to keep from going back into the nightmares. Of course, there are sleep disorders, like sleep apnea, with a physical basis, but these are the exceptions to the rule. Generally, our patients say after yet another horrid day, "My brain won't turn off." It is true. A brain moving too fast cannot readily be stopped.

This patient was 55, retired on a disability from factory work, and divorced from a husband who had since died. She had moved to stay with her daughter and son-in-law six years ago, to take care of her autistic then 10-year-old granddaughter. The resident explained to me that she had spent a lifetime taking care of others and that it was hard to turn it around.

As always, I replied intuitively, if only to hear my own first impression, "Well we need to find out how to release her from some of this guilt!" The patient replied, "And find out how I'm not sleeping, just rolling around!"

I was delighted with how her first reply went straight to the point. I could just see her rolling around. "So you have trouble falling asleep?" "Yes, and waking up early, for a couple of years." Now, she took me right to the change that had brought on her trouble. "I never used to have trouble sleeping in my apartment before I came here. It had big open windows. I miss the fresh air and hearing the owls! I'm angry at moving up here and losing my freedom. I take care of an autistic granddaughter."

She was so direct. How could such a blunt individual get herself out of a free situation into a trap? I responded, "So it was kind of a sacrifice?" "Well," she said, "my mother passed away, whom I had been taking care of, so it was kind of unanimous, because it was draining them." "So, it was kind of unanimous," a most telling phrase, indeed. It had been a kind of vote, in which she voted along with everybody else, even against herself!

In other words, the unanimous vote is that she should step in and relieve her daughter and son-in-law of the burden of care of their autistic daughter. Surely, the parents vote in favor of being relieved, and our patient votes as if she has no choice but to agree.

Certainly, I needed to understand this vote. "I kept finding I was angry all the time." "At the parents?" "There's nothing I can do about it. I'm on disability (from factory injuries), so I am doing nothing." Thus, she justifies taking on the autistic granddaughter as her burden. Immediately, she gave me the countercurrent in an offhand remark, "I don't really like knitting this sweater!" As if to say, she really is opposed to some aspects of the role of grandmother.

I say "countercurrent" because she is admitting an objection to fulfilling the role of a stock grandmother who knits sweaters! Yet she seems to argue against herself to put down her objection as it arises. "I am doing nothing" (implying that "I have no rights to decline the job").

"Do I hear correctly a tendency to push yourself, get angry, and then find it hard to sleep?" "I never thought of it!" Now that reply surprised me, but I knew enough about selective inattention to believe her. She just hadn't added up the sequences.

As I am wont to do, I naturalized the sequence for her, saying, "Two-thirty a.m. is the right time to fall asleep when you're mad." She rejoined, "My granddaughter never stops talking. I can be ready to shoot her. Usually, by evening, I am ready to cut off my ears!" "Or cut out her tongue?" I ventured. "No, I'd rather harm myself. I already did this enabling a husband. I'm still mad at him. He died last year."

"I have dreams of yelling at him, but he never says a word!" I reply, "It's maybe even harder to take care of an autistic girl and her parents." "I'm filing bankruptcy, for buying gifts and splurging on them." Now, I was truly surprised again. She was making quite a virtue out of giving, and at her own expense! I noted that it sounded like a potlatch. She replied, "I *feel* selfish."

"I guess you're supposed to be a self-sacrifice. As in the myth of the doctor. You're full of it." She laughed here at my slip, which nearly implied she was full of shit. But, of course, she knew she was, from her project of self-sacrifice. I laughed too and said, "Well, not shit exactly, but it builds up." "My daughter is full of it too! She always walks away mad. I can't tell when she's angry at me." "She's farther along than you! So we know why you don't sleep! Shall we see about your dreams? I bet they fairly shout out the situation." "Yes," she answered, "I've had a recurrent dream for a year (the length of her insomnia). It has to do with work, in a factory."

I'm going to leave off the narrative here, as interesting as the dream material is. It finally led to going upstairs in the house with a tornado coming! Speaking of walking right into an eruption! My point in concluding this chapter is not about how to use dreams to map the situation, but rather the nature of the situation that brings about anxiety.

This one is typical. The patient is agreeing to a terrible exchange. We contained it for a year with antianxiety agents to allow sleep. Often, we can do no better, because the patient is not ready or willing to face her predicament. This patient was more than ready.

Biopsychosocial Containment

Our Potlatch Grandma had a year of containment in the clinic with antianxiety agents, which helped her contain her nightmares, and her panic by day. These helped her to stay in her role as caretaker for her autistic granddaughter, without decompensating. On the other hand, they did nothing to lessen her pushing herself into a very unequal exchange of giving far too much, until her anger burst out. In other words, she was playing Mrs. Jekyll, and turning into Mrs. Hyde. The move from her free space in her beautiful apartment with the owls into the contained space as servant of the extended family set loose forces that even our powerful drugs could not contain. So, after a year of this partially successful psychopharmacology, she was brought to me in the Brief Psychotherapy Clinic for an assessment of the whole situation. This allowed us to see what she was walking into, psychologically, and socially, as in the old meaning of danger I quoted as an epigraph: *Danger.* Subject to the jurisdiction of... "You stand within his danger" (*Merchant of Venice* IV, 1, 175). This allowed our patient to step back from crossing over this line into abject servitude, and thus cut back her rage and panic tremendously. This simple step is what I mean by biopsychosocial containment in the full sense of the term.

CHAPTER 2
Depression as a Signal of Defeat

defeat. From defait, p.p. of F. defaire, to undo, from VL. disfacere for deficere. In ME. To undo, destroy, etc., mil. sense being later, e.g., not in Shakespeare.

down. With downcast cf. dejected.... To down tools is a good example of the E. power of forming verbs from preps.; cf. to out (an opponent), to up (and speak). (Weekley, 1967)

We list depression as an illness in DSM-IV, which it is, in the sense of being something that is *nonfunctional about a mood* (American Psychiatric Association, 1994). It is a disorder of mood. Moods are either compatible with order, or they bring about disorder. Thus, I never object when a patient or doctor tells me that the patient has a depressive illness, and explains that it is caused by biochemical defects, which are inherited and run in families. This is partly true, as science has demonstrated, but I do not leave it there.

I also take depression as a signal of defeat. From this perspective, which has a long development starting with Freud (1917/1975g) in psychoanalysis, the mechanism of depression, as Bibring (1953) wrote in his classic paper, is profoundly simple. When the patient's ideal can no longer be sustained, he collapses into defeat. He or she is dejected, undone, destroyed.

Of course, there are degrees of this condition, to which the English language is tuned. Thus, when I want to introduce the subject of giving up to a patient, I will simply say, "What is getting you down?" That is mild enough for most patients to turn over in their minds. Often, they will say, "I don't know," and often they will have some notion. In the former case,

21

I will simply note, "You haven't given yourself much time to consider it!" The humor of this will often ease the patient into some consideration.

The Ideal of the Helping Professions

If you want to follow a clear line of inquiry about what has gotten the patient down, you have to form a clear idea of his ideal, then you can trace its demise. It will help you to understand that the number of ideals is actually few.

In chapter 1 we discussed the ideal of service, which collapsing, brings about what Malan (1979) called "the helping profession syndrome." Essentially, this is anxiety as a signal that helping is threatened, and depression as a signal that helping is defeated. Often, the patient whose life is devoted to helping will have a mixture of the two signals, because some of his or her attempts are on the verge of failing, and some already have failed.

This syndrome is essentially the same in all of the helping professions, such as medicine, ministry, or teaching, or in the informal professions in any service bureau, or in mothering or fathering. Secretaries and receptionists have it, and so do psychotherapists. Any person who sees herself as in service to being of help will be vulnerable to its failure. Thus, you will recall the Case of the Potlatch Grandma, who had a considerable ideal of generosity, which drew her over the limit of giving, without getting much back. She was anxious that she couldn't keep up her ideal, and she was angry that it didn't draw to her considerations for her service. Anxiety and anger are deeply allied in the English language through the old root of enge- which means to *narrow* in Old High German, which they have in common. To be narrowed is to set up mighty signals, with forebodings of eruption. But to be gotten down is also a mighty signal, because we might not be able to get up again to serve our cause. Morale can disappear. That was the case with our Grandma, who had gone into bankruptcy as a result of excessive service to her granddaughter, daughter, and son-in-law.

The Ideal of Control

Control is an even greater ideal for most of our patients. It overlaps with the ideal of helping, since controlling an outcome can be so helpful, as in medicine or in mothering. Yet controlling also takes other guises, warlike as well as peaceful. I can hardly think of a patient in the last month who was not espousing some form of control. Scientists control things, technology controls things, military force controls things. Bureaucracy controls everything! Its form is so universal that you cannot tell a pharmacy from an airline from a school when you place a call. Each puts you on hold with the same message system.

As I wrote in the introduction to part I, "Containment," there seems to be nothing which cannot be controlled in the minds of the public. If it is out of control, science will soon bring it under control. It is hard to say who believes more in control in our clinic, the patients or the doctors. Both think there is a technique for everything that the patient might complain of, from misery at work to misery in relationship, from anxious moods to depressive moods, and so forth.

Of course, the control lags the promises, for it is only the chief ideal of our time, and often cannot deliver. Any ideal which is purporting to do so much is going to set up a lot of anxiety and a lot of depression. Its claims are inflated (Jung, 1916/1953), and will have to be deflated. That is a frightening prospect, and it gets people down.

The Nonlinearity of Depression

Depression is something that strikes our patients out of the blue, so to speak. It comes on insidiously, or it comes on suddenly. There seems to be no apparent logic to it. The patients often say, "I shouldn't be depressed." Certainly, it can be brought on by nearly any illness known to man. As Bibring (1953) argued, it is a state of inhibition, which closely allies itself to any state of fatigue, boredom, and demoralization. I *always* consider that a good medical history is necessary with any case of anxiety or depression, and I *always* consider getting laboratory screening of the CBC (complete blood count), chem. 7 (electrolytes, blood urea nitrogen, creatinine, glucose), and TSH (thyroid stimulating hormone). Even when a psychodynamic mechanism for depression is obvious, I consider whether there might also be, for example, an anemia, or a diabetes, or a hypothyroidism.

But why does depression usually appear out of the blue in our patients? If Bibring (1953) is right about the garden-variety mechanism of depression, which involves the collapse of an ideal, why are so few patients (or doctors!) aware of what is going on?

I think this has a great deal to do with the nonlinearity of the appearance of depression. By this I mean that the patient's lifeline of morale or vigor or vitality just takes a sudden drop. The reason for this is because control can be willed up to a certain point. Will can keep up morale by more effort, more technique, more trying harder. What *else* is this country about?

In other words, the ideal of control calls incessantly for more will. When it flags in its results, like Avis it tries harder. This gets our patient through medical school, or any kind of school these days, all of which pile on the quantity. But the end of schooling is only the beginning of more of this piling on of quantity in the professions. Hours worked, numbers generated, papers written: this is what gets you qualified in a profession. Yet there is no relief from it at home: the house that is always in need of repair, the places to take the children, the social events that require attendance for work or school or church. There is no end to it (Brooks, 2004).

A typical patient told me a typical dream about his terror of not keeping up: he dreamt that the weeds in his yard had grown three feet, despite the weed killer he had used. By day, he had lists of things to do, by night, he worried that he might not keep up.

Suddenly, such a patient might give up. One more thing might be one too many. A bad conference with the boss might signal to him that, despite all his efforts, he was going to be let go. A bad fight with his wife might signal to him that, in spite of all his efforts, she was leaving! In other words, his ideal of control might suddenly become unbelievable. His faith might collapse. As his load increases in quantity, his response of more effort continues to rise. However, when his ideal of control by will is suddenly disconfirmed, his nonlinear response is a collapse into defeat.

The Ideal of Perfection

It is bad enough to control a mounting load by mounting effort. It is worse when the patient believes in perfecting everything, because then there are no shortcuts. Every detail must be right, and thus the natural correction is ruled out.

A doctor in an emergency room practices triage whenever he is in danger of being flooded. He takes the life-threatening emergencies at once, and next he takes the illnesses that will get worse without treatment, and last he takes the things that will go on the same whether he sees them or not.

This triage is precisely what a perfectionist cannot practice in his life. Everything requires a complete effort. There is no distinguishing a grave matter from a large matter from a small matter. The patient is incapable of making this distinction. He just has lists in which everything is essential. Indeed, trying to distinguish the essential from the inessential would terrify him— he might miss something.

All he can do is meet increasing loads with increasing effort. If he were a resident in the Oakland County Hospital Emergency Room for one 12-hour shift, he would soon go into a panic, because he could not keep up with the volume of ill patients, coronaries suddenly wheeled in, and auto accidents wheeling in patients close to death. Not long after his panic would come the collapse into defeat which is depression.

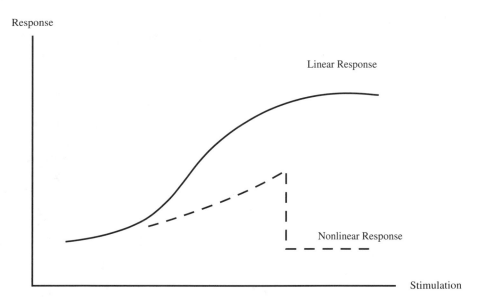

Fig. 2.1 The nonlinearity of depression.

But, somehow, his policy works for most other loads. Indeed, I find it is the policy of almost all of our patients. Control and achieving perfection is what they are up to. How did this get selected? Weber (1904/1958) argued that the discipline for it came from the Protestant religion, such as the method book of Methodists, which kept track of sins on one side of the page, and contributions across from it. A person's worth could be reckoned from this moral ledger.

Weber (1904/1958) argued that this method of quantity was taken over by bureaucracy. A hundred years ago bureaucracy was a relatively new institution, adopted by governments for carrying out its mandates, by ensuring that everyone followed its rules. The collection of taxes, the maintenance of armies, and later on such programs as Social Security, depended upon it.

What has happened in a hundred years is that every other major institution has adopted bureaucratic authority to control its outcomes: businesses, universities, schools, professional accreditation, you name it. Everything has a correct procedure, and more of it is needed to become qualified. Our patients have been selected by every institution they have met, all of which operate in the same way. If they haven't made control and perfection their own ideals, they have been disqualified. The *pressure of reality*, as Wallace Stevens (1942/1997) put it, is simply overwhelming, and they bow to it.

Control and Grief, Perfection and Grief

Grief hasn't much of a chance in this climate of control and perfectionism. It interferes with mounting effort. For a loss calls for grieving, and grieving is time out. In this moral climate, grief is a lack of what our patients, and doctors, call positive emotion. *Mind Over Mood* (Greenberger & Padesky, 1995) is the single most important book in the clinic, and it teaches how to distract oneself from negative emotions that make one nonfunctional. It has become our Bible.

The general result is that losses are not grieved, because the pressure of reality will not let up to allow it. Freud (1917/1975g), in "Mourning and Melancholia," argued that grief becomes pathological when the patient has rage at the object lost. Because he is so guilty at being so angry at this lost object, he cannot be angry, only sad. Thus, he cries, and cannot stop. This screens out the anger. It is called melancholia, and it is pathological grieving. Because he cannot be angry at the lost one, he cannot separate from her. Instead, he becomes her as a way of holding onto her, often showing the same characteristics of the one lost.

Our patients are full of losses like this which they are stuck to, such as a divorce rate that is greater than 50%, deaths, failing children, or being disqualified in professions. In general, we contain the depression from getting too bad, with *Mind Over Mood*, antidepressants, and, if necessary, electroshock treatment. Our patients must go on. Indeed, they demand it, and others are impatient for them to stop crying about their losses. They are even told that crying is selfish! Thus, simple grief has no room to turn its back on the world. All our patients feel pulled to rush back from simple grief, and we can help them *not* to do that.

Is There a Floor under the Treatment?

Despite our best efforts to contain depression, some of our patients fall right through the floor. Life becomes so unbearably painful that they elect to kill themselves to get out of it. We are continually having to put ourselves on guard against it. Indeed, my chief job in supervising our trainees is to watch out for this.

The usual effort by the resident or psychologist to read the danger of suicide is inadequate. Why is this? I think it is chiefly because the situation as presented by the patient in the consulting room is taken at face value. This happens in so many ways: The patient is asked if he is suicidal. He may not be just now, but this is hardly his condition at two in the morning, or last week, or next week. He is asked if he has a plan for suicide. Often, he won't tell if he has one or not.

This is why the one thing I must supply as the backup in every assessment, and in many later sessions, is to get a reading on how bad things can really get. I have explained in my introduction to part I, "Containment," that I attempt to get as close as I can to the patient's worst moments, or hours. I try to imagine it with him or her. I want to add something further to that account.

Not only must I imagine it with the patient, but I must also imagine what has allowed him or her to survive to that point. This is because the patient's survival might depend upon a few threads: take them away and he is gone. This is a totally nonlinear situation. Today, his wife has not left him, and he is not suicidal. Tonight, she has had enough, and his one reason to continue living in so much pain is gone.

Following Havens (1965, 1967), I supply both an imagination of how bad it gets, *and* I supply an imagination of what keeps the patient from doing him- or herself in. I will say something like this: "It is this painful, but you are still here. What allows you to keep going?" If the patient is not very forthcoming, I will note that most people can keep going if they have hope of coming out of it, if they don't want to hurt people they love, and if they have a religious faith. This is likely to call up some recognition of the patient's few stays against complete despair.

With so many of our patients being chronically depressed and chronically suicidal, I do not want to be continually pestering them for their suicidal ideation. After all, they mostly *have* it. It is much better, simply, to ask how bad it has been in the interval since you saw them last, and how have they managed to survive. From this, we can espy and estimate what props could disappear!

For example, I saw a patient last week who is doing badly in high school, and is quite depressed about it. She is one of these good girls whose entire esteem stands or falls on her having a scholastic performance that will please her parents. That is what holds her up, and is her sole hope for having a life of her own. In every other department, like friends, sports, interests, there is little going on. I asked her how bad she felt about her bad semester, and what I would see if I saw her at her darkest moments? She mentioned crying, and going to bed, and pointedly denied any suicidal ideation.

This week she tried to shoot herself, after going off in the morning to summer school, and reassuring her mother she was fine. Now how did we miss it? Well, it certainly could be she already had a desperate plan when I saw her, and she just didn't *want* me to know, and take away the ace up the sleeve for getting out of despair. Also, summer school could have dealt out another blow to her fragile confidence. Following Kernberg et al.'s (1968) policy about all depressed patients, I had told her it was up to her to let us know if things got worse, for we wouldn't know unless she told us if they had worsened and she had crossed the line into more pain than she could bear. Yet she didn't call us.

I suspect it was her dire policy of perfection by control. If she was in control, that is, of doing well in her studies, she was in an okay mood. If her perfect procedures faltered, she could be totally shattered. I think she crossed the line.

I will close this chapter on the containment of depression, and its signal of defeat, with a very subtle case, mixed up between motives to die, and motives not to die, in a very uneasy alliance. This kind of reading can be very tricky, and always shifting, especially when the patient is hugely connected to a family member who already committed suicide. The way has been lined to death, and it can be very tempting to go down it.

The Case of the Sister of the Dead Pilot

It was the beginning of the second semester when she came to us, depressed. Fortunately, I had a whole hour to see her in consultation in the Brief Psychotherapy Clinic. Less time would not have sufficed in this case.

The rough outline of the history was this. She had been depressed since the previous summer at a family reunion. Everyone had ignored the absence of her brother who had died the year before by suicide. She alone seemed to notice he was gone. This was probably because she was the most like him in rebellion against her father. Everyone else was a white sheep lined up with the father, but these two were black sheep, one of whom had already taken his life.

Of course, I asked how bad it had gotten since the reunion. She told me that one dark night in the fall she had nearly driven off the road. She was at the very split second of doing it. What had kept her back? She was on the way to her big brother's, and he did care about her, and he would have been enormously pained: that had held her.

Then again at Thanksgiving, another family get-together, the pain in her gut at the dinner table became unbearable. She didn't know why. I asked her to sit with it, and the feeling, of course, was a world in thought (Balzac, 1835/1946, p. 165). It turned out that the pain was about her father, presiding over the dinner as if nothing were wrong, this, the father, who had refused a loan to her brother just before he died. She sat there at dinner enraged with her father.

But she also continued to feel the pain of it. It would not go away. I could see she was almost totally identified with her dead brother, as Freud (1917/1975g) argued was the center of pathological grief. Like her brother, she felt totally rejected by her father, and like her brother, she felt murderous rage. In so many ways, she was carrying her brother on her back, and the weight of the two of them was taking her down.

What I had to do to estimate her chances was see if I could divide her from her brother in some way that would make a difference, and lead to a different trajectory. Already, I had the tie to the older brother that had saved her once, and could save her again. But I was not altogether sure it was strong enough to hold her, not only because of her near total identification with her dead brother, but also because it was compounded by guilt. When she had heard that her brother had been turned down by her father for the loan, and sold his experimental airplane, she had been alarmed. She knew it was his dearest thing. That night she dreamt he had killed himself. Yet she dismissed the dream, and didn't call him. Soon after, he killed himself.

So I said to her, you're still here, but how will anyone know if you cross the line from bearable pain to unbearable pain? Well, she said, my older brother might know if he heard a change in my voice! Yes, I replied, but what if he misses it? Here, she cried, and admitted that might be more than she could stand.

It was time to end the interview. I noted that she was still near the edge of catastrophe, and needed more than the ear of her older brother to get through. Could she agree to call us, also? That would give her one other way to hold on. She wept, I think, in gratitude, and promised me she would.

This, of course, was not the end of danger. Just as he had refused the loan to her brother, her father refused to pay for her psychotherapy! This brought her back to the edge, but we knew exactly what it meant to her, and arranged for a fee reduction in the clinic. Gradually, she got her psychotherapy aimed precisely at the mechanism of pathological grief, and she was able to let go of being her brother going down his road of death. In the meanwhile, we had constructed this reliable ground floor to contain her, while this essential work of grieving was carried out.

CHAPTER 3

The Compensations for Unbearable Anxiety and Depression

Once any human being crosses the line into an eruption of unbearable anxiety or into a collapse of unbearable depression, a compensatory defense will come into play (A. Freud, 1936/1966), or, if you prefer, a security operation (Sullivan, 1956). If this defense or security operation continues, it gradually rigidifies into the patient's character (Reich, 1931, 1949), or personality, or idiom (Coren, 2001). It is a rigid one-sidedness, in terror of what it has dissociated. Jung called it the persona, or an identification with a god (Jung, 1916/1953).

It has the virtue of allowing the patient to go on, and not give up altogether on his or her dream (Gustafson, 1997). It seems to be mammalian in origin. A threatened mammal will increase its REM sleep when confronted with a dilemma it cannot find its way through; for example, as a rat does in a maze. If the increased effort fails, the animal gives up, and his immune system falls apart, and he is likely to die. Thus, a completely misleading dream of oneself has at least the virtue of keeping up morale, and thus effort (Thurber, 1942/1986). For example, the patient will keep dreaming of a beautiful woman coming to him (James, 1903/2003). In this way, the illusion of security (Sullivan, 1956) can be more important than actual accuracy about what will work. Of course the latter is preferable in the long run, namely, increased REM *and* accuracy about the dilemma.

In any event, a threatened animal will carry out some dissociative move to get rid of overwhelming signals of anxiety or depression. The temporary advantage for morale, however, is often canceled by the disadvantage of becoming rigidly one-sided, as in avoidance, or as in overeating. Thus, we are continually called upon to contain these compensatory defenses. They become ruinous in themselves.

One-Sided Operations Set Off by a Single Step

It is not necessary at this point to have a theoretical discussion about what sets off a defense, whether it be the anxiety or depression about the conflict between instinct and superego, or the insecurity with one's fellows, or what I would prefer to say, that human beings are profoundly tuned to exchange with others going badly. The reader may turn to my "Theoretical Scaffolding" in chapter 18, for such consideration. Obviously, these formulations are closely related.

What I want to delineate here is the array of one-sided operations by the patient which we are called upon to contain for their ruinous trajectories. I also want to emphasize that a single wrong step can bring them back into full force. This is well-known in alcoholism, and discussed acutely by Bateson (1971). Bateson emphasizes how vulnerable the alcoholic is to a single thought, such as, "I can control my drinking." This step sets him off on a binge of uncontrolled drinking. Conversely, the reverse first step, "I admit I am powerless before alcohol and have to depend upon a higher power," allows him not to fall for the temptation of his hubris, or fantasy of being on top of things like drinking.

I think the other common dynamics of compensation have the same kind of bifurcation between a disastrous first step which cannot be controlled and a sound first step which will contain the compensatory run to ruin. I described them at length in my previous book, *The Common Dynamics of Psychiatry* (1999), and I will outline them here with an eye to how we may best contain them. It is a paradox that many patients prefer to keep their compensations as a distraction from true distress, while others are able to give them up and face their anxiety and depression as signals of what is wrong.

The Common Dynamics of Psychiatry

In the mid-1970s, when psychoanalysis retained a theoretical hold on psychiatry, we would divide pathology into neurotic and psychotic, or minor and major, with a borderline group between them. I still think this pattern is highly orienting (Gabbard, 1994) for what we need to be ready for, if we want to contain these rampant compensatory processes.

Minor Pathology

The minor or neurotic defenses fall into four patterns: hysterical, or histrionic as we now call it, avoidant, obsessive-compulsive, and perverse.

Histrionic   Histrionic defenses invent a drama as a diversion, and, indeed, the root word here is *histrio-*, Latin for actor. The diverting drama can be interpersonal, such as throwing a tantrum, or more somatic, such as getting numb feet. It can be an exaggeration, or an absence. It can have elements of both, such as in Freud's (1895) case of Lucy (Breuer & Freud, 1893–1895/1975), who complained of the smell of burnt pudding, and of an inability to smell anything else. This was a somatizing complaint, as we like to say, but it operated powerfully upon her boss with whom she was in love. Thus it was both somatic and interpersonal in its force. Once such a move is successful in organizing its little theater free of anxiety and depression, by distraction as dissociation, and in compelling the household and the doctor to come pay attention, it may be very difficult to stop. The ingenious step runs away with the show, as happened with several of the other cases in *Studies on Hysteria* (Breuer & Freud, 1893–1895), namely Anna A and Frau Emmy. These used to be called primary and secondary gains; primary to reduce unbearable signals, and secondary to recruit advantages with other people. Indeed, the containment of histrionic maneuvers still turns on recognizing the two gains: seeing what anxiety or depression became unbearable, and seeing what advantages have been recruited by the histrionics. The reader may refer to my case of "Basilar Artery Migraine," for a carefully studied version (Gustafson, 1995b, 1999). The recognition of the unbearable feeling the patient is running from helps her to bear and contain it more simply, and the recognition of the recruitment of the household and of doctors helps to minimize these advantages by not playing into them and thus not reinforcing them. The aim, as Balint (1968) put it, is to allow regression in the service of recognition, which tends to quiet things down when the patient is understood, and to disallow regression in the service of gratification, which tends to heat things up and make them increasingly demanding with every gratification. The first is a benign regression, and the second is a malignant regression (Balint, 1968), and there are often elements of both, if the doctor allows him- or herself to meet special demands, such as for excessive phone calls, sessions, or drugs.

Avoidance   I will be simpler with the subsequent defenses, because they have a similar way of taking off from a discovery by the patient that they reduce unbearable anxiety or depression, and recruit gratifications with the household or the office or with doctors. Avoidance is dissociation by avoiding the situation which arouses the anxiety or depression. In this way, it is even simpler than histrionics, which avoids *and* distracts. It has a similar career once it proves successful, just as histrionics proves successful. My favorite case of malignant avoidance is *Bartleby the Scrivener*, by Melville (1853/1986; discussed in Gustafson, 1992). Bartleby discovered the enormous power of a single phrase, "I prefer not to." Our cast of avoiders simply follows his first step. Of course, we don't have to go along with it. A simple step against "I prefer not to" is what I always pose to these patients as evenly as possible: "If you want out of this, you will have to expose yourself to what you fear." That is *the* treatment of avoidance, namely, exposure therapy (Marks, 1987). In the meanwhile, we *contain* it by not rewarding its power over us, and leaving the responsibility for facing it to the patient, if he chooses. At least we do not make it worse, which is a kind of containment.

Obsessive-Compulsiveness   Obsessions are worries, such as, "What if I took up that knife?" Compulsions are distractions, such as "I will wash my hands." Some patients have just the worries. Every detail becomes an occasion to worry about the bad outcome. Paradoxically, the worrying process reduces the terror, by keeping the patient so busy with the details, so that like Hamlet (Shakespeare, 1604/1969b), he can lose track of the action. Thus, either the compulsive ritual and the worry ritual sidetrack the patient from the terror.

On the other hand, either ritual, of thought or of action, once discovered as a distraction can proceed to take over more and more of the patient's life. Therefore, we are called upon to help contain it. Containment works the same way, as with avoidance or histrionics, namely, by exposure to what is painful if you cease worrying or distracting, and by reducing the reinforcement of dragging other people into it.

Perverse Relatedness   Perversity entered the literature of neurosis through Freud's (1913/1975d) discussion of perversion. By perversion, Freud meant the use of a part-object, such as fetish toward a foot, for the whole sexual object. The detour avoids the anxiety, and despair, of the patient's failed attempt at a relationship between whole persons, by substituting an object that can be *manipulated* to release orgasm.

Ironically, this "technique" has been generalized by advertising to discover an entire culture of gratification by objects in place of relations between whole persons. The consumer is back in "control" of his or her own gratification by fantasy, using an endless array of material objects as part-objects.

Even more ironically, this "technique" can be utilized in a nonsexual way as "control" of the object by one's own agenda, at the expense of the other's agenda. Isn't that what histrionics forces upon the spouse or the doctor? Or obsessions? Or avoidance? In this precise sense, all secondary gain is a kind of a me first, at the *expense* of the object, which is what Freud meant by secondary gain.

All of our patients practice it *heavily*. Having had a bad day, they will be histrionic, avoidant, obsessive, or worse, which we shall get to next, and make their partner pay for it, or their children, or whomever is available! Thus, they are compensated for their suffering, and forget their anxiety and despair. If the television has not supplied enough perversity of satisfaction, this will supply the remainder.

Containment of this rampant compensatory process is impossible, in a culture of entertainment as distraction (Postman, 1985), devoted to little else. Our doctors recommend it to the patients, for they also recommend it to themselves. As for the interpersonal aspect of perversity, I cannot think of a single one of our patients who is not involved in a perverse relationship, in which each party takes turns inflicting punishment upon the other. If it isn't with the spouse, it is with the children, or the parents, or the extended family, or with all of the above. Someone is always suffering at someone else's expense. It is true that we can sometimes reduce this *punishing process* in individual, couples, and family therapy, but it is very difficult work and takes us into the next three sections of this book.

Just to contain it, and not let it take up more of the patient's life, is quite a trick. Yesterday, I saw a patient with a resident, who was the object of continual tirades by her husband as soon as he got home from work, all evening, all weekend, and so on. She couldn't leave him and support herself and her children. I just said, "Well, can you go out the door for a break?" "No," she said, "He follows me!" "What," I said, "if you go to the neighbors?" She admitted he wouldn't want to be seen doing it!

Borderline Pathology

There is truly a continuum between neurotic and psychotic, minor and major compensations. As Sullivan (1956) described so well, histrionics slides into the borderline in grand hysteria, avoidance into schizophrenia in the in-the-corner lifestyle, and obsessive-compulsiveness slides into paranoia. However, there are three lines of defense that are borderline from the start, that is, verging on psychosis, namely, alcohol and drug dependence, narcissistic and antisocial operations, and borderline personality maneuvers. That is because they not only avoid and distract from the pressure of reality, they attack it head on, and attempt to destroy it. This is the cardinal characteristic of psychosis, the literal and symbolic attack of reality per se (Bion, 1967). However, as Bion argued, psychosis is never 100%. There are all degrees of it, and hence this borderline region.

Alcohol and Drug Dependence   Alcohol and drug dependence attacks reality by substituting an intoxicated state for it. Of course, a certain amount of this is nearly universal. It is the day in and day out substitution of intoxication for reality that we are talking about.

The gist of it is very primitive, as Bateson (1971) explained with a beautiful logic. If the patient has made himself impossibly tense with willing himself into a narrow life, the potion releases him from will and lets down his tension. If he is not to continue this, he needs a different way to let down his will, which Alcoholics Anonymous (AA) provides by endless confession.

Narcissistic and Antisocial Operations   Here is another crude attack on reality by a different means, namely, taking revenge. Indeed, as Winnicott (1971) showed, every child does it when hurt, by forcing compensation, stealing, or setting fires. Narcissism is just a subtler version, by forcing tribute, admiration, attention. As Winnicott (1971) argued, the containment is simple, and well-known to every good parent. First, put your foot down to stop its momentum, and get the child out of securing advantages by revenge, as in tantrums, and then seek to understand the hurt that drove it. Usually, the thing is attempted in reverse order, and this makes it infinitely worse, by intermittent reinforcement, and fills up our child psychiatry clinics with little else. Containment of antisocial and narcissistic claims in adults works in exactly the same way: some blocking of its success, sometimes by the police, and then reaching to the pain that drives it.

Borderline Personality Maneuvers   This is, perhaps, the crudest thing known to man or woman, for destroying reality: threaten to kill yourself, or hurt yourself, and everyone will come running. It works so well that it represents half of our on-call system, and half of our hospitalizations. Linehan (1993) figured out the countermeasure: Don't give in to it, teach a different trick for getting attention, besides self-destruction. Enlist a network, or list, of other things to do.

Major Pathology

There are three defenses even more primitive than the three in the borderline region, namely, negative therapeutic reaction, mania, and psychosis itself.

Negative Therapeutic Reaction   This one is really terrible. Every success turns into catastrophe. Nothing is more powerful for destroying the morale of a doctor, for his or her best turns out worst! Why? Because of guilt. The patient cannot allow himself to succeed. It is tantamount to killing someone, like his father. Freud had it himself, and couldn't go to Rome, because that was admitting he had surpassed his father like Hannibal conquering the Eternal City (Freud, 1900/1975a). Its containment is relatively simple: tell the patient not to succeed, or, at least, limit it. Thus, Freud denied himself his satisfaction as conqueror. Of course, our patients must deny themselves infinitely more, being greater prisoners of guilt.

Mania   This one is fight-or-flight from depression. It is very difficult to contain, because its euphoria is release from misery. We try to contain it anyway, with the hospital and drugs, before it destroys the patient or his relations. Often, it eats up every dollar, every connection, every advantage. There is little use talking with it, when it is so powerful. Generally, the patient agrees to be curbed *only after* he has done a lot of harm to his milieu. This is like "hitting bottom" in alcoholism. Things are so bad he may finally admit his destructiveness, and take our drugs.

Psychosis   This is the final act of desperation against reality. Invent yourself as a god, pursued by demons. Of course, you do not do it consciously. It erupts from the unconscious so long deprived of any grandeur (Gustafson, 1967, 1999). Thus, it comes naturally to those who have no means left (Havens, 2000).

You can't argue with a god, except to tell him he might want to sleep a little and be less tormented by the demons. However, your very offer leads him to think you must be a demon yourself trying to come near him. Therefore, it is essential to keep your distance and your offers as simple as possible. "Would he like something to help him sleep? Would she like something to reduce her anxiety? Would he or she feel safer in the hospital?"

In Summary: The Logic of a Containing Step

Of course, there is a great deal more to say about any of these topics. Books have been written on each one. My reason for going through them rapidly is to show you how the logic of containment is a constant. This logic comes through in that any particular defense is a variation of containment and is the pattern that connects them (Bateson, 1972).

Thus, I propose to save the reader a great deal of time in learning about containment of compensatory forces. Always, it is a matter of reducing the anxiety or depression that drives them, and reducing the reinforcement that selects an advantage for them in the patient's milieu. If the reader would like to pursue any one topic in further depth, he or she may turn to Sullivan's (1956) *Clinical Studies in Psychiatry* or my *Common Dynamics of Psychiatry* (1999). It is a timeless subject, in the sense that 50 years has changed nothing in how they work their temporary advantages for the patient, while tending to swallow up his life. Sullivan is considered out of date, but he is absolutely not in his astute management of these runaway dynamics of compensation. It is a lost art that I am trying to bring back. Our residents are fascinated by it.

Finally, closing this chapter, I will give you what is called a "Mock Board Exam" in our business of psychiatry to show you the failure of imagination that is routine in our best residents because of their training. This is my central point in this chapter. You cannot contain a desperate condition if you can't imagine how bad it is. If you underestimate it, then it will have the upper hand, and will shock you because you are unready for its actual power. A "Mock Board Exam" in psychiatry is a training exercise to simulate an actual "Board Exam" that qualifies a psychiatrist for his or her specialty. The "Board" is the American Board of Psychiatry and Neurology. The routine is a strict half-hour interview of an actual patient by the resident, followed by a half-hour divided between the resident's presentation of his or her findings, diagnosis, and treatment and a cross-examination of this presentation by the faculty psychiatrist.

A Mock Board Exam of Psychiatry

The patient for this exam was an attractive and intelligent woman of about 40, married, with five children, a relatively unusual case on our inpatient service, because she looked so well, and had so many social advantages. Of course, this too leads to dangers, when the surface persona and the depths are out of joint. The interviewer is apt to be taken by the surface and never get into the shadow side that got her hospitalized. That is indeed what happened in this interview, yet I do not think any of our other residents would have done any better. The resident being examined asked all the right questions, but that is not a sufficient procedure.

Essentially, the tale that he got was that she had been hospitalized three times in 3 months, two for cutting, and the third with us for a suicide attempt. He even learned that she had a long period of stability of about 20 years, preceded by a stormy adolescence. At that time, she had confided a sexual abuse from her stepfather. She had become anorexic and bulimic, and she took many street drugs, including psychedelics, cocaine, and marijuana. Somehow, she managed to marry a very stable guy, and have five children doing well, or so it appeared. All of this came apart when they decided 6 months ago there would be no more kids and no more moves to new houses.

I was impressed with the clarity of this history, so far. Of course, now I would get to see how he zeroed in on the relevant dangers, which needed to be contained. Of course, our interviewer asked a few questions about the suicide attempt. What he found out was that she called her therapist saying she was about to take an overdose, and the therapist called the police, and the patient tried to take the overdose in front of them. From this vignette, the interviewer concluded that suicide was not a serious threat. It was obviously histrionic, for attention.

Next, he turned to the regression to cutting, and not eating, and binge-ing, in which she went back 25 years from age 40 to age 15. He learned that she also had fallen back into the memories of her sexual abuse. All of this followed from the fateful decision to stop having more children and buy-ing houses, and, generally, no longer staying very busy with this maternal project.

Essentially, he asked her a number of questions that showed his famil-iarity with posttraumatic stress disorder (PTSD), and elicited the usual findings of flashbacks, nightmares, startle responses, and hypervigilance, but a lack of agoraphobia. He also knew to ask about hallucinations, and delusions, to rule out psychosis. She only replied she had conversations in her head. This was dropped.

He finished up his half-hour exam with a mini-mental status exam, which was normal, and asked a couple of questions about her medical his-tory, which seemed to be nil.

The presentation was orderly, listing diagnoses on Axis I of eating dis-order, PTSD, major depression, and borderline personality disorder on Axis II. Treatment would continue the Zoloft and Seroquel, and include behavioral programs for each of the Axis I and II diagnoses, that is, for the eating disorder, PTSD, depression, and borderline personality disorder.

What Was Missing

My cross-examination of this interview and presentation was very simple in keeping to a single point, with several aspects. The dangers needing to be contained were suicide, borderline self-destruction, regression into PTSD, and possible psychosis. With respect to each of these dangers, we simply did not know how it stood with the patient. We did not know how dire any of these dangers actually got. Yes, the suicide attempt was orches-trated for her to be saved, but this hardly told us about her worst hours. Yes, she had PTSD, but what emotions had been aroused that were unbearable? Yes, she did not have the formal phenomena of psychosis, but how strange did things get?

Because these difficulties were not imagined by the resident, the patient remained a smiling, seductive lady, and never got disturbed so we could see what her disturbance was really about, and how far afield it took her. We could hardly manage without knowing these things, and yet this type of examination is what is routinely performed.

PART II

Selective Inattention Revised

The argument of part I of this book is the step of containment of anxiety, depression, and the compensatory defenses. One aspect of this argument is that patients tend to have little idea of how they make themselves anxious or depressed, or how they allow these two signals to become unbearable, and thus set off the compensatory defenses. In other words, they have *selective inattention* (Sullivan, 1956; Gustafson, 1986/1997a, chap. 6) *for where they are going.*

Now we consider how they take the step of revising their own selective inattention. This will help them from generating their own psychopathology, which is difficult to contain (part I). Also, this revision will open up all the other possibilities for going elsewhere (parts II, III, and IV)!

In other words, this next step is the one on which *pivots* the entire divide or bifurcation between psychopathology and well-being. This certainly was Sullivan's belief about selective inattention, and it is also mine borrowed from him (Havens, 1976/1993). Yet, I have also added something to Sullivan's belief. I have added that the *crucial thing missed* by typical patients is their *exchange* with the world. They will tend to ask only a little for their huge effort, and then feel wronged. Conversely, they will ask a great deal for their small effort and then feel wronged. Either way, it is a bad deal. As every further step repeats the first step, they will be increasingly in the wrong, until their anxiety erupts, or their depression collapses them. Finally, their defenses will be set off by this fiasco, and attempt to compensate them for being so badly received.

The reader will recall that Robert Louis Stevenson's famous character (1886/1985), Dr. Jekyll, is the main type who asks only a little for his huge effort. Once he has gone too far on this trajectory, he becomes very anxious and very depressed, and Mr. Hyde erupts out the back gate at midnight, unstoppable, and runs over anyone in his way and takes whatever he wants. Mr. Hyde has compensated Dr. Jekyll.

The reverse is the type who asks too much for his small effort, and gets those around him to feel, greatly, like putting him in his place. Usually, this means the patient has been hurt, and then allowed to be *spoiled* (Winnicott, 1971). This is the trajectory of all our patients who turn a defense into a way of life and thus put upon their spouses and children, their coworkers and doctors, and so forth. Thus, we discussed the minor, or neurotic, defenses like histrionics and avoidance, and obsessive–compulsiveness and perverse relatedness, which turn out to be quite a trial for those around the patient who must endure them! Then, we discussed the borderline defenses of alcohol and drug dependence, antisocial and narcissistic operations, and borderline personality maneuvers. These are obvious trials for those around the patient from the get go. Finally, we discussed the major or psychotic defenses which are violent attacks on reality via guilt or mania or psychosis, quite like those of Mr. Hyde.

This array of all of psychopathology in terms of being increasingly in the wrong about exchange begs a question. Why is this so? Why is the human being not able to pay attention to it, and so be self-correcting? Why is this apt, increasingly, to take over his or her entire existence?

Our clinic has hardly a case but this one case. Of course, there are a few exceptions that result from medical illnesses. Otherwise, our cases are a legion of humanity claiming either too little or too much for themselves with the world. Everything follows from being wrong in the first step of the claim, and it just runs away into a career. Why?

This is not a local aberration of our clinic. Look at any psychotherapy text like Wachtel's (1993) from New York City or Coren's (2001) from Oxford, England. Wachtel and Coren parade the same legion of humanity. They have the meek, and they have the proud (Coren, 2001, p. 23; Wachtel, 1993, pp. 20–21). Each patient sets off on the wrong first step (lack of claim or excessive claim) and ends up on a road to hell, while thinking he or she is heading in the right direction. The patient is not trying to repeat, yet he or she ends up repeating this trajectory.

Why is this pervasive? Wachtel (1993) argued that every piece of psychopathology goes around in vicious circles. The more gentle and giving and thus meek the patient, the more he or she will build up rage, and finally lose it (Wachtel, p. 20). The more proud and narcissistic and forcing the patient, the more he or she will build up doubt about being truly accepted (Wachtel, p. 21). Thus, either too little a claim or too much a claim will set off its opposite. This will shake the patient, and return him or her to starting over in the same way.

Wachtel also argues that the origin of the vicious cycle in childhood is important, but that once under way it is self-perpetuating as described, and also perpetuated by what he calls "accomplices" who feed it, such as the dominating who keep the meek in place, and the meek who provide the audience for the dominating. Thus, as Wachtel notes, his explanation is very much in the interpersonal tradition of psychoanalysis, while being very compatible with behaviorism and family therapy.

I don't disagree with Wachtel at all, but I would go farther. Biology is also important. As Werner (1989) and her colleagues (Werner & Smith, 1992, 1998) demonstrated in the only prospective, 40-year study of over 600 children from prenatal care, constitution also matters. Some children from very disturbed families (one-third of the study) sit in it and get worse, while some children from the same families go out the back door and find a better exchange for their gifts. The "sensitive dependence" of this first step, of acquiescence, or of going elsewhere, is absolutely profound over a 40-year follow-up! A million repetitions of the first step lead to a totally different trajectory, between terrible psychopathology and remarkable well-being.

Yet I would not leave the explanation there, with biology and with interpersonal dynamics. This leaves out the social or systemic dynamics that are probably even more powerful. Consider this, which Marx (1844/1975) held to be the center of capitalism. Actually, it is the center of any modern state, or any accumulation of power, which results in a hierarchy. Such hierarchies have run the world for 3,000 to 6,000 years (McNeill, 1963).

In any such dynamo, which tends to take over its neighbors, there is a profound inequality of exchange of labor from the top to the bottom. You can observe it in whatever department you are in. Those at the bottom put in long hours and get the least back. Those at the top may also put in long hours, but the *return* is 10 or 100 times greater. This is what Marx called the exchange rate of labor. It is profound in itself, but it does not stop there.

Those at the top of a hierarchy not only get a multiple of the exchange rate at the bottom, financially, but they also get it time wise, and esteem wise. Their time is more valuable by the minute, and their esteem is more valuable for exchange in all other realms, such as getting seated at a restaurant or selecting marital partners.

This too is why our patients make claims in line with their place in the hierarchy. They know their own exchange value, in this logic of the external grid. Indeed, their eyes tend to be on their place on this grid, alone.

This selects the claim they make, hugely, unless they have a constitution that is resolute and will ask for better, and unless they have a world elsewhere (Poirier, 1966/1985) that will validate such a counterclaim to the usual rule of the world.

Such individuation is not usual. The vast legions orient externally. They know their score. They heed their lessons. Freire (1970) called it a *Director Culture*. The term is apt: it means that human beings take direction, and ignore their own signals. They go into a "culture of silence" when directed. They lose their own internal grid of feeling (Gustafson, 1997, chap. 10), which could tell them something is going in a bad direction for them. They take their external rating as the truth about themselves. They seem to have little defense against it.

Indeed, the patients who most misread the exchange they are going to get are the ones who get in the most trouble. This is a disaster of selective inattention. Immediately, three patients come to mind who are absolutely typical. The first is a false self lady, whose exchange with the world is to sell real estate by crowing about it. The second is a minister whose righteousness is so great that his wife calls him "Planet Harry." The third is a lawyer who works 80 or 100 hours a week and is considered invaluable in his specialty, but has no other life. All of these people are inflated in their claims, by being able to promote themselves in one hierarchy or another, while being otherwise insufferable. Things are not going to go well for them.

Oddly, a little old lady who has almost no claim on the hierarchy of money but her Social Security, is going to do very well because she loves to walk and take in all of the glory of an early morning. She is rich in exchange on a daily basis.

That will serve for an introduction to our subject of reading exchanges, or the lack of it in selective inattention, and the profound consequences from getting the first step wrong. It is truly a biopsychosocial set of forces that brings about the misreading, so that it is nearly universal and pandemic in the modern world.

The three chapters of this subject divide as follows. Chapter 4 is about the possibility of schooling against a compensatory claim that is false. For example, we can school against avoidance, and it is the main thing we can do for that false claim. Chapter 5 is about backing up the history from an inflated idea of exchange, which only ends up badly deflated. Chapter 6 is about going forward to read exchanges that are coming, but distorted by hopes in work or in love that are often wrong.

CHAPTER **4**

Schooling against False Claims

To some extent it is possible to school some of our patients who compensate themselves with claims that will not hold up. For example, the famous schooling of alcoholics in Alcoholics Anonymous (AA) (Bateson, 1971) turns on the first step. "Try some controlled drinking," says AA, and the alcoholic tries and cannot limit it himself. "Instead," says AA, "admit you are helpless to control drinking, and turn yourself over to a Higher Power."

This is an extraordinary school, for its teaching is about a difference that makes all the difference (Bateson, 1972). Namely, it teaches one wrong step is perpetual hell, and one right step is salvation. Of course, clarity of this difference in a single step is difficult to arrive at and difficult to sustain. In the first place, the alcoholic may deny the failure of controlled drinking through countless disasters, until one is bad enough that he or she hits bottom. In the second place, the alcoholic may go through a period of sobriety and forget that he or she cannot control drinking and fall off the wagon of trust in a Higher Power. In the third place, the alcoholic may not be able to tolerate the dynamics of AA, with its endless confessional. The school itself may repulse the alcoholic.

The same limitations apply to all the other schoolings of the defenses. The patient may not be ready to admit failure of his claim. The patient may get it for a while and forget. The patient may not be able to stand the dogma or didactics of the school. When schooling works, the patient gives up a grandiose claim for a fairer and more equal exchange. Thus, in AA, he or she is no better than anyone else.

A Survey of Schooling

It is interesting *which* defenses lend themselves to didactic lessons. Among the minor or neurotic defenses, avoidance and obsessive-compulsiveness respond to exposure therapy (Marks, 1987). Among the borderline defenses, alcoholism responds to AA (Bateson, 1971), antisocial activities to jail (Winnicott, 1971), and borderline activities to dialectical behavior therapy (Linehan, 1993). Among the major or psychotic defenses, psychosis responds in its chronic phases to exposure therapy as well (White, 1989). By and large, OCD, bipolar II disorder, and schizophrenia act as if hard-wired and require drugs for containment plus community support programs.

What is the pattern that connects these successes? In general, out and out antisocial compensations will get worse and worse, until someone puts his or her foot down (Winnicott, 1971). The subtler defenses do not respond, because they take such a detour for their compensatory fantasy that it cannot be hunted down (Freud, 1915/1975f). Thus, histrionics is too elusive in its game of illness. Perversity is also a secret. Guilt is often a secret to the patient him- or herself. Mania, or fight-flight, runs so fast it cannot be caught up with. Thus, there are no classes against these compensations. It takes an astute doctor to track down their devious ways, or, as Freud (1915/1975f) put it, circumventions of repression.

I am not saying anything new about exposure therapy. It just works simply, against a simple avoidance, in the neurotic form, or against what White (1989) called the "in-the-corner lifestyle" of schizophrenia. We just cannot do without our behavior therapists and community support people to encourage these people out of their corners, but of course, they have to agree to leave their corners.

Similarly, we cannot do without AA or its equivalents for the replacement of drink with something else, namely, confession. Nor can we do without jails and other punishments for antisocials. Nor can we do without dialectical behavior therapy to school our borderlines in a replacement of self-destruction. We simply have to give all of these people attention, *against* their destruction, and *for* something else! Every psychiatry clinic is armed by assistants for these operations. It is a truism.

What is usually not said in the manuals for these schools is that the patients also resist them mightily, so they surreptitiously act like the patients with the subtler defenses. They are subtle with their simplicity. Our borderlines go to school for a while, and then they don't. Our avoiders face things a bit, and then they don't. And so forth. In other words, schooling looks a little better in the short run than it is in the long run. As Freud said, quoting an old Austrian wit, "Nothing is half so great as it first appears" (Breuer & Freud, 1893–1895/1975). The battle of schooling goes on incessantly in our clinic. It is difficult to keep our avoidant and anti-social patients in society, for it sorely limits their scope, and this is depressing. So, they are always disappearing on us, and resuming life in fantasy. In general, a "God" is likely to live on the edge of town, and not in the middle of the market (Jones, 1923/1951).

Schooling and Dilemmas

In the mid-1990s, I was invited to a tiny colloquium for a week on obsessive–compulsive disorder with about seven of the world's experts on the subject. I was to represent the psychodynamic perspective, while the seven others represented objective–descriptive psychiatry, in terms of behaviorism, like Isaac Marks, or in terms of psychopharmacology, like John Greist. Each of us had a turn to present a paper for discussion, which was to go into a book as the latest scientific knowledge on the subject. The book was never published, but the encounter was interesting, between the seven of them and myself. My paper (Gustafson, unpublished) was called "The Ecology of OCD," and it is still available from me. Theirs were about the well-known treatments of OCD, from exposure therapy to selective serotonin reuptake inhibitors (SSRI) to neurosurgical oblation.

My approach to them was as one biologist to another:

> What you see when you are looking at some phenomenon in biology depends profoundly on the lens you have available or which you prefer. For example, biologists with electron microscopes see organelles, while biologists with the naked eye see gross anatomy, while biologists with the extension of their eyes provided by their feet can see whole ecosystems. The lens creates a field with a certain grain and extent, while it obscures other fields. Thus, the electron microscope takes you inside the cell boundary, but closes you out from seeing objects larger than the cell. (Gustafson, unpublished, p. 1)

Essentially, to line up the argument of the whole paper, I told them that their biochemical and behavioral lens was entirely accurate: what you have in OCD is an incredible delay or distraction operation, tangled up in a million details. The only way to break it up is with a "null-function" (Selvini Palazzoli, 1980) which just *stops* what is going on in one broad stroke. It is like clearing out a garden overgrown rankly with weeds. Thus, exposure to anxiety and SSRI drugs allow something new to start over.

I proposed, however, that this biology looks very different when you have a lens to see the patient's relation to his or her milieu. Here you see that patients with obsessional difficulties are selected by a variety of composts, which bring about a brisk growth:

Delay as a form seems to be called out for countless uses (Gustafson, unpublished, p. 18). I cited the snugness of a meaningless rich life (Melville, 1853/1986), cold bureaucratic heartlessness (Tolstoy, 1886/1986), academic twittery (Carroll, 1865/1985), and the climate of being degraded or degrading someone else (Erikson, 1958). All of these milieus select a creature who will sit on the sidelines, and multiply distractions.

Of course, I was speaking to practical men, so I backed up the perspective provided by my social lens with citing the last six cases I consulted to on the inpatient service. They were patients caught up in dilemmas, who could not make up their minds, until they finally went crazy and had to be hospitalized, with extreme anxiety or depressive collapse, and classical obsessions and compulsions. A typical one was a man who worked 16 hours a day, and who, to please his wife, bought a grand old Victorian house that was falling apart from the roof to the basement. Now, he couldn't work less than 16 hours a day, but then he could make no progress on house repairs. You can imagine how the tension rose with his wife, and his sense of failure compounded daily.

Now, this *dilemma* would not go away with an SSRI, if the anxiety and depression were more contained, nor would exposure to the avoided repairs get him very far either. The repair of the bathtub drain would advance his cause with his wife, while 10 other things dear to her fell apart even as he knelt in the bathtub! His *trajectory* would be to get into more and more trouble, and the signals would try to signal this to him before he broke down. It was simply an untenable situation. This, I argued, was the typical situation between an obsessional patient and his social milieu; namely, a dilemma, in which he was unable to decide which way to go. He just perseverated on his list, and distracted himself with rituals.

I therefore proposed that facing dilemmas with the milieu was of absolute importance to a practical doctor. Immediately, after I finished my argument, there were no questions, and my colleagues literally turned their backs on me to resume conversations with each other that they were obviously more comfortable with.

I had run into another aspect of social biology, namely, that modern group life is made up of collections of specialists who are comfortable feeding each other details. Aristotle (336–322 BC/1991) was right: if you don't give them one more (n + 1) of their details, you are disqualified from the group. The group *literally* closed by turning their backs upon me. So, I was grateful for another lesson in social biology.

Dilemmas and Selective Inattention

So, here is a beautiful example of selective inattention (Sullivan, 1956, chap. 3). My colleagues were only going to look through the lens shared by their group, because their membership in the group depended upon this restriction. Similarly, my patient was going to look only through the lens of his wife, that he had to undertake a massive rebuilding of her Victorian house, in order to be accepted.

So caught up in his belonging, he did not even conceive of an opposition. He was caught up in the *lemma* or preliminary assumption of a proof that constructed her world of prodigious details. Thus, he missed the other *lemma* of his need to work 16 hours a day. The two projects were simply irreconcilable in a 24-hour day.

This is why I say that facing the *di-lemma* the patient is walking into is absolutely necessary. He will not see it as a whole (Gustafson, 1995a, 1995b). He will see his wife's world, and his own will disappear. He will see his own world, and his wife's will disappear. As Riemann (cited in Kaku, 1994, p. 36) argued about the bookworms on the crumpled sheet of paper, the great forces build up where the paper is crumpled. On one side of the crumple, you cannot even imagine there is another side to what you are looking at. Now, that is an adequate picture of why selective inattention is a pandemic among patients in Flatland (Abbott, 1884/1984).

That is because almost all of them are engaged in building a niche for themselves in a profession that is like my colleagues at the colloquium; namely, a huge and prodigious buildup of details on a very specialized subject. This *lemma* or preliminary assumption for constructing a professional world will block out every other consideration which originates in other worlds, like those of their wives or children. Naturally, trouble will build up, and erupt, or collapse them.

The Routine Simplicity of Seeing the Dilemma the Patient Is Walking into, and Has Selective Inattention for

So, this is my problem with schooling against a defense like avoidance or schizophrenia. It is useful to get the patient *out* of the corner, but he misses everything he runs *into*. As usual, the prepositions tell the story of motion on a surface the patient cannot imagine. It will get him *out,* but what will he collide *with*? Allow me a few examples of a prolific host I might offer. In one of my books on dilemmas (1995a, p. 348), I counted 48 terms in the English language for different nuances of dilemma. Like the Eskimos with nuances of snow, we have got to reckon with our milieu. I will take you on a very short tour of the inpatient service on a Sunday, and the outpatient clinic on a Monday.

I had to make rounds on our inpatient service last Sunday and saw about 15 patients, two of whom actually wanted to talk with me, which took 5 minutes each, very brief psychotherapy. The first was a very astute lady of about 85, who began asking me if I knew anything about measles? Now, that was odd. I said I really didn't, but what prompted her to ask? Well, her daughter had had a terrible rash and died 10 years ago of the measles. She began to cry. How terrible it is to die after your own child. Immediately, she pointed to a painting by Renoir she had hung in her room, of a man admiring a woman. I said, "Isn't it beautiful, and notice there is a double in the background of the same admiration of a man for a woman!" "Oh," she said, "I never noticed that." Well, that was enough for her. She had her grief, and she had her beauty. The world of the first was too much for her, and the world of the second saved her. Such was her di-lemma.

The second patient was a young man about 30, who had never caught on in life, and had a considerable drinking problem. I asked him if he wanted to talk about anything? He said he was thinking about a wedding he was scheduled to go to soon, but might not because his nasty brother would be there. I said, "What is your inclination?" He replied, "I'd like to go. I think I will call my father and ask if my brother is going too. If he is going too, I will still go, and yet keep my distance from him." He thanked me, and left. The nurse present said to me, "Is that all? I can't believe it." I replied that he got some company with his dilemma, and that was all he needed to figure it out himself.

On to the clinic on Monday, where a schizophrenic patient was being encouraged to go to the community support house and put up with the anxiety (exposure therapy). That was okay with him. What bothered him was a female patient there who wanted him to go to a movie. He was avoiding her, and feeling terrible. Yet, he didn't want to feel trapped with her in a movie house as in a terrible machine. Such was his di-lemma. Well, it never occurred to him that there was any other possibility, between yes to her offer, and no to her offer (Anthony, 1976). So I said, "Well, what if you proposed to do something else with her?" "Oh yes," he said, "I can just invite her over to my apartment where I am more comfortable." So, that is all it took for him to figure it out himself. Yet, you would have to understand the endless array of dilemmas to be ready for this quick step of very brief psychotherapy. The patient would never think of it.

Now for a final note on a series of patients of my own on a Monday afternoon for a further window into this routine simplicity of dilemmas which are missed. The first did not understand why his wife and daughter endlessly connived to take advantage of him, and of his money. The second did not understand why her reasonable suggestions got her assaulted in her bureaucracy. The third did not understand why a very attractive man with a Renaissance array of interests kept her at arm's length from a sexual relationship. The fourth did not understand why his career as an assistant professor just under way might get in trouble if he put his foot down on a grant to be the principal investigator, and set aside his mentor? It is simple routine that patients, and persons in general, see only half of the world, the half they want, or the half others want. *They need you to see the two halves together, so they can decide what to conserve, and what to give up.* Human beings are ill equipped to do this for themselves, making a mess of it in general.

Often the patient comes unprepared to face any of this and just wants drugs to feel better. This isn't necessarily bad. As Pies argues (Pies & Gustafson, 2004), feeling better may allow the patient to face his dilemmas later, when he is less overwhelmed.

THE CASE OF A DOLL'S HOUSE, OR A LIFE LIE

Here is a very simple case which I consulted to in my Brief Psychotherapy Clinic concerning avoidance, for which nonavoidance, or exposure schooling, would not suffice. It is so simple, and yet too much for a didactic approach. The patient was already dying of didacticism, as was the case with Nora, the wife in Ibsen's play *A Doll House* (1879/1961).

Her staff therapist had spent a year and a half with her on her missing identity. She was like a doll in a correct marriage, while having flings by night with men she met as a waitress. The question was "How is she to have a satisfying relationship?"

So, I said to her, "You have a dilemma." She replied that she could not stay faithful in this marriage because it was boring, but she could not leave either because she couldn't make it on her own emotionally or financially. Even more desperately, she could not support her 2-year-old son and he would get an attachment disorder like hers. (Here she put a fist to her head, in the most drastic version of self-accusation, or guilt, of Gustafson's sign. The gesture is quite unconscious and consists of one or more fingers pointed at the head [Gustafson, 1992, 1995a, 1995b, 1999]). Also, she might only end up molding herself to new men, in the endless cycle of mating.

Here I was actually relieved. I had been expecting only a person playing a part, wearing a mask, and yet here she was, so real. So I was quite direct myself. I said, "Well, you mold yourself to everybody, and you eventually erupt out the back door. Why not be more disagreeable sooner?" This made her laugh with relief.

But back she came to her husband, saying, "I don't need him as a father." "Yes," I answered, "but how are you going to be a different person who doesn't go along with such things?" "Oh," she said, "the initial anxiety is so great I have to please them." "Oh," I said, "you are an Irish politician." This made her laugh again. "So," I said, "how are you going to handle the anxiety of not being agreeable?"

"You know," she said, "the second meeting with a person is worse than the first. I charm them in the first, and I have to fulfill the promise in the second." Here, her therapist put in, very cogently, that her real mom died when she was an infant, and her dad spent nearly 2 years looking for a new mom, and so she got passed around, on trial, as it were, so her anxiety to please made a lot of sense.

She volunteered, "His (her father's) mom finally took me." Her therapist countered, "It was weird for her being passed around." She answered, "My father's new wife took him away, and wouldn't have me." Here, she took her marriage ring on and off, unconsciously. So, I put in, "You *did* connect, but you had great anxiety about being accepted."

All right, I thought, it all makes sense, but what is she willing to do about it? I asked her, "You are in the old story, being *agreeable* to be *adopted*, but what now?" She answered that she had some capacity to disagree, telling a girlfriend she was full of crap. I felt it was time to drop into a dream if she could. She had a very simple one. She left her husband, and couldn't come back, because he was with someone else. She met another man, like her first boyfriend who was not kind. I asked her about him. She told me he was mean to her in public, but this gave her an out. She could always leave. Here she was gleeful.

She went on from here to tell me about why she likes her second job as a massage therapist. She especially likes the tough truck drivers. She can have fun, and not get attached. The second sessions with them are excruciating, because she fears she can't keep up the pleasing. I said, "It might be interesting with your therapist to miss an appointment on purpose to screw up, and see if she can tolerate it." Here, she laughed and laughed, the hardest of all.

We were coming to an end, so I said, "Tell me something bad about you so I can reject you." She said, "I feel very bad I didn't make my sister-in-law the godmother of my child." Here, she got very nervous with her hands on the cord of her microphone (of attachment). "She ended the relationship right there!" "So," I replied, "you exploded the situation right there." "Yes," she answered, "I'm glad. I can't stand the perfect little wife."

It was time for a final remark due from me, as Winnicott (1971) used to put it. I said, "The perfect little Madonna is a setup for rebellion." I told her about Nora in Ibsen's play. She answered, "Do you have to create a tragedy to have an end with somebody?" *Now, that went to the heart of the matter.* So I replied, "Maybe you could lower yourself more intelligently? I think you have a sense of fun." Fostering her sense of humor, I added, "I'll think of someone who has too high an idea of me so I can lower it." She answered, "I have a shocking sense of humor!" And so we left it there, but for my letter, which ran as follows:

> We addressed two questions. The first was how to have satisfying long-term relationships. The answer is straightforward but difficult. You have to avoid the step of molding yourself to give the other what he or she has in mind, but rather be willing to let them know things about you that are different or even disagreeable and bear the anxiety that they might not adopt you. You could think of it as a test of them!
>
> Otherwise, you get into a life lie, as Ibsen would put it, which can only erupt, sooner or later, into a rebellion that gets you punished or dropped.
>
> Paradoxically, you might get stronger by practicing blunders to test people. It is terrible to be in too high a position, in terror of being found out to be lower. Actually, you have found it a relief to be lower, for there is no farther to go! Indeed, that is why you like mean men, for you have an excuse to get out of being trapped. How happy you were to know you could get rid of me in an hour!
>
> The second question is the dilemma of your marriage, which, *for now*, is insoluble. You'll act out in rebellion of living in the doll's house, but you are likely to be in greater danger of throwing yourself to the wind, and your son with you. I would be for leaving this dilemma alone, for now, until you get much farther along on the first question of being a real person, consistently.

A Final Note on the Case of a Doll's House or a Life Lie

The patient went against my advice on her dilemma, and left her husband, yet I saw her soon after at the couple's therapist down the hall, and I do not know the outcome. The point is whether there is something between yes and no, as E. J. Anthony (1976) put it as being the dilemma of all adolescents. I would be glad if she didn't have to live as a doll in a doll's house, or if she didn't have to live with mean men to feel free to be herself. Thus, pure yes is bad, and pure no is bad, and something between is my hope for her. That is not something to be didactic about, but something for her to play with, being herself, and yet being adopted after all.

CHAPTER 5
Backing Up the History from Disaster

Sullivan (1954) was one who found that getting the history straight was itself the treatment.

> Thus, we try to proceed along the general lines of getting some notion of what stands in the way of successful living for the person, quite certain that if we can clear away the obstacles, everything else *will take care of itself.* So true is that, that in well over twenty-five years.... I have never found myself called upon to "cure" anybody. *The patients took care of that, once I had done the necessary brush-clearing, and so on....* The brute fact is that man is so extraordinarily adaptive that, given any chance of making a reasonably adequate analysis of the situation, he is quite likely to stumble into a series of experiments which will gradually approximate more successful living (pp. 238–239; emphasis added).

Yet, he will usually not do this adaptive thing without help. Why not? The next paragraph explains it as follows:

> There are a great many things that cannot be changed quickly, simply because the anxiety which the patient undergoes in presenting the relevant facts is so great, and because nothing can be learned by him until that anxiety is lessened. In other words, a person must feel fairly safe in order to make use of anywhere near 100 percent of his abilities. *If he feels extremely insecure, he will be unable to present adequately the simplest propositions, and unable to benefit from its discussion* (Sullivan, 1954, p. 238; emphasis added).

55

Very anxious patients cannot and will not bring the simplest of histories into focus, because it takes away their security operation which allows them to function at all. So, they keep things in a fog, and do not learn anything about their trajectory to misery (Sullivan, 1956, chap. 3). So how is the patient to become secure enough to see the simple thing he or she is doing wrong? Probably, it takes a borrowing from the therapist of a perspective that there is another way to do things. As Prochaska and colleagues (Prochaska, DiClemente, & Norcross, 1992; Prochaska & Norcross, 2001) have demonstrated, there can be a long delay before this happens. They show the previous stages of precontemplation, contemplation, and preparation, before action, and a stage of maintenance after action. Before action is a gradual admission of having things wrong, and after action is an admission of slipping back into having things wrong. Ancient assumptions may loosen very slowly. That was Balint's (1952) argument about the paranoid and depressive positions and Reich's (1949) about encrusted character armor.

It seems to me that all of this is correct, but that it is more abstract than necessary. It seems to me that the anxiety discussed by Sullivan, and the covering up described by Sullivan, and the gradual admission of these things described by Prochaska and colleagues, has to do with the specific matter of exchange. Our patients have got their exchange, both in work and in love, screwed up. That, in turn, always goes back to childhood, as argued so clearly by Malan (1976, 1979). On the other hand, this fundamental misstep in exchange is always played upon the current realities of what it means to work and what it means to have a relationship of love. If the therapist lacks an adequate idea of how to deal equably in work and love, in our modern circumstances, the patient is going to have a terrible time catching on to something sensible. Let us be entirely specific with two cases that are typical in our clinic.

The Case of the Antihero in a Vacuum

The dynamics of this case are simple avoidance. An assistant professor is simply not doing his work. Thus, he is in danger, eventually, of being caught up with. That was why he was presented to me a year ago. I considered it a disaster in the making and looked to see how we could back up from where it was going. The most remarkable finding to me was not the avoidance. After watching my peers at Harvard College and Harvard Medical School wait until Thanksgiving to start working, I knew all about it. It is commonplace.

What interested me about this man was his delight in being found out. After about a half-hour of our consultation, he said, "My whole worth is in being an academic, so this is going to be a spectacular defeat." I replied that he was surely blowing it up. He laughed for the first time, and said, "I must be a drama queen." I agreed it was self-sabotage, dropping the queen part. He said, "So I am autosaboteur!" I said, "You are lucky to come to this clinic. This clinic is all self-sabotage!" I said it always led to depression. He said, "Really! We sit on the precipice of a revelation."

The second half-hour concerned the specifics of how he arranged to fail. Essentially, he foundered without deadlines. The game was, "I'll do it later." The history behind the game was that he was the most talented student probably ever seen in his small town. Unfortunately, this led to a neglect of him, a kind of structureless existence. This history explained his delight in being found out. As he commented, "Everyone needs approval." I commented, "You can't blame a dog for lying on its back winning the world record of his small town."

But what to do about it? Did he have to walk into this vacuum of being all on his own as an assistant professor? It seemed a setup to fail. Backing up from this outcome, I asked him about graduate school and found out that his professor had met with him every day to set his agenda. It worked marvelously so why not do it again? If this university did not supply it, why not arrange for it to be supplied? My letter to him summarized our discussion as follows:

> Dr. _____ and you ask me the same question. What is the mechanism of this self-sabotage, which leads to dark days in history as in 1999, and as the trajectory is leading again even now?
>
> As I said to you, it is always everywhere the same (scalar invariance as chaos theory puts it), and we could start anywhere and find the same thing. This seemed to cheer you up right away, and show us some of your buoyancy of spirit, that this drama could be elucidated as well as its antihero!
>
> So, you chose to start with the present, and 400 days in a row are always the same futility, and trying to get back to the paper only turns into distracting yourself and even lying on the floor of your office! Why? What the _____ is going on the same every day?
>
> Very simply, your slight motivation to work at your research on your own collapses. By yourself, you cannot make yourself do it. Or vice versa, you need somebody to set you tasks every day, as your advisor did for you to get you out of black futility in finishing your thesis. Otherwise, the dog gives up and regresses, almost to a fetal position.
>
> Of course, it is an old story that goes back to your childhood, as the sixth child of a meatpacker and his wife with little attention left

for their sixth, and even less for academic matters. This was especially so for a boy who won all the records in academics in his little town without even trying. So, he never got attention to help him develop discipline, by parents putting their foot down, so he could learn to do it for himself.

So, here we have the Archimedean standpoint after all on your history: why it cycles endlessly when you are alone with it, and why it gets somewhere when you get firm attention to deadlines from the outside.

So, what to do with this clarity on the history (bifurcation, as we say in mathematics)? One step leads by endless repetition of its futility straight into black hell.

Nearly a year later, a colleague was away and I happened to be the attending in the regular clinic of his resident doctor. I had hardly seen the patient since our consultation. He seemed very glad to see me. I asked why? He said it was because I had recognized the tragedy of where he was going. And what had happened? Not very much. He was getting by, but had so many projects getting farther and farther behind, that he just wanted to leave town and start over somewhere else.

I told him I was just finishing a book, namely, this one, which concerned the determination of forces by the geometry or folding of a sheet of a paper, as argued by Riemann (cited in Kaku, 1994). I showed him his own case, of a simple bifurcation of the paper between his present vacuum, and his previous fertility. "Oh," he said, "you mean basins of attraction!" I agreed that was it.

But he really lacked an Archimedean standpoint as he had put it in the consultation. Archimedes had half-joked that he could lift the entire world with his levers. Our patient could discuss the two regions separated by a bifurcation beautifully, but lacked the standpoint to lever himself into the previous region. I agreed. I arranged for him to see one of our behavioral coaches. She might not meet with him everyday like his old mentor, but she might be able to set up the structure to put him back into the previous basin which was so constructive for him, in contrast to the present basin which is so destructive for him. This clarity about the history had been neglected for a year, and now maybe it was going to be taken seriously.

An Opposite Case of Service

A typical tale of a patient of ours in the reverse error has gone like this. Instead of avoiding, he pours out effort.

His childhood is only slightly better known to us than the last patient. Both parents worked as scientists. Our patient was expected to do well in school, which he mostly did. This was under considerable pressure, however, as his mother talked of him as a future president! Instead of making this great claim on the world his own, he lived in dread of failure. He worried ceaselessly just about keeping up.

Both work and love have been plagued by this positioning. In love, he has had three long relationships. The first two ended in his being left for another man. The third, which we have followed along with him for several years is with a woman who has severe medical problems.

He seems to work very hard to help her out, but he seems, also, to be unable to object to anything with her. She gets defensive, quickly, and he falls silent. Recently, he has had fantasies of another woman, and become suicidal over them. When we discussed this fantasy as a natural compensation for his mounting frustration, he replied that he could not afford such fantasy as it had contributed to the explosion of one of his previous relationships.

Work seems to go a little better, but he is ceaselessly worried about it too. He was fired from two previous jobs in which he thought he had provided good work. In the present job, he survives nervously, and especially when the boss calls on him to organize special projects which seem impossible to carry out. The dilemma feels terrible, as with the present girlfriend: He tries to do the impossible as asked by the boss, and is ready to be discarded, or he tells him frankly that the thing cannot be done, and is ready to be dismissed at once. With our help, he was able to decide what to do in such a dilemma, and he decided to tell the boss that the project could not be done. He preferred to be executed now, rather than to put in a false claim, and be executed later. To his surprise, his professional opinion was accepted, and he was relieved.

However, the entire case runs on nervously for all concerned. A failure of either the relationship or the job could be fatal. Both are posed as last chances by him. He either proves his worth on these two projects of work and love, respectively, or he is finished.

Of course, we have told him that we cannot proceed on the knife's edge. He needs to be responsible to let us know if things are feeling perilous again. He is reluctant to agree to this and give up his exit from life when he feels he has to take it, and when he fears we might force the hospital upon him. Cautiously, we have agreed that we are willing to negotiate an alternative in such situations when it is possible.

The danger runs on, but, at least, we are *oriented* to a way out of it, and we convey this to him, and he becomes a little better about what he agrees to. He is prevailingly vulnerable to attempting too much in the way of service, which is what Malan (1979) called the helping profession syndrome. This builds up rage, which terrifies him, and is turned into suicidal ideation. So, we are continually pointing to an exchange with the company or girlfriend which is more equable. As Malan argued, this is usually easier for such patients to negotiate at work, because it is less personal, and so it goes (Vonnegut, 1969) with this patient. The personal version at home is more fraught with fear, and so he tends to keep up his security operation there of trying harder.

When Revising Selective Inattention Comes Much Quicker

I have deliberately provided two cases which are taking years to revise selective inattention about the claim of the first step, for Sullivan was right about profound insecurity. When all you have got is an illusory idea about dealing with the world, what, after all, are you going to put in its place?

Yet there are patients who are quite the opposite and quick to make a turn to a different claim on the world. It is interesting how befuddled they can be on their own, and seem totally lost.

The Case of the Missing Kangaroo

This young woman of about 30 was seen in our regular outpatient clinic by a resident and myself in an intake evaluation for having no motivation. She seemed half asleep, and yet her eyes betrayed a considerable alertness. I could see how quickly they looked in different directions as into different worlds. She had no evident psychopathology, and she was pleasant enough. She just wasn't all there. The resident thought she had attention deficit disorder. I guessed she was a kind of sleeper, with a lot of potential, and proposed we take an hour in my Brief Psychotherapy Clinic to consider her situation in more depth. She readily agreed. So we began our hour. The resident presented her as a person having difficulty paying attention and as a person with a certain anger. "Who cares?" seemed to be her motto. When I asked her what she wanted from my consultation, she said, "Make me happy!"

I liked this challenge from her, and replied, "Well, fine, let us see, first, what makes you unhappy!" Quickly, she took me back to her family of origin. Her parents seemed to get along, but suddenly divorced when she was 14. She went to live with her father and his parents. Her reaction? None.

So, it was all a great mystery, her childhood, and her adulthood of lethargy. I said, "Let's see when you are happy." She replied, "I get up fine every morning." Now that was astonishing. "So, what happens?" She answered in the most precise English I have ever heard, "I am *spoken to* at work, and then I feel stupid, and then I go blank." She explained that this meant she got criticized at work in her secretarial position, and she could find no way to defend herself.

"Oh," I said, "You always put your tail between your legs?" "No," she said. "At home, I would never cower like this. I have been very sharp tongued at home." She went on to explain that she was quite like her Grandma. She even struck her fiancé!

Now, she veered in the opposite direction and told me about being picked on at school. More than halfway through the hour, I got to the point. I said, "You can either lose it, or go silent. Why the latter at work?" She gave it right back to me, "I don't want to blow up at work!" Here she showed me exactly what she meant by pressing her lips tightly together. "Yes," I said, "Things could jump out!"

Now I summarized my diagnosis: "You put up with things, not to have things bust out!" Now, she added that this is quite how she puts up with mother, as in shopping. "I just take it." I replied, "Take it, and get lethargic." She continued with a story about her mother bugging her about going out on Christmas Eve. She just moved away!

Fifteen minutes left, I summarized: "You take things, not to floor people like your Grandma did. You seal your lips. You cower. Not to let open the floodgates." We were at a beautiful place to drop into a dream, as Winnicott (1971) would have it, and so I asked her if she dreamt about this?

"Yes," she answered, "I dreamt about a kangaroo!" She explained that the dream was of visiting a coworker, who warned her about a problem with kangaroos. She went out, nevertheless, to look around, and saw one out of the corner of her eye. Next she knew it jumped on her back, and let go some emission. She wiped it off with a mitten, "Yuck!"

The second half of the dream was about going to the house she had just bought with her fiancé, only to find another friend taking over her bathroom with all her makeup stuff.

Time was short, so I just exclaimed, "*Another* intrusion!" I could only ask one question, "What about kangaroos?" She explained that kangaroos were mean, and kangaroos jump. All of a sudden, she knew what it meant. This is what happens to her at work. Here, she moved her whole body, as to get out of the way, not just her eyes! I simply said, "The very problem that brought you here, a picture of what to be ready for. Unexpected meanness!"

Time was up. I told her I would summarize my reply about her happiness, or unhappiness in a letter, and I sent her the letter as follows:

> Dear _____:
> I believe many mysteries fell into place for you and Dr. _____,
> about your happiness and unhappiness, moodiness, and difficulties

with concentration. You go around the same cycle at work, with your mother, with your fiancé. Essentially, you get put upon, as at work by criticism of errors in a demeaning way, and just shut down, and "cower" as you put it, steeling yourself against erupting in anger. This leads to inability to think about what actually you did wrong, or maybe not wrong, and lethargy, coming down from your natural buoyancy that begins the day.

Your pair of dreams puts it this way: It's like being jumped from behind by a mean kangaroo who has an emission on your back, or as if your friend took over your house!

So what to do? I believe you will need some practice finding a middle way, between cowering and letting out rage like the Grandma _____. Cowering is miserable, losing your natural happiness to lethargy. Letting loose is too destructive to your work and to the people you love. We can take one situation at a time, and help you locate your feelings about it, before they get too big, and help you decide upon a measured response. That is the way to happiness!

We have had only one session in the three months since the consultation, and she seems very clear about how she wants to deal with the kangaroos at work. Expect it! Be ready to speak up! Why so quick? She was already quite conversant with her two extremes, herself cowering, herself as a mean kangaroo. The balance has been long prepared. Someone just had to pay attention, and this allowed her to pay attention to herself. Without it, she would have stayed in a fog, as Sullivan (1956) would say.

CHAPTER 6

Walking Forward to Read the Exchanges in Work and Love

If I were to say that human beings walk forward with their eyes closed, you would say that I was exaggerating. They do see something, even if they miss a lot. They see their hopes and their fears. Thus, they are highly selective in their attention. The more insecure they are, the less they see. That was Sullivan's (1954) argument, which we discussed in the last chapter. Such a step based on such a seeing usually leads to a mess. If you see half the world that others want you to see, you lose track of your own needs. If you see half the world that you want to see, you lose track of the demands of others which are necessary for you to meet. This was difficult enough 60 years ago in Sullivan's day.

Iteration

The tendency to repeat, even if in increasing error, was called the *repetition compulsion* by Freud (1920/1975i). I do not believe I have heard the term in 30 years. Mathematically, there is a simpler way to put it which is called iteration (Gleick, 1988). Let y equal the result of any function performed upon x, or $y = f(x)$. For example, if the function is to take 1 from x, then $y = x - 1$. Iteration means to take any result of y and repeat the same function. Thus, $y_2 = f(y_1)$. For example, if $x = 10$, and the function is to take 1 from x, then y_2 will be 9, and y_3 will be 8, until $y_{10} = 0$. After 10, successive y's will become successively negative to negative infinity.

Thus, iteration of a single step sets in motion a trajectory which has a tendency. This tendency may be to converge on a huge number like infinity, or upon zero, or it may fluctuate in a pattern which looks chaotic, but turns out to be a beautiful design called a fractal. This is not the place to explain what functions lead to what in a mathematical world. The reader may turn to Gleick's (1988) book, or any other book on chaos theory.

Iteration in the Modern World

Rather, I would like to turn to the kind of iteration which is typical of our patients. I believe it is only an exaggeration of the iteration of the average citizen. Swenson (2003) argues that this iteration is to add more and more to what the person is already doing. Thus $y = x + 1$. Iterate this simple function, that is, add one more to whatever you have gotten, and you have got a trajectory toward infinity, or as Swenson (2003) puts it, more of everything faster and faster. It looks like Charlie Chaplin on the assembly line in *Modern Times*. Canetti (1960/1984) called it an increase pack.

Up to a point, more and more is accomplished, while the body gets more and more selectively attentive to more numbers. Do this in every compartment of your life and you are the modern citizen par excellence. At a certain point, however, you are, as Swenson puts it, maxed out, overloaded, and finally burned out (100%, 120%, and 140% of ordinary capacity).

Suddenly, you begin to get anxiety and anger, depression and exhaustion. This is not only true of the individual citizen. It is true of any system which fails to read the relation as Swenson argues between load put upon it and its limits. You see it nowadays in electrical grids which go into brownout, and airline scheduling which goes into overbooking, and nearly every production that our patients are involved in. If they work for the hospital, they have increasing quotas of patients, or if they work for the widget manufacturer, increasing quotas of widgets, or if they are trying to get a degree in anything, increasing quotas of reading. It simply is a runaway of numbers that is required.

This puts our citizen in a dilemma. Keep up and go into overload. Don't keep up and be let go. This is nearly universal in our patients who remain in the ordinary economy. Those who cannot keep up and are let go fall into a nether world of welfare and disability and homelessness. This is poverty.

Margin

There are certainly huge sectors of the world, and of our own country, in which the dilemma is extremely strict. Keep up increasing quotas and go into overload, or don't and be let go. Strangely, there are many sectors in the wealthier world in which the dilemma has room in it to negotiate, and yet it is overlooked. This is a selective inattention which is very likely to make you ill.

Swenson suggests that there is a space which is *potential* between our load and our limits. This is only the case when we decide what is absolutely essential as in triage in medicine where we divide the catastrophic from the serious from the unserious. Every window of time, from one minute to 1 hour to 1 day to 1 week, and so on, is an opportunity to sort out the emergent from the unnecessary, and what is in between.

Swenson particularly addresses himself to doctors. Certainly, they are driven by quotas. However, to get in a given number of patients, say in an hour, or a day, or a week, they do have a *potential* to decide how much is given on each case. The less that is given per case, the more margin of *reserve* is left, in any time window, for the *unexpected*. Patients, and administration, are always adding to this estimate, so a reserve is absolutely necessary to keep from being pushed too far.

A Single Step for Conserving Presence

Swenson (unpublished) gives a long series of recommendations, what he calls "Guarding Sustainability and Restoring Margin." Thus, 10 essentials for him begin with:

> Recommendation one, tame technology, recommendation two, selectively disconnect, recommendation three, define/defend boundaries, recommendation four, say no, recommendation five, cultivate simplicity and contentment, recommendation six, control debt, recommendation seven, nourish relationships, recommendation eight, slow the pace, eliminate hurry, recommendation nine, decompress intensity, recommendation ten, get sufficient rest and sleep.

He goes on usefully with long lists of things to do to reduce the load, and increase the margin. Yet the lists epitomize the problem, for they constitute the load and leave no room. Our patients are essentially people carrying a set of lists, for the office, for the house, for the children, for the extended family, and even for the vacation which may take even more work. Every time they turn around they are handed another list. And they are supposed to say yes.

Is it possible to be ready for this epidemic at every turn? The social dynamo is ready to run away with you at every step you take. If you fall into such a step, you can feel ill at once. I do. I am extremely alert to it.

Most people are less alert to their own signals, so the dynamo carries them a considerable distance before they wake up to what is wrong. By then, they are likely to be literally ill.

Here is my countermeasure to the general tendency of selective inattention to runaway loading. For any time interval, 5 minutes, or an hour, or a day, or longer, I first contemplate the window of time without doing anything. Then I decide from among the myriad things I might do in that interval to do one thing. This reverses the general tendency to be caught up in content (the lists). Content or lists put in the foreground blocks out a view of the available space and time. Therefore, I reverse it, and contemplate the available space and time. The container comes first, and the contained second (Bion, 1970). I am always out to protect the container. In a sense, the container is me. It *is* me in the smallest increment, or infinitesimal.

I would like to emphasize that this reading is not in the service of pure selfishness. I am not out simply to say no, just as I am not out simply to say yes. This reading is *in the service of clearing the field.* I want to see how big it is and how long it is, and I want to have an exchange which feels right, with no hurry, and plenty of room and time around it, to be prepared for the unexpected. Thus, it is *a step in the service of presence.*

I agree with Lévi-Strauss (Gustafson, 1997, chap. 10) that the origin of man is in relatively equal exchange. In aboriginal society, or what Lévi-Strauss (Charbonnier, 1959) called the cold engine, this is what man was selected for. The recent dynamo of the hot engine is but a flicker of time against this perpetual background.

In a relatively equal exchange, the internal grid of the body has as much force as the external grid of the society. I ask for something, and I give something. Indeed, Lévi-Strauss argues that music is a play of the internal grid of the body's rhythms upon the external grid of the society's values. Mythology has the same structure. I cannot take us afar here, so the reader may refer to my chapter on Lévi-Strauss, and to Lévi-Strauss (1964/1983) himself.

My point is this: In a heated up world, increasing its quotas of the required every hour, the external grid is going to get a lot more force than the internal grid. The conscious mind will get busier and busier at every iteration $(x + 1)$ on this external grid. The man will run faster and faster, as in John Cleese's movie, *Clockwise.* Cleese plays a headmaster in a kind of airport control tower overlooking a school. He epitomizes the imposition of an external grid upon everyone under him. Thus, in those under him, the internal grid will get weaker and weaker $(x - 1)$ at every step, so the members of the school gradually become less and less present. They are ever busier in what is imposed upon them, and ever more absent in their own feelings.

Thus, the simplicity of the countermeasure is to decline the lists as the first consideration, and the first consideration is the next interval of time that I have. This is the external grid I give myself. It is relatively equal to the internal grid of my needs. Thus, it is an infinitesimal form of the ancient exchange of equality.

Sullivan (1956) could not have posed this problem of selective inattention 60 years ago. The take-off of the external grid in numbers was just under way. Now, it is to be expected in every interaction. Somebody is about to run into you with a list of things you do not want to do. That somebody is also not going to have any attention left over from his lists to pay any attention back to you in return. That is why you must be contemplating your next interval of time, so *you* can decide what little to put into it, and not have this person take it over with their business, and give you hardly a glance. That is my simple step of readiness to set my own exchange, and not have it set for me by everyone I meet. Let us now see how this plays out in the realms of work and love, respectively.

Exchange in the Realm of Work

I am most familiar with the realm of work in our own clinic, and I am quite confident from listening to our patients that the same dynamo runs in their place as in ours in this new universe of ours. Therefore, I will use our clinic as a general model of what humanity is up against.

I get a list of patients to see with their residents at the rate of about three to eight per hour. Five seems about average. That computes as about 10 minutes per case, with 10 minutes left over for me to lie on my couch in the margin or reserve I set aside for myself.

How then do I set my step into these 5 offices in an hour in such a way that exchange is satisfactory? Basically, I divide the 10-minute window into two halves of a single container. In the first 5 minutes I watch the patient and resident interact. I am looking for signals of distress, especially with the fingers and feet, or the eyes. In these peripheral portals much is let out unconsciously, while the center of the body is held rigidly in place, and self-consciously.

By 5 minutes I ask if the patient or resident has any question for me. This signals that I am not there just to take it in, but to give back, and yet to give back a reply, by and large, to a single question. I am not going to allow either patient or resident to run on anymore, for I will put them off for the next session. Thus, I am already preparing my exit at the halfway point.

If I do not know the patient well, or if I know the patient well and that he or she is in continual danger, I will take the single question as one of containing disaster. I will ask the patient how he has been at his worst, and how he has made it through. "Above all, do no harm," wrote Hippocrates. "Above all, be alert to harm that is close at hand," I write here as my chief duty in the exchange, the single thing I put into the container I am defending so carefully.

If there is no such disaster at hand, I can entertain a question of why things are going as they are going. This usually means backing up the history from the bad point it has come to, or forwarding the history to the dilemma that is coming. Usually, there has been selective inattention backwards, and forwards, and so I can usually give a clear reply to what has been missed, simply by listening to the patient for what has been left out. As Sullivan (1954, 1956) put it, the patient can be counted on to give less than an adequate history, and the resident also. So, I have a simple reply to give to a simple question, which is unforeseen by the patient and resident. This is a mutual satisfaction. Also, it takes only half of the interval, so there is no hurry. In general, I want the job to take about half of the time interval, because I never want to be jarred by the unexpected. It is a little theater, with a clear entrance and a clear exit, and plenty of room to cope with what is necessary.

The Exchange of Mr. and Mrs. Everyman at Work

We are all vulnerable to getting our little theater at work completely wrong. We all have these little 10-minute windows in which to do things. We can start late. We can attempt too much. We can end late. Iterate this 10-minute interval and its excessive content all day long, and we are going to finish the day tense and exhausted.

Then a compensatory step is also possible. Having put out too much for each client or patient, we may begin to get our backs up, and give a lot less. People get mad at us, and we feel guilty. Now we are tense, exhausted, *and* guilty. It is not a good state to go home in.

We are completely out of rhythm. We have put out too much, and then we have put out too little. It is a very jarring music between the internal grid and the external grid. It is like hitting too early and hitting too late on the tennis court. It feels bad.

The Exchange of Mr. and Mrs. Everyman at Home

Now, we go home. All we want is a break. We want to disappear, into music, or eating, or going fishing. Yet our spouses have a whole list of things for us to do, with dinner, shopping, the kids, and the house. Now we are in danger of getting fouled up again. We can attempt the list, and lose ourselves. We can compensate ourselves in taking a break, and anger our spouse.

The chances of righting this imbalance either way are not very good. Usually what happens is that each of the marital partners takes up some of the list, and some of the break. This division of labor is understandable, but keeps the two in different worlds. Iterate this a million times and you have got what Rose (1984) called "parallel lives." There is little left of mutual pleasures.

Righting the Wrong of the Everymans

Again, we come back to the fundamental problem of what is attempted in a given interval of time. If we watch it all day, and have satisfactory exchanges, we come home in balance. If we attempt a little in the intervals of time at home, we do not have to disappear on our spouses to compensate ourselves. We can play at our mutual pleasures.

One more thing. There is a pretty good chance that one or both partners will have disappeared in any given evening. Therefore, even if you have managed your *own* exchanges, your spouse will have been overwhelmed by something, and be unable to be present, until she can recover. Or this may be true of you. There is no getting around this but to let time pass and your spouse or yourself recover. So often, you are on your own. This is modern life. Unfortunately, everyman has a tendency to punish (Dicks, 1967; Donovan, 2003) when he is ready to enjoy himself and his wife is done in, and vice versa. This makes a bad situation worse, which would have righted itself in time. The only way out of it is to accept what is going to be the case, from your day, and from your night.

Your Partner's Troubles Are Your Own, A Typical Case

Marriage is a very simple business in theory: arrange as much mutual pleasure as you can, and arrange as little perversity as you can in which the pleasure of one is the misery of the other (Gustafson, 1999, chap. 11), and, finally, punish as little as possible for the other not fulfilling your ideal (Dicks, 1967; Donovan, 2003).

In actuality, most of these criteria are poorly upheld. Generally, the interests of one are the downfall of the other. Usually, this is overlooked. The following is an hour's consultation in my Brief Psychotherapy Clinic to face things *before* they become impossible.

This woman was brought to me by her staff psychologist after 13 visits. The challenge of the case was that her partner was considering giving up her not so lucrative law practice for going into a seminary in Chicago. Our patient was worrying about it, and compensating herself with too much eating and too much gambling.

What she felt was that her partner, already lacking in bringing in money, was going to get worse. She, a stalwart of Dutch heritage, would hold up her own in her business, and her partner would not. She had a dream about it, which went as follows:

It was 2 days after her 47th birthday, in which she was feeling, "I can't count on my life as I know it." A very precise phrase of the English language, I thought, and surely the burden of the dream.

She dreamt there were "Nazilike men invading our land." She and her partner and a baby and a black Labrador were at home. Meanwhile, everyone in the neighborhood seemed to be walking down the railroad tracks. Four of them, German speaking, asked to be let in. They wanted to use the toilet, but our patient was afraid to let them out of her sight. Her parents came along with their dogs, urging her to take flight with everyone else.

She was disappointed in her father's advice, to leave her house, so secure, for this flight, but she decided she had better do it. She thought of killing herself first, but she did not want to hurt her family. What about the dog food? Forty pounds? Luckily, they had "The Load Hog" her father had given her to take it in. There seemed to be room for everything in it. They would join the masses after all.

The dream was about as harshly metaphorical as it seemed. My letter to the patient put it as such:

Dear _____:

Your dream is a big one, showing in its motion the fork in the road: You could hold fast to your house, in the face of invasion probably set off by _____'s path into the seminary. You could back down, and be practical in the business sense of going into debt with the masses, but this would abandon your entire project of being self-sufficient as a stout Dutch woman. Outer practicality, following your father, could let go your project of being stalwart which is of great emotional importance.

There is more about being 47, and something about a baby which we didn't get to, which you and _____ may want to go into as well. I enjoyed seeing you so much, with your morning papers, and your determination not to let go of life as you have known it. I hope to see you again in a year.

Certainly, the dream portrays a dire predicament, a dilemma in the extreme of her ancestors in Holland, staying put, or fleeing the Nazi invasion. I really couldn't tell which was worse. At least, we could face that it would be bad either way. At least, we could pay attention to the suffering of staying or the suffering of going. The rest had to be up to her.

This is what I meant when I wrote, "Generally, the interests of one are the downfall of the other." It is possible, however, to have a close look at the dilemma between two totally different trajectories (worlds) and decide which is better and which is worse. That is what we just walked forward to consider.

PART III

The Opposing Current Navigated

Humanity is selected for one-sidedness. It selects itself for one-sidedness. Nowadays, the operative word is *control*. I cannot think of a term that our patients respond to with more agreement. Their chief complaints are about lack of control, and their treatment plans are phrased almost totally in terms of giving control back to them again. That, presumably, would be a satisfied population.

Certainly, it would be a more secure population. Control, literally, is about the only way to secure an income. Get yourself a specialized procedure in controlling something, and a credential to make it official that you are qualified in it by a Board of Something, and you have a secure niche. Everything is run like this, from cosmetology to neurosurgery.

Yet these security operations, as Sullivan (1954) put it, leave aside a great deal which is beyond security. As we have seen in parts I and II, of this book, our patients push themselves so far to belong that the body becomes overtaxed and begins to signal alarm and collapse and arranges compensations that are highly inconvenient for taking care of business. We end up containing the signals, and we end up pointing out the selective inattention for walking right into such extreme states of mind.

Yet the natural correction of this one-sided bent for security is always arising in the body. For example, I recall a patient in the last week who complained of recent panic. I asked where it arose, and found out that it was after she had gone to see *Fahrenheit 911*, indeed, precisely, after she had tried to sleep, and woke up thinking of the suffering of children in

Iraq. She was in a helpless rage about it, and this erupted into panic, which she had never had before. I asked her what else had been bothering her lately and she replied that she was very angry in her job as a faculty secretary. Her boss, the chairman of a department, had told her she had to open a website for a new faculty hiring, on top of all her excessive duties. This, too, put her in a helpless rage, for she felt that the labor of this project would be pointless and ignored, and yet she had to comply.

Therefore, I told her that the cause of her panic was her inability to contain her helpless rage. She answered that she didn't want to have any such thing. She just wanted to have positive feelings. I supposed that her childhood had contained all too much of the negative feelings. She answered that her father had the rage, and she had the helplessness facing him.

Here we were at the very bifurcation at which we have just arrived in this book. On one side, the call for containment of overwhelming signals walked into unwittingly, and on the other side, the possibility of taking these signals as a current that needs to be ridden. I gave her the choice. She could take our psychotropic medications to dampen her panic, or she could take her anger as something necessary to come to terms with, or she could do some of both. What advantage, she objected, could there possibly be to getting conversant with her anger? I said that anger, modulated, might get her somewhere in objecting to things that were objectionable, like this war in Iraq and like this chairman in her face. Now that interested her. I told her to get a journal and write down the situation at the end of each day, and then the dream that replied to her situation. Thus, we could get the best X-ray or set of X-rays like a CT scan of her difficulty, making use of her anger in a constructive way.

So I will see her again soon and we will begin trying to navigate with this opposing current of objection. Obviously, she is fearful of it running away with her, as it ran away with her father. It has that risk. So how do I propose to have the benefit without the danger? This is the territory of which Winnicott (1971) and Balint (1968) have been my masters, as I described in my first book (Gustafson, 1986/1997, chaps. 7, 8). Both of them understood very clearly the diagnostic and the therapeutic problem.

The diagnostic problem is in deciding which patients benefit from being put more deeply in touch with their own deep feelings, vs. which patients get worse from the very same procedure. Balint (1968) called it the distinction between benign and malignant regression. In a benign regression, the patient goes backward into childhood feelings long dissociated in order to have them "recognized." The patient asks no more than to be understood. Conversely, in a malignant regression, the patient becomes more and more demanding of gratification the more his feelings are understood. The more he is given of understanding, the worse he behaves. Most of our borderline patients behave in this malignant way, obviously, but there are many other more subtle dangers we will discuss in part III. For example, some patients behave benignly *and* malignantly, depending upon how they are managed.

The therapeutic problem can be stated in relatively simple terms, but it can be difficult to bear with. The opposing current will always be arising, whenever the main current is getting in trouble, as with the main current of subservience in our departmental secretary. As Jung (1916/1953) put it, the psyche will balance itself in relatively healthy patients when given its chance. The chance we are speaking of is recognition of the force of feeling in such a way that the patient quiets down by being understood. This allows the feeling to be turned back toward its objects in the world in relatively modulated terms, such as in assertion, as opposed to explosion. Conceptually, that is a very simple step. Once gotten under way, it is what Balint (1968) called "a new beginning." The patient feels like a new being, in that she is able to trust her own instincts as reliable guides to reacting to a difficult world. This is a great advantage in flexibility, compared to having her feelings merely contained so they do not destroy things.

My actual procedure in consultations of 1 hour in my Brief Psychotherapy Clinic follow Winnicott (1971). I open by clarifying the question I am being asked. This would be something like the question about panic in our departmental secretary. What is it from, and what to do about it? If possible, about half way through, I will take what Winnicott (1971) called a "drop" into a dream, simply because it gives a beautiful map of the whole situation. Finally, I will come up to the surface with a summary and a conclusion. Winnicott (1965) called the whole procedure "meeting the challenge of the case." A letter summarizing the chief findings of the hour will follow.

Part III of this book will consist chiefly of a set of consultations on the three opposing currents most commonly met with in our clinic. Chapter 7 will be about "The Opposing Current to Receptiveness," chapter 8, "The Opposing Current to Pushing," and chapter 9, "The Opposing Current to Guilt." Each chapter will have a pair of my consultations in my Brief Psychotherapy Clinic for contrast, to allow a discussion of the diagnostic and therapeutic challenges which they pose for us.

I would add only one more point in closing this Introduction. The world of security is a relatively static world. The world of the opposing current is a relatively fluid world. It is exciting, and fresh, while it is also potentially dangerous. Those who would navigate it with their patients are involved in a kind of crossing over from the old world to a new world, which is full of sudden departures, and quickly rising storms, and strange discoveries (Gustafson, 1987). It is a world of nonlinear changes, compared to the linear containment of the old world. This kind of work is a marvelous privilege, which needs to be earned by time at sea under good captains.

CHAPTER 7

The Opposing Current to Receptiveness

This is a chapter about what happens to women. Mostly, it is about what happens to women because of their gift of receptiveness. Men with this gift get into similar trouble. It is also about the opposing current to receptiveness, which leads elsewhere, and out of the trap. It is simply true that kindness gets taken advantage of, although it need not be so if measures can be set up to prevent this from occurring.

That is why our behaviorist colleagues have such an opportunity to teach assertiveness, which helps and is a move in the right direction. Certainly, the reader will hear me bringing up the possibility of assertion, against the patient being badly used. My argument is that assertiveness is good. My argument is also that something more fierce is called for. My argument is that being fierce is profoundly unsettling for a nice person.

Why fierce? As the two following cases will, I think, illustrate, the forces pulling a kind person into making a sacrifice of her life are often tremendous. An equal and opposite force is going to need some of the primitive quality of ferocity. It is a battle for one's own existence.

How then is a basically nice person to ride such a primitive current from within, take advantage of its benefits, but without inflicting harm? Often, such a person feels compelled to be nice in reaction to cruelty.

Often, there has been nothing in between. Thus, it is a huge relief when somebody shows up who is evidently kind, and evidently fierce in a constructive way. Winnicott (1971) had precisely this quality. He made it his job during World War II in England to give radio broadcasts addressed to young mothers telling them that hating your infant had a hundred causes (1949/1957)! Later (Winnicott, 1947/1958), he called it "objective hatred,"

by which he meant that anybody in the situation of serving the ruthless-
ness of an infant would end up with a great deal of hatred. The same is the
case in every helping profession. The challenge is to have it, and contain it,
and not act it out, yet, to put one's foot down.

Listening and imagining the two cases that follow, the reader may get
the feeling of a doctor putting his foot down, and of two patients following
suit. That is fundamental. However, much more is going on. Let us see.

The Case of a Reasonable Woman

This woman in her 40s was brought to me in Brief Psychotherapy Clinic by
one of our trainee psychologists who had the patient in group therapy. She
was presented to me as a person stuck, both in love and in work. She
wanted to be close, but kept up a mask. The group felt her to be aloof. She
wanted to be effective at work, but had quit a series of jobs, or, as in the
last one, been fired. She wanted to be a strong player.

She began on the work side. She grew up in a city out east with what she
called a Calvinist ethic. Namely, if you were honest, you did well. She did
well, but then she moved here with her second husband. Here, things
seemed to go differently. A girl insulted her on in a petty way, and she
didn't know what to do, and finally quit. She seemed to be the bearer of a
certain religious and business culture in which respect was a given. Here,
she was taken aback.

And about closeness? She began directly with her mother, of whom she
said, "She was never affectionate nor present. When I competed, no one
was there." By contrast, her sister was sickly, allergic, and angry, and took it
out on our patient. Mother would say, "She can't help it." Our patient
would say, "But what about me?" Here, she began to cry.

A quarter of an hour into the interview, now, I could summarize and
tell her that her two problems were one. Being hurt, or abused, she had no
way to protect herself. This summary seemed to open up the entire file on
this subject. Immediately, she thought of her second marriage, in which
the 14-year-old stepdaughter by her husband's first marriage was simply
awful to her. This almost split them up, but she got just enough backing
from her husband to survive it. Thus, she had handled one version of the
old story.

What version did she want to address next? Here, she turned back to
her last job. She got a fairly high-ranking position, but there seemed to be
no work to do. Her boss seemed to be one of those women who did not
want to be interrupted. So, she just floundered. She would have liked to
have a direct conversation, but she feared it. She would have liked to go to

the boss above her boss, but she feared that too. Hanging her head a bit, she said, "I sound foolish."

I was *not* impressed by her foolishness. After all, her dilemma seemed to be quite real. If she went along like this, she would be disqualified. If she challenged, she might also be disqualified. I really could not tell which was the worse alternative. So, foolish she was not. I was more struck by her amazement. She could not quite believe the malevolence of her boss.

Like so many of our patients, she had a faith in being reasonable. This was supposed to get a return. It didn't. Then, she just froze. She didn't seem to know that the world is unreasonable. For a while, back east, she had found an unusual business culture in which reason seemed to rule. Now that it didn't, here, she seemed in shock.

Therefore, I told her that her problem was not in reading the situation foolishly. Her problem was in feeling it was her fault. Yes, this reminded her of her first marriage. Her husband was very entitled in his demands, and she made herself the loser.

More than halfway through our hour for the consultation, I felt the mounting evidence against her position. Being reasonable, she got bullied, by her sister, by her first husband, by her stepdaughter, by her jobs here. I did not need any more examples. I did need to see if she could move against it. So, I told her she was forever in a bullying process. She had the short end of the stick, and somebody else always had the long end of the stick. This turns out badly.

I told her she had only one problem, and this was it, in 6 or 60 versions. I told her I had been afraid when I first saw her. Oh no, I had thought, another nice person, reasonable, expecting others to be reasonable, unready for the next battle, and going to take blame for it.

So what did she want to do about it? Her response was to recall the stepdaughter again, and her husband getting depressed, and she getting depressed. She didn't want to burden the group with this. Hence, their impression of her as being aloof.

Did she not have a network of friends? Yes, she did, but one in particular goes on for hours about her own troubles. When our patient tries to change the subject, her friend is indignant at being cut off. Two hours for the friend, but not 1 minute for her! Now that is the short end of the stick, indeed.

Finally, she laughed and said it was time to stand up for herself. She wanted to break out. But the friend might not speak to her again. I replied, "So, don't do it." She laughed again, and said, simply, "Shit!" I commented that some people have to have their 2 hours or they *will* quit. She replied that her husband listens, and she listens. I allowed that there are such people!

We were running out of time, but the opposing current seemed also to be up and running. "Here," she said, "I've got another situation for you." This was about her younger brother, always acknowledged by the parents, while our patient was not acknowledged. Mother said of her, "Never a stitch of trouble." A year ago, she proposed a gift to her parents, but this rich brother would not contribute. Now, the nerve, for he's bought a diamond for them and expects her to pay too! Not very equal.

So, what did she want to do? She didn't want to pay, and she didn't want to refuse and have him not speak to her for a year. I told her she didn't want either, and she laughed and told me he talked nonstop during his visit last year. I noted that some people were determined to come out on top. I offered to send her more of these people for her education. She laughed. Her eyes were wide open. I told her she got to consider using some of her own power in a measured way. She liked that. I told her it wasn't foolproof, but we'd have to stop there, and I'd send my summary in a letter, which went as follows:

Dear _____:

It's always the same dilemma coming, so you get a million more chances to freeze, or to do something more to your liking. Essentially, you walk over and over into a situation of being bullied, and you are shocked and tend just to hold on and hope it will improve, and it almost always gets worse. That's what happens when you take the short end of the stick, and the other guy's got the long end of the stick.

For example, you first proposed to discuss the last job, with the shaky boss 2 years older than you like your sister. From the first step in, she is trying to disqualify you, so she can prevail. *Before* you are wrecked by this, and overwhelmed with terrible feelings, you get to consider: Do I prefer to sit tight and hope she will be merciful? Do I prefer to run the risk of talking honestly with her, or with the boss above her (knowing I may get really attacked in the face), or do I decline the game?

For example, you finally proposed the problem of your brother refusing to help you with your gift idea to your parents, and then insisting you contribute to his gift. If you go along, you are taking the short end of the stick. If you refuse, he won't talk to you for a year. Well, what would I do? I would tell him my dilemma, and ask him what he thinks about it?

We discussed other examples, like your first marriage, your husband's daughter, and the friends who want to talk for 2 hours, and change the subject when you take your turn for a minute. And the original version of your sister being awful, and your mother saying it could not be helped. But it is always the same dilemma, and so you get to consider in the past, present, and future what you prefer to do *before* you are frozen (overwhelmed).

I enjoyed seeing you very much, and would be glad to see you again later for a follow-up and see how it's going for you.

The Opposing Current Is a Kind of Wellspring

In the 1950s, Milgram (1963/1973) and Asch (1955) did some startling experiments in social psychology that showed the power of the group to turn an individual on or off. They found that a single *ally* is usually necessary for an individual to continue to hold an opinion against the opinion of the group, even when the experimenter sets up the group to be dead wrong, and the individual wholly right.

My interview could be said to vindicate this finding. The ally effect makes all the difference. She lacked an ally when bullied by her sister. She got some support from her husband when bullied by her stepdaughter. She got plenty of support from me as this interview went along. Her own opposition to being bullied flows as the backing goes. By the conclusion, she is truly in motion, and laughing, and showing some spirit.

Of course, I'd better not send this opposition into a foolish battle, right or wrong. I send her into a dilemma, running risks, but running risks of her own choice, and ready for others to be wholly out for themselves at her expense. Neither will I have her running it in dead earnest. Serious people are so flat footed. I'll have her seeing the absurdity of the claim of others as laughable so they won't amaze or shock or mortify her. She can enter with her own claim, pause, survey.

Her old way was what Brenman (1952) called moral masochism, or arranging to come out in the wrong. The opposing current to moral masochism is always moral sadism, or arranging to come out in the right. I would have her midway between these two.

However, the general tendency that follows from the force of the group is that the individual well of feeling, and claim, and imagination, is the limiting condition. By and large, it dries up our patients with its multiplying requirements to fit in. Over time, they become more and more impoverished. That is why I am called upon to get it flowing again, by backing it, and this before turning it back to make its claim upon the world. What about transference? As Reich (1949) argued, it is usually frozen solid and thus unavailable until the flow of opposing current has gotten going. Then, the patient's poor exchange with the world will be felt as coming also from the therapist.

The Case of the Woman Who Could Help Everyone

The following case is more complicated, because I had to have the knowledge of the dynamics of grief, and of antisocial reactions, and of families, to help the patient get over her mystification. I also had to have knowledge of separation-individuation, so held up here between a mother and a son. I had to know something about what allows separation to flow as an opposing current.

This patient was presented to me in Brief Psychotherapy Clinic for depression, obviously related to her son in his 20s who was having a very hard time with both manic and extremely depressed moods and an inability to sustain relationships and jobs. The resident knew that the past was very heavy in the present, in that the young man's father had killed himself when the boy was 4. The mother, our patient, had moved on quickly. What's the use of thinking about it, it's over, was all her attitude. She had to make a living, take care of her two young children, and be responsible. The resident, however, wanted to know if a better understanding of the past could make a difference in the present.

Immediately, our patient confirmed how the past did impinge on the present, for her son was now the same age as his father when he killed himself. It was a huge, heartbreaking stress. Could it happen again, I asked myself? I said to her that talking about the past might reduce the heartache, and she said, "Whose heartache?" That seemed to be a very telling remark, for the two of them were so mixed up together.

I asked her to tell me more about her son. She told me that he seemed to have little reaction at the time of the suicide of his father. By 13, he showed a certain rage by breaking doors, but taking him to several psychologists and psychiatrists led nowhere. He wouldn't talk, or no one seemed to know how to get him to talk. I said he was 4 going on 13. She said he was wanting to be friends at 25. He wanted to protect her!

The situation now was that he had a psychologist and a girlfriend. These two and his mother seemed to think he ought to go into the hospital and take psychotropic medications, but the young man was reluctant and fearful from an involuntary commitment 4 years earlier. He rather wanted to move in with her and her second husband. They refused. She felt badly about it, but she and her husband could not take him in again.

He broke things when angry. He tried to rule when she went out. He wouldn't let his sister go out. He objected to television, telling them that families should interact and not watch television. To me, he sounded like a lawgiver, and quite the double of his father. To me, this was what happened in a grief that was unresolved. He became the father he lost (Freud, 1917/ 1975g). He would show his mother and sister and stepfather what's what.

Essentially, he had been this way all along since his father died. His moods ruled. His mother and stepfather picked their battles with him carefully. So, he was somewhat socialized when he was not at home.

With a quarter of an hour left, I asked her what one thing she wanted to ask me. She answered that she needed to find some way that this would not take over her whole life. All his emotions seem to get into her. She said she "felt his feelings." I agreed that they were pretty unseparated.

Now, she rubbed her hands on the chair, and told me she had been getting better at standing up to him, but now it all seemed so sad, he so intelligent, so handsome, his life ruined. Yet, she did not feel she should put up with his impositions. And he might not get better. I could see how she identified with his hopelessness, and thus how she was in a tremendous amount of pain. Just as he was identified with his father, the lawgiver, she was identified with her son. This, the classic melancholia Freud (1917/1975g) talked about, which has not let go the lost person, but clings to him by identification, by becoming him.

Strangely, at the end, we talked about the father, and his mad family, who were still intruding upon our patient with all their needs. I asked her to describe her one-time husband. She said he was a medical student, never responsible at home, out for fun, probably promiscuous. She did all the work, he studied. And gallivanted. Yet he was the proud papa of his boy, liked to take him around and show him off. Like an image of himself. A carbon copy, a spitting image. She suspected something when he gave away his golf clubs. She asked him to get help, but he claimed he was not depressed. Then he killed himself, and she went back to work a week later.

My letter to her follows. Note that the father and son have the same name.

> Dear _____:
>
> I believe the questions for my reply from you and Dr. _____ come to this: Is coming to terms with the past important to the present? Is there relief for your heartache about _____? In other words, what is the diagnosis of what went wrong? And what is the treatment?
>
> It seems to me that the past *is* the present. In other words, _____, your husband ruled at his pleasure, and you did all the work. _____, your son, continues the same game. He will be the lawgiver, and you are supposed to pick up the pieces and make it work. This is where capable people like yourself get in trouble, taking all this responsibility for others. After all, many others are only going to take responsibility for themselves if it is *asked* of them.

Now, is it too late to ask this of _____, your son? I don't know without asking him myself, or watching you ask it of him. Shall we try it? Clearly, a part of him is asking for the past to be dealt with, but also, clearly, a part of him only wants or is willing to be the mad lawgiver for others, and thus hold onto his father by *being* his father. What happens depends upon which part of him is bigger, and whether the sane part can be called upon to be responsible?

Which brings me back to you. You plunged ahead 1 week after the suicide of _____, your husband, so you really never faced up to your feelings about what happened. Similarly, you plunge ahead in the present to do things, which also misses your feelings about the second tragedy of _____, your son. So there is a lot of pain and anger and dread and several other feelings as well to be faced up to, to let go of this double heartache of the _____s, father and son.

The Opposing Current in Pathological Grief

Grief like this runs on forever when the antisocial protest of it is allowed. Therefore, I took a very simple step of backing our patient against the takeover by her son, which followed the example of her husband (Selvini-Palazzoli, Cirillo, Selvini, & Sorrentino, 1989). This stance was tested strongly. When the son came to a session with his mother, our patient, he refused to talk about himself, only his mother and her problems, and walked out the front door right into our nearby meadow. The police were called, but I declined to put them in pursuit. Since then, our patient has been relatively firm about when he can come over, and what he can do at home, and he has behaved like a better citizen.

In other words, she is behaving more separately from him, and he more separately from his father. I am sure the testing is not over.

CHAPTER **8**

The Opposing Current to Pushing

This chapter is about what happens to men. It happens to men because they are endlessly pushing. They are endlessly pushing because they are selected in contests for this single quality. When there is a scarcity of niche spaces, there is a fierce contest for them (Gustafson & Cooper, 1990).

> Power in human societies is granted to leaders who promise to maintain the traditional niches or even to expand them. In this endeavor, two *stratagems* are open to leaders that might be called further changes in the niche: *Technical ingenuity,* which produces more goods and services, or *trade.* When these eventually fail to satisfy, as they are bound to in populations of unchanged breeding strategy, only a single stratagem remains, that of *taking land from other peoples by force* (Colinvaux, 1983, p. 4).

Of course, everyone knows that women have been drawn into this poem of force (Weil, 1937/1993), for taking and holding territory, in every different specialization. Thus, the push to control has a tendency to take over their lives too, if they work in any hierarchy at all, from elementary school to running Hewlett-Packard.

So, there is a general tendency in our population for pushing to get ahead in an endless series of contests, which determine who gets to hold the niche-space. This one-sidedness in the exterior milieu has an overwhelming tendency to cut off the interior milieu. Everyone is busy getting ahead, and no one is at home. Canetti (1960/1984) called it "the increase pack," which is always in emergency session. It tends to be an increase of materialism, and its servants carry lists of what the materials require of them, as I described fully in chapter 6, "Walking Forward to Read the Exchanges in Work and Love."

Is there an opposing current that can rise from within to get a man, or a woman, out of this perpetual race? Yes, there is a simple step out of it that puts you into another flow. It is an ancient move, which is well known to all the great religious traditions. In China, the Empire was served by the Confucian tradition of rules. The step out of the exterior world, into the interior world, was called Taoism. Its most vivid teacher was Chuang Tzu, who lived about 300 BC, wrote prolifically (Legge, 1891/1962), and who was translated brilliantly by Thomas Merton (1965). See, for example, "The Active Life" (pp. 141–142), which describes being caught up and compelled to move by the social machine.

Probably, the most common version of this move from action to meditation in our society, is Christian prayer, but Christianity itself tends to pull a person outwardly into endless service. As Jung argued in "The Difference Between Eastern and Western Thinking" (1939/1971), the West tends to put God outside, to be bowed down to, while the East tends to put God inside, to be listened to. This is the great attraction in the 20th century back to the East, which takes popular form now in, for example, mindfulness meditation. Just stop acting, and pay attention to the breath! That's it. This operates as a null function (Selvini-Palazzoli, 1980) to cancel out the exterior world at one stroke, and let in the interior world.

A Little More Complexity to Letting in Receptiveness

This is all well and good for getting out of the race. By itself, however, it will not suffice. For example, there is a tendency to use mindfulness meditation as a kind of break from the race, now to be run back to again. Really getting free of its compelling machinery is much harder.

Consider Freud's argument of what drives it, namely, what he called "the Oedipus complex" (Freud, 1913/1975d). Basically, he argued that man has in him a drive to kill his father and marry his mother, like the famous Oedipus himself. Nowadays, you hardly hear of this formulation without scorn. Yet, the two cases that follow will show how ferocious it really is, and only a fool will deny it. Why is it denied? Modern man believes himself to be rational. He likes to think he is only interested in control.

One of our residents who was having a reading tutorial with me asked me what I meant about the dream of a man (Gustafson, 1999), and why it is a fearful thing? I said it is because such a dream is not just a hope, but an entire journey with many dangers, such as described by Jung (1916/1953) and Campbell (1949). In other words, the man/boy has to find his objection to his father's house, leave it to seek his own and battle the dragon, and bring back the ring for his own wife. Campbell (1949), following James Joyce, called it "the monomyth." So much can go wrong! This is not welcome news for those who believe in progress as a linear path.

The resident thought of his own struggle here, and remarked upon his preference for a light and airy house, in contradistinction to the huge displays of wealth of his parents. "Why," he asked, "do they resent my kind of house?" "Because," I answered, "you reject theirs. As Winnicott said, 'Children grow up over their parents' dead bodies.' They pick up the violence in your departure from theirs!" "Indeed," he said, "they want me to buy theirs for half price, and I will not!"

This led to his next question about a patient of his with fibromyalgia. She has put herself on a slippery slope by paying half the mortgage on her partner's house with no legal rights in it. The partner is the kind of woman who asks our patient's opinion about where the cloth for polishing the silverware should go, and promptly discards that opinion for her own better one. Thus, our patient is a prisoner in her partner's house, disqualified in her opinions, and anxiously clinging to this insecurity. Of course, this is a copy of her relationship to her mother, and is thus the female version of the Oedipus complex. Some wit once called it "The Edifice complex" and that is quite true. You sit as a prisoner in your mother's dwelling place, and it becomes your own grave. Your own body becomes a rigid and tense vessel within that house by clinging to it. Or for a boy/man, in your father's dwelling place. Thus, acquiescence is very dangerous.

But departure is the opposing current and is equally dangerous. The Oedipal myth is but one variation of "the monomyth," and it is a variation which is disastrous. You really had better not literally kill your father and marry your mother and bring down the plague upon Thebes.

I wrote a chapter called "A Digression Upon the Tragedy of *Oedipus Rex*," to argue how one gets past this dilemma (Gustafson, 1992). Essentially, I said that the group you belong to will make you its servant, and that you have to go out the back door to a world elsewhere to find your own wellspring (Thoreau, 1854/1947). In other words, acquiescence in the group is the descending slope of tragedy, and the departure is the ascending slope of comedy and thus its happy ending.

That was a little romantic (Tate, 1999) of me, but not such a bad thing in a younger man for making his own way. Now I would say that the Edifice Complex is not transcended by being in, or out, of society. I go back to the aboriginal point of view (Gustafson, 1997b, chap. 10) to say that every berry you pick up can have something fresh to eat in it, and something rotten not to eat in it, and the key is to slice between the two. From this perspective, every little thing you deal with is likely to be "mixed up" (Rushdie, 1994). When you are ready for this, you are your own man. Let us see how this works out with two young men seen in the Brief Psychotherapy Clinic.

The Case of the Vortex

This young man came to me in quite a lather. The resident told me that the man felt like he was alternately in hot and cold showers with his wife. The story, familiar enough, was that he had struck her a half year ago in a fit of jealousy, which prompted her to get him out of the house. Since then they saw each other mostly over their exchange of the little son, and now she was threatening divorce. The night of admission to the hospital, he felt it was all over, and was close to walking off the end of the dock on the lake on campus, laptop and all.

Now, he took over the interview completely, as he takes over everything with his wife, and with everyone else, and went into a long ramble, fairly hysterical, about how she helps him, how she hurts him, how she should tell him what to do, "Just Go." I asked him if I might interrupt him, to ask him one question, "Why does it go wrong?"

This started up another long ramble, about having to protect himself, losing his temper, liking to be in excitement, screaming "stupid" at his wife, "I don't know why, I can't stop." I noted he did get on a roll. This started him up again, how he had the same problem screaming "stupid" at his first wife. She left him. "Why did she drop you?" I simply asked. "You were mean to her too?" Yes, he agreed, and he talked too much too.

Already halfway through our allotted hour, I simply said, "Yes, you can be overwhelming." He replied, "I develop dependency. Someone once told me, 'You're like a vortex.' I love my sense of self." This struck me as extraordinarily apt as a characterization of this spinning dervish of a man. I said, "People have trouble living with vortices. What if you left off being a vortex, and left space for other people to be themselves?"

He said he didn't know how. I said that life would be a mess as a vortex. He said it *was* a mess. "I just give, give, give … with no reserves." I replied, "Let's see how you might have a new direction. Let's begin with shorter answers, and not spinning off. What next?"

The remainder of the hour was roughly about holding him to brief answers. He told me he wanted to make an honorable life as a social worker. I had to halt him again, and tell him that brevity was a practice.

What could go wrong with his honorable hope? His presence destabilized his wife. I asked if he could be in the same city without upsetting her? "Why does it bother her so much?" he exclaimed in amazement. "Maybe I should let her go, if I love her?"

I said, "It could be that it won't go." "And 35 other women," he added. "I don't know why? It's so degrading to be dependent, and get no love." Now, he burst into sobbing, saying, "She *is* my family ... I am so sorry. I'm not sure I can stop my anger, calling her 'stupid.'" I agreed it was bad.

What if he were not involved? It was boring and empty. He was a wonderful father, but he was not a wonderful husband. I agreed. So, I summarized our findings, essentially, that this vortex would not work. I gave a simple answer to his question. If he remained overwhelming, he would have no relationship. That's why I stopped him, over and over, his turn, my turn, so I did not go crazy! This would have to be his practice, if he wanted a relationship. He replied that he did this very thing, one day this week, by not calling her, a big surprise to her. I agreed it was a start, and I got his address to send the following letter:

> Dear _____:
>
> The diagnosis is the process of the "vortex" as you put it, which swamps other people and gets you rejected. The alternative is calmer and slower and simpler, and allows an exchange which is not onerous, but a question and a reply. The question is how to have a simpler life? The answer is by practicing it. The trouble is that you will be drawn back into the thrill of being accepted, and the despair of being rejected—"hot and cold showers," as you put it exactly.
>
> The same applies to your relationship with us. We too have limits, and have to leave you until next week, until we discuss the next crisis.

Oedipus Pollutes the City Until He Is Stopped

Perhaps, it will now be evident how right Freud's diagnosis can be with certain men. This man was neglected by his parents as a boy, because they were too busy in their lives as schoolteachers. Like Oedipus abandoned on the hillside because of his club foot (Oedipus in Greek means literally that), this Oedipus grew up with a considerable force to make his claim, namely, himself as vortex. Winnicott (1971) was right to show how many Oedipal triangular problems are driven from an abandonment at an earlier age. This is also evident in Freud's Rat Man (1909/1975b) and Wolf Man (1918/1975h).

The antisocial protest of such a claim tends to overwhelm the container, so the young man runs over father and mother, man and woman. Thus, he pollutes everything, as in the pollution of Thebes by the crimes of Oedipus. So, it was with the Vortex Man.

The opposing current is absolutely crucial, and is but a single step, repeated as I did over and over in this hour. I interrupted him and made space for myself. I obliged him to be receptive to me. Sullivan (1954, chap. 10, pp. 220–225) liked to say that the entire problem of interviewing is to know how to make transitions. With such a forceful, oblivious patient as this, a smooth transition is not forceful enough to stop his rushing forward. I had to get him to come to a full stop. Thus, I began by asking him questions like "Why does it go wrong?" which obliged him to pause, for he had no idea, and had never stopped long enough to consider anything but his own harangue. Later, I just said, "Hold it. Why not do something different?" And still later, "Why did she drop you? You can be mean to her. You can be overwhelming." Finally, I made it absolutely clear that his running on, of which he was so enamored, was itself what was wrong: "People have trouble living with a vortex." And, "To stop is a practice." And, finally, "*That* is why I stop you, so we can have my turn, your turn, or I will go crazy." My letter just put it in writing.

The result was dramatic When I came into the resident's office for the next visit, he stood up, and bowed, and shook my hand. He had decided I was right, and that meant he had to stop hounding his wife to see him, to answer his calls, to prolong visits over the child. Over the next 3 months, he gradually got *her* point of view. She only wanted the child, and *not* him, but was willing for him to be the good father. This led to a lot of grief, that it was too late to win her back. He grieved that *he* was the cause of being turned away. He moved into an apartment on campus, which was very spartan. He wrote poetry in his journal, and lived as a kind of monk. He worked two jobs to support his family. Finally, he decided to go back to his home state, and asked me for a letter summarizing our work with him, which went as follows:

> Dear _____:
>
> Dr._____told me after our last session that you wanted a concluding letter from me. This is fine with me, as I am glad to summarize what I think you have accomplished in these three months since I met with you and Dr. _____ on _____. At that time, as my letter remarks, I was most struck by your "vortex" of nonstop talking which leaves no room

for anybody else. I could well understand why your wife was determined to get away from the "vortex."

Since then you have slowed yourself down a great deal, which
indeed gives room for others to exist in their own right, and which
allows you to see their position apart from your self-interest. Of
course, this is and has been very painful for you, because you see it
is *too late* to be accepted or let in very far, when you have run over
somebody like this (your wife). So, you have been grieving your
previous motion, and have been conceiving a different role for
yourself, which allows give and take with others.

I wish you well in your return to _____ and hope you
will keep us posted on developments. I enjoyed seeing this other
side of you emerge, with your childhood elephant.

The doctor here wields a scalpel like a surgeon, who in turn, is the
quintessential aboriginal man. He cuts decisively between what is ill, and
what is well, or, as we discussed earlier, between the part of the berry that
is rotten and the part that is vital (Lévi-Strauss, 1964/1983). This allows
his patient to do it for himself, to distinguish between what is bad about
himself and what is good about himself. The elephant alluded to in the letter is one which appeared in a dream for him to take care of.

The Case of the Robber Robbed

The following case is similar in having all the classical Oedipal elements:
the early abandonment, the antisocial claim that overwhelms others and
pollutes his environment, and the forcing of women, and the robbing of
men, and delight in both. The difference is that the patient also has a
receptive current opposed to his forcing current. Therefore, I do not need
to make room for the receptive current, as I did in the previous case, which
was so crude in its primitive pushing. This case is primitive enough, as you
will now see. What would a man do for a beautiful woman?

This patient was presented to me in the Brief Psychotherapy Clinic after
he had to leave college for a severe depression in which he lost 60 pounds
after a breakup with a young woman he was in love with. He lost her to a
rival older man. He did not seem to be able to give her up. The question to
me from the staff psychiatrist was what would allow him to begin to give
her up? He had a remarkable dream about it that he wanted to tell me.
I don't believe I've ever been presented with a dream within 8 minutes of
starting such a consultation. It was a beauty, and the patient was eager to
drop into it at once.

A Triptych Dream of Power In and Power Out

As such epic dreams often are in three scenes like a triptych painting in three frames (Gustafson, 2000; Jung, 1944/1974b), so was this one. In the first frame or scene, the patient wakes up within the dream with the electrical power in the house gone out. He goes to check the circuit breaker and runs into a beautiful woman half undressed and has sexual activity with her.

In the second frame or scene, he wakes up in the same place with the power out again. This time he is not himself, but himself in the third person standing over himself: a he not an *I*. This time he enters the house downstairs in the dark and walks upstairs to stand over his bed looking at himself as an object. He feels what he is looking at, namely a man short of breath, in a panic, with no ability to make a noise, and utterly robbed of any strength to move at all.

Strikingly, as he tells the second scene, he leans forward toward me. I say, "Your power was out," and he smiles at being understood. He proceeds to tell me a third scene. He wakes up in the old bedroom he had when he was about 9 or 10 years old. He walks to the bathroom where he runs into the beautiful girl again half naked, face to face, and has some sort of sexual actions after she takes him to his present room in the house. He then hears his mother's voice in the hall and wakes up worried.

I asked him to tell me whatever he could figure out himself about the dream so far. He began with the man, himself, standing over himself, and said, "I felt like I was the burglar!" As a child, he had literally been on the receiving end of a burglary like this, and now he was *also* on the active end. This middle panel of the dream was so powerful that, after he had it 2 weeks ago, and, after his friends left from a visit, he became convinced that someone was breaking in the house and went to check the doors downstairs about 15 times!

Already, something was due from me, as Winnicott (1971) liked to say, and I explained that he was stuck in the dream as if he were at the mercy of a robber, and so he was having great trouble getting out of that position. Someone, I added, whose power was in. Still, he didn't know what I meant, so I noted that he did have a rival. Ah, yes, now he understood, and exclaimed he'd like to slaughter the guy. Yes, I said, there could be a burglar of your relationship. "You've been robbed!" Now, he became very upset and exclaimed, "It never should have happened!"

Now he felt so angry, and noted that he had a really bad temper, and leaned forward once again. I asked him about the rival, and he told me that the guy was a very rich man who showed his old girlfriend all about town. I noted that he had lost to a sugar daddy, and he seemed to feel all the more angry, while reassuring me that he would control it and not get physical.

I noted that he was trying to contain his rage as best he could, and he explained to me that he was quite capable of being a very dirty player as he actually was in hockey with elbows and other rough shots. I allowed there was much satisfaction in this, to have your power in, but in the dream his power was both in and out, as he played both parts. Immediately, he told me how he was taking revenge on his girlfriend by dating her best friend and thus robbing her. Not only that, he was visiting her mother, and winning her over to his cause, and robbing his girlfriend of her mother's loyalty. I commented that persons in a passive, losing position often take an active position and make the other feel the position of being a passive victim (Weiss & Sampson, 1986). He could drink to that, and leaned forward toward me once again!

Now, he looked very sad, so I asked him about it. He looked down, as if ashamed. He explained that he didn't like his girlfriend's girlfriend, so he was really leading her on, and thus using her badly. I commented that his revenge made him sad, and thus he was a burglar with a conscience.

I told him I felt bad about my robberies too. So, he was a sad, embarrassed robber. His staff doctor put in that the old girlfriend keeps calling him, to invite him to try again. He is reluctant to get back into a losing game. He has been an undercover robber since he lost her.

I commented, "Burglars are usually people wronged." He said, "Wrong? Or wrong*ed*?" I said, "Wrong*ed*." I explained how Malcolm X became a robber after his father was murdered when he was 5. Now, he became quite disturbed. I left out something that happened when I first walked into the room. He had said, "I've seen this guy before (namely, me)." Now, he explained that he did multiple *wrong* things as a boy, including many vandalisms. He is sure I was a guy who once chased him! I assured him, like Freud did with the Rat Man (1909/1975b), that I was not the guy who chased him. I told him, however, that the dream called out to connect to the past, of how he was wronged as a child, and went wrong in taking revenge in robberies.

He told me that his parents opened a store when he was 5 and he hardly saw them. He was put in the care of his grandparents and became the scourge of the school, always in the principal's office for one infraction or another. I told him that was what children always did when they were wronged, forcing the attention they had been robbed of. What notice did he lack? "Of my parents you are going to say," he allowed. Now he looked very, very sad, and sat forward toward me once again. Now he was a little paranoid and suggested I was putting that into his head. I told him I had no such intention, but I did notice that his girlfriend had withdrawn her notice. He did allow that he hated to lose, and that he felt helpless. I allowed that power out was a very bad feeling, and he wanted his power to be back in. Indeed, that happened in the third scene of the dream! Time was running short, and I did not want to leave him on the downward going slope of the middle scene of the dream, of power out lying helpless at the mercy of the robber standing over him (Winnicott, 1971).

With 5 minutes left, I asked him what we had missed. He seemed very puzzled about the beautiful young woman he met face to face twice in the dream, because he did not recognize her, dark hair, about 5 foot 6, just up to his chest level? I asked him if I could borrow her? He said, "Not if you rob her from me!" and said it was his girlfriend, but with dark hair. I said that such images were usually composites. Oh, he understood that, for he had taken multiple girls. I said, "You dream of the ultimate, having all of them you want." I got his address, to send him the following letter. He said, finally, "When I walk out of here, I'll know where I've seen you before!" Once again he sat forward.

Dear _____:

Your dream is a marvelously accurate instrument, and it replies precisely to Dr. _____'s question about where you are stuck and what it would take to get you unstuck. Indeed, it already moves away from _____'s game in which you lose, to the composite beauty face to face right behind you, and leading you from your childhood room to a more adult company.

The stuck point with _____ is from the pain of losing, and its urge to take revenge by making her feel in the losing position in the love triangle, via her mother and via her best friend. Yet the burglar, you, has a conscience about this revenge, and you feel sad, pained, guilty, and embarrassed about being stuck on revenge and hurting an innocent person. Maybe you will now let that go.

But the dream also points to a deeper and older sticking point, namely, yourself as the child, terrified by the burglar, paralyzed, unable to speak, immobile, with your power out. You have yet to face your pain at 5 or 6, because you were able to draw attention to yourself and do battle, over and over, even if it got you in perpetual trouble. Such acting out bypasses your losing position as a child, who feels unattended to, and is driven to force attention.

I am confident that your subsequent dreams will clarify further this earlier sticking point. The price is to face the pain of it.

I look forward to seeing you again further down the road with Dr. _____, when the two of you are ready for a follow-up consultation.

Conclusion

What more needs to be said about such a graphic dream? The dreamer had several more sessions, and gave up the girlfriend's girlfriend and mother as revenge on the girlfriend, and gave her up too, and seemed no longer to be depressed. It seems we met the challenge of the case (Winnicott, 1965).

What needs to be said is what allowed this resolution of his crisis. He really was in a serious pathological grief reaction (Freud, 1917/1975g), which cost him 60 pounds. As Freud argued, the key to these matters is not so much the sadness, which is evident, but the rage. For fear of it, the patient clings to the object. We weathered his rage, and made sense of it to him. Then, he decided that he did not want to inflict it on the innocent parties. Then he allowed that he had lost, and would have to try elsewhere, as in the final scene of the dream which brings him back to his own bedroom. The cure is thus presented in the dream, and he takes it.

But the opposing current is also important to this resolution. He gets to feel what it is like to be wrong*ed*, and what it is like to *inflict* wrong. He has enough capacity to be receptive to the wronged party, so prominent in the middle scene of the dream, that he can feel his own pain in being wronged, and that of others he is wronging, and so he lets go of the terrible urge to revenge.

CHAPTER 9

The Opposing Current to Guilt

Guilt is a difficult subject to unwind, because of the very matter we discussed in chapter 8, "The Case of the Robber Robbed." Namely, the *wrong* are always those who were also *wronged*. Usually, the patient is mixed up about this.

Generally, what happens is that a person who has been wronged has a claim to make against the world (Winnicott, 1971). This claim to set things right again often makes matters worse. The Robber Robbed took revenge on his girlfriend via her girlfriend and mother. This only made him feel more and more guilty for the harm he was inflicting.

We shall see that the claim to set things right can run many different and twisted courses, which get more and more complicated in time. The longer they go on, the more confused the patient gets about himself. Often, he has a vague notion about something unfair having happened to him, and he has a vague notion that he is not altogether good himself. Left in this state of moral confusion, he is apt to get depressed (Bibring, 1953). He is doubly wrong, for he is not arranging his due, and he is full of punishment for others.

Brenman (1952) called this moral masochism. Some days in the clinic, I feel as though I see nothing else all day long. I see a long line of patients who seem cheated by their lives. They seem to know little about making better deals for themselves. They also seem full of resentment. I have to watch out that they do not take it out on me! They suffer and they punish for it. As Brenman (1952) argued, the shadow side of moral masochism is always a kind of moral sadism.

Is there a simple opposing current to such mounting complications? Yes, there is, and it is strangely little known. Winnicott (1971) invented it and showed its beautiful line of simplicity from a single step. What he always did with a very guilty patient was to admit that the patient did bad things, of which he was indeed guilty, but that this always arose from being cheated. He always reached back to this, the engine of the revenge. This moves the patient to his pain and unmet need, and to the absurd way in which his claim for himself is forced back upon the world. This allows a different avenue for the claim to proceed upon.

Now we proceed to two cases presented to me in the Brief Psychotherapy Clinic. In the first, the patient is caught trying to get justice out of his violent family. In the second, the patient is caught in a beautiful romance. Both are impossible claims, which keep the self-punishment going.

A Case of Seeking Justice from a Violent Family

The resident presented a man who was depressed 8 years after the death of his father, who had been a tyrant. Such a melancholia, of pathological grief, always turns on difficulty with anger (Freud, 1917/1975g). Not being able to accept the anger, the patient stays stuck to the father.

I asked him to tell me about himself and his father. He was the oldest of three boys, never close to the father. One brother followed the father in his sporting interests, and became a kind of double of him. Another opposed him, and got his violence. Our patient cleaved to his mother, and stayed as clear of his father as he could.

This worked to a certain extent, until college when he married young, and ended up divorced. This was not accepted by his parents. He married again, and his wife had a difficult pregnancy complicated by illness, and his parents acted as if he and his wife were conceiving a bastard. From then on, he held a grudge. There was no financial help with the medical bills or with college. Since he wasn't the orthodox Catholic son, he was on the outs. "That's why I'm angry," he said. Immediately, he countered it with, "I'm mad at myself." Thus, he demonstrated the knot he was tied up in.

I noted at once his undoing of his anger, turning it against himself. He replied that he wanted to be able to be mad at his father, for giving him so little. It was very difficult, however, just to be mad at him and hurt. Knowing he had a dream to tell me, I felt we had reached the time to drop into it. It would show us his full difficulty (Winnicott, 1971).

A Dream of Father Tearing Off Mother's Nose

This was the dream. He and his mother and father were sitting in the kitchen in the house he grew up in, yet he was now his own adult age. They were eating, but there was anxiety in the air. His father was going off in a rant, yelling at his mother and at him. The dishes rattled. Then, the father just reached across the table and tore his mother's nose off. She just sat there crying, bleeding. His father just threw the nose away. I could see our patient breathing hard now as he told this terrible detail. He tried to go back to sleep, but he felt angry at himself, for he had not done anything about it.

Defending him, I said, "Who in the hell knows what to do in such a situation!" He replied, "I should have noticed what was building up and prevented it." I replied, "So let us face what it is like to be in this terror."

I went on to say that they were trying to have a meal, perhaps, to reconcile, perhaps, a ceremony of reconciliation. He agreed it was something like that. I suggested we walk through it.

He feels afraid from the outset. His father is raving, and it is the precursor to violence. He eats fast, hoping to get out of there as soon as possible. He notes that he did nothing to set his father off. He did not put his elbows on the table. He tried not to be noticed at all.

Then, suddenly, his father reaches with his right hand across the table and rips off his mother's nose! He cannot believe it. He cannot believe he did that to mom. He is astonished. Then, he feels an urge to smash his father's face in. "A nose for a nose," I respond. He replies, "But we would fight and I just would get hurt. But just to smash his face in, the dumb son of a bitch, you don't get to do that to mom!" I say his tremendous rage makes sense. He says this is how he felt as a child, but he also felt he wasn't big enough to take his father on directly.

We had 5 minutes left. I had time for one comment. I only said that the dream spoke of an attempt at reconciliation, but showed, instead, an exaggeration of his father's violence in the most dramatic form possible. Why? Because he still underestimated what he was up against, and thus found himself guilty for not opposing an overwhelming force. I said, "You look at his malice right in the face."

His reply brought up a crucial point. His father was on his deathbed in the hospital, but our patient refused to go see him. Why? Father wanted to say he was sorry. Our patient refused to give him a chance. Here, he rubbed his nose, and held his neck. I said, "You didn't want to." He said, "Light appears!" By this, he meant, now, that he could see in the light of the dream why he refused. I felt we had struck at the heart of the matter, and got his address for the following brief letter.

Dear _____:

Your dream gives the key to where you are stuck: your father rips off your mother's nose. Instead of facing your feelings at this terror and horror, you tend to veer off into blaming yourself for not doing the right thing. Now you begin to understand why you did not go to him in his last hours so he could apologize and get off easy, when the overwhelming urge is to bash his face in. Makes sense doesn't it?

The opposing current is the full light on the situation in which he did not defend his mother. In this light, there is a step taken to accept himself. He can be acquitted on the evidence of his own dream.

Guilt from Romance: Bipolar Dynamics

I intended to write of several cases in which the patient had a grand romance. I wanted to show how this inflation had to come down to earth, because its claim was too great. The guilt is not about rage, as in the last case, but it is about being extravagant (Binswanger, 1967).

I had two cases in particular in which this romance became psychotic, and ran wildly into manic heights. Both did get back down to reality. I wrote up the consultations that did help them achieve some grounding. However, both patients were empty without their romance. When they read my summary, both became disturbed and one outright manic and psychotic again.

This is why the bipolar cases with both manic and depressed phases never can be counted on to settle once and for all. If the entire meaning of your existence is in a fantasy, as of romance in the sexual sense, or of romance in the broader sense of being a hero like Walter Mitty (Thurber, 1942/1986), then the renouncing of it is tantamount to giving up all you have to offer. You give it up, and you drag yourself around like a dead man (Gustafson, 1999, chaps. 21, 22). Read an account of your previous thrills and you are in danger of taking them up again.

I understand that such bipolarity is supposed by most psychiatrists to be driven by biological rhythms that have no meaning per se. Such a perspective could not explain how hungry these patients are for meaning, and how my accounts of their previous meaning may trigger them quickly into manic flights of psychosis.

Paradise Spell

Also, our patients live in a country which is rife with this tendency. Brooks (2004) has a final chapter in *On Paradise Drive* called "A History of

Imagination" in which he explains the entire drivenness of this country: "America, after all, was born in a frenzy of imagination" (p. 248). Brooks calls this "the horizon mentality" (p. 267), "a fruition myth" (p. 268), and "a Paradise Spell" (p. 263).

This really is a deep and mystical longing (p. 265). But this "utopian fire" is really dangerous too: "So hope instigates, but it also lures. It arouses the most amazing energies, but it produces its own set of awful temptations" (p. 278).

On the Western Circuit

Europe has this fever too. You can see it in a story like *Youth* by Conrad (1898/1966) or *On the Western Circuit* by Hardy (1891/1988). In each story, a young person gets on a run under the *spell* of a beautiful image luring him toward the horizon. Take all of these people across the Atlantic, and you have got a whole country racing for the Promised Land. This is not to deny the biological aspect of mania. Indeed, I am talking about a selection of it in the Darwinian scope of an entire population.

The Opposing Current to Psychic Inflation

I withdrew the two manic cases from my book, interesting as they were for the illustration of guilt from manic flights. The reader may read amply of such cases in my *Common Dynamics* (1999, chaps. 21, 22).

This, however, opens up space for the kind of case that is more typical in our entire population that Brooks is writing about. It also begs the question of what is necessary to get out of the rush to the horizon that is selected in an immigrant nation?

I will state the opposing current to this rush in general and then illustrate it with a case. In general, you must have some substance if you are going to slow down. If you are empty, slowing down will only put you into a panic about being alone and left behind by the group, or into an empty depression. In general, this deceleration will be tolerated and even fulfilled if there is an inner wealth that has been neglected (Birkerts, 1999; Thoreau, 1854/1947, 2000). The trouble with this gift is that there is a comedown to be taken with it. When you come back to the world with your inner wealth, you are going to have to come to terms with getting much less of an exchange than in Paradise. If you have a comic capacity (Bergson, 1900/1980), this can be fruitful and even delightful.

One more word about guilt in the general population. When the tendency is to rush for the horizon, the ideals may be flimsy, and the results paltry. This was Mark Twain's main subject, as in *Huckleberry Finn*

(1885/1962) or *Roughing It* (1872/1980). Shams (Henry, 1973) abound in such spaces, and a sham is somebody who tells you a little truth, while hiding most of the truth, and claiming he has told you the whole truth. That is a sham, or what Twain (1885/1962) called, more forgivingly, a "stretcher" (a stretched truth). Being a sham is a setup for guilt, because you are claiming a lot with little to give, and luring the other person into a bad deal for him. Thus, we have a very guilty population, guilty as charged.

A Case of Jumping 40 Years in One Second

This patient had a devil of a time with shams in his youth, looking always for the beautiful combination of imagination and soundness, but he could never find it. Mostly, people lacked imagination and were dull, and they lacked soundness and were shaky. If they had imagination, they were not sound. If they were sound, they lacked imagination. He just couldn't figure it out. Why was it so (Anderson, 1921/1986)? Of course, he was just a youth, and lacked perspective about the population on the run. Such a population would bifurcate or split imagination from soundness, leaving soundness behind, racing for the horizon in California. He was just caught up in the middle of the pack (Canetti, 1960/1984), which bewildered him in its prevailing tendency for increasing at an ever faster rate in ever greater numbers.

I saw him in the clinic after he had meditated on this subject long and hard for 40 years. Thus, he had done the work of preparation, which made him ready for a jump (Prochaska et al., 1992; Prochaska & Norcross, 2001). This came in a dream of two images, or panels, or what is called a diptych in art.

In the first panel, he dreamt of making love to a beautiful woman in the air over her canvas which was bright red and lay on the floor.

In the second panel, he was in a café in Paris trying to order a supper, and unable to muster a word of French. The owner came over and touched him on the shoulder and offered to help him choose a dish (Voltaire, 1759/1949). The owner went to a table and sat down with a strange man, and came back with a fish that would take three plates to hold up. It was a flounder (a fish as flat as can be), but it had whiskers (like a goat), and two little patches (like a patched coat), one of blue and one of green. The dreamer knew at once it was a scapegoat flounder, and declined the dish.

Between the first panel and the second panel, he jumped 40 years in 1 second. The first panel was his youthful self playing out the dream of having a beautiful double for a wife. She was an artist, and he was making love to her in the air! Such a thing has to fall out of the air because of its extravagant elevation (Binswanger, 1967).

The red canvas was very puzzling to him. He thought it alluded to Jackson Pollock and his painting on canvases on the floor, by dropping or splashing paint on them. The beauty would be Pollock's wife, who promoted him to much fame, based on very little, until he crashed drunk into a tree. Such is the comedown, tragically, of a much inflated fellow. But why the brilliant red canvas? At first we could make no headway on it, except that the precise color was one of his own shirts. So, he too seemed to be guilty of claiming the entire paradise for himself, and setting himself up for a tragic end as bad as that of Pollock. So, a dire warning of tragedy.

The second panel was himself again at 24 in Paris, where he actually had a supper of a grilled Dover sole 40 years ago. Only this time, in this second, he seems ready to read the exchange. The fish three times too big and utterly flat like a playing card and having whiskers like a goat, or scapegoat, and two little patches, merely of color, one green and one blue, is read at once as a sham, and he declines it. He has managed to find an opposing current to psychic inflation and its guilt that brings about a tragic end. The opposing current is comical and encompasses the whole situation and the deal or exchange.

In this way, the release for him is like the release of the man in "The Case of Seeking Justice in a Violent Family." That man also got a picture of the whole situation when his father tore off his mother's nose and threw it away at the dinner table. The mood there was terrifying, but it also had an absurdity built into it, a reductio ad absurdum of the proposition that he had no right to his rage. He got a right to his rage in 1 second of this image of the whole situation.

In the present case, the release is also tremendous, absurd, and straightforwardly comic in its presentation of sham help. In 1 second, he goes from his youth to his wisdom, from being fooled by his own claim, to being fully aware of the deal.

The fish is a kind of summary of 40 years of social experience. A history of many floundering people, usually scapegoats, with a little bit of color in two little patches of blue and of green, but otherwise flat as a playing card, inflated in length and breadth to cover three plates! This too is a reductio ad absurdum as for the previous dreamer, but its spirit is comical and thus, accepting. He can laugh, and decline the fish

Thus, the opposing current to guilt is a picture of the whole situation which allows the dreamer to adjudicate his claim in the air, and bring it down to earth, where it can be fairly read. That is the way out of guilt, by justice being given. It is also the way to surmount an impasse, which is our subject in part IV of this book, to which we now turn.

PART IV
Impasse Surmounted

An impasse is a cul-de-sac, a mountaineering term for an apparent passage that comes up against the mountain and allows no way through. I have borrowed it as a metaphor for the places that psychotherapy gets stuck routinely.

These blind alleys turn out to have a very simple, but crucial structure, whether in relationships like marriage, or in work, or developmentally. It first became clear to me from Donovan's (2003) portrait of where marriages get stuck. He called it "the fight," by which he meant the couple that is stuck always has the same fight over and over again. They continually take the wrong step, and head back into it again. The step is this. Each partner has an ideal which is projected onto the other in courtship. However, the partner always turns out not to be that ideal, after all, and is punished for it (Dicks, 1967). This is "the fight" which is the marital impasse.

For example, a wife projects onto her husband that he is the great communicator missing in her childhood. However, she swamps him with her lists of topics, he bogs down, and then she punishes him with her anger. Conversely, he projects onto his wife that she is the support for his simple enjoyment of himself missing in his childhood. However, she is always on his case with her lists, and he is enraged, and punishes her with his anger.

So long as the partner has to fulfill the ideal, of what was missed in childhood, the punishment rages on in a perpetual dead-end. The way out is simple, but arduous, as in most difficulties of mountaineering. Each has to back out of forcing the idea on the other. This occurs, usually slowly, by an understanding of where the ideal came from, and how meaningful it is, and how tempting it is to force upon the spouse. At once, it is accepted, but no longer forced. That is the single step that surmounts "the fight." I say it is a single step, because it is often present in infinitesimal form, as a moment of truth, from the very beginning of the attempts to negotiate. Usually, this moment is a comical one.

Sullivan (1956, pp. 243–246) gives a memorable example of two women in a control battle over the details of household life. Each grinds the other down over the minutest matters, like who has the better idea of what to do with coffee grounds. One day they are running to outdo each other in entertaining the guests and collide head on in the kitchen doorway, and burst out laughing. For a moment, the contest is equally absurd. That moment extended is a trajectory which can surmount "the fight." That is our subject of chapter 10, "The Relationship or Marital Impasse."

One of the most useful aspects of the concept of marital impasse is for admitting when it is truly impassable. This can save a huge amount of time and agony. Yesterday, I was seeing a young college student with one of our trainee psychologists, who was trying to help him reconcile his long-standing bitterness with his parents. Essentially, he said he was home for the summer only because they paid for his college. He mowed the grass, and watched his separate TV, and that was about it. The exchange was about as minimal as you could ask for. The psychologist was concerned about the eruptions of punishing anger from the young man's side, and from the parents' side.

The parents were obviously bitter that their son turned his back on them. He was obviously bitter that they had never taken any interest in his interests whatsoever. The line of the Beatles' song, "She's leaving home after living alone for so many years," flashed through my mind. Here is a family impasse which is of quite the same structure as a marital impasse.

I summarized the standoff, with its eruptions, and the young man said, "Of course, it's always been that way!" He gratefully smiled and looked at the psychologist to see if she got it. I said it would probably run on as before. I could see no way to reduce the bitterness accumulated for his lifetime, and that he might prefer to put his efforts in some more fruitful direction. He shook my hand with much relief. Thus, the subject of the marital and family impasse is equally one of recognizing what is to be given up on, and it is of recognizing what it is that can be surmounted.

The work impasse turns out to have a nearly identical structure. An idea or a dream of oneself propels the young person down a path into a discipline which turns out to be more of a trap. Yesterday, I saw a young man who is quite typical of what happens. After an adolescence of drugs and alcohol and petty antisocial activities, he had foreseen security for himself as a parole officer. Only, he turns out to hate it. It is a dreary routine of filling out papers, and going to court, and going back to the office to hear more complaints from the former prisoners. He plods through it in a state of apathy.

The previous day I saw a young woman in the same career who is surprisingly lively, only nervous as can be with her hands, and with twisting her head one way and then the other on her shoulders. She cannot decide where to go on in the business, whether or not she should get a Ph.D. in forensic psychology and become a professor, which would have its free passage in and out of the narrow confines of the system. Or should she drop it, and go into graduate school in education, so she could have children for her subjects, and so she could have her summers off. Interestingly, she had missed two appointments with me, and barely made this one 15 minutes late, after the receptionist had told her she would be charged if she canceled late. She was exceedingly apologetic to me, and now we had our half-hour left, and she asked if she should come back? Now, her head was really twisting one way and the other, and she noted the pain at the base of her neck. I laughed and said, "Well, here you are, trying to be on both sides of town at once, rushing around in the parole office, and being here to sit with me!" Rather than decide, she was putting it into my hands. I was giving it back to her to decide about coming for herself, as the very step out of her impasse she needs to take, namely, to accept that she has to give something up (i.e., be on one path, or another, not both at once). It's too hard on the neck.

Of course, this is the general structure of the work impasse, and of surmounting it. How to be *in* the discipline to meet its qualifications, and yet to be *out* of the discipline in taking your own beautiful dream of your *own* work. What lasts beautifully is being on both sides of the bifurcation between being wholly an insider and wholly an outsider. If you are wholly an insider, you become a hostage to its ever increasing load, and tempo, and repetition. It is merely a replication of procedures, which is so arid that you dry up. If you are wholly an outsider, who insists on her dream of her own work, and will not do *their* work, you will be disqualified and cast out. As in "the fight" of marriage, the fight of work is surmounted by seeing both sides of the fight and their ideals and their punishments, and being ready to balance the force from without and the force from within.

The art of doing this involves imagining the available time and space before you decide to do anything. This window of time can be a minute, or 10 minutes, or an hour, or a day, and so forth. If you imagine this container first, you can watch for the demand from without, and consider it, and you can watch for the demand from within, and consider it, and then decide what the exchange will be. This is the infinitesimal step, which, if repeated, becomes a trajectory of a balanced being, ready for the dangerous forces, outside or inside. It's like the minimal window of time in tennis of a single exchange of shots. You will be present for it, freely, if you imagine both the force coming at you, and the force you are preparing in order to send the ball back the other way. If you lose the perspective that sees both forces, you will surely lose the point (unless your opponent falters at the same challenge first).

So, this is our subject for chapter 11, "The Work Impasse." Again, we will attend both to the impasse as a limit, which may be a trap with no outlet, and which may be surmounted, with imagination.

Finally, my surveying of the marital and family impasse, and the work impasse, led me to consider the impasses of development, such as described in Erikson's (1950) eight stages of man: basic trust vs. basic mistrust; autonomy vs. shame and doubt; initiative vs. guilt; industry vs. inferiority; identity vs. role confusion; intimacy vs. isolation; generativity vs. stagnation; ego integrity vs. despair.

The first question I had to ask myself was why I never spent much time thinking about these eight stages? These stages all seem more or less accurate about what needs to be considered as you get older. Practically speaking, I don't think in these terms. Why not?

I think it is because there is a simpler structure generating these as variations on a deeper theme. Chapter 12, "The Developmental Impasse," will unfold the entire music, but I can submit a small song here that will prefigure the argument. It goes like this. Every stage is a variant about the exchange between the internal milieu and the external milieu. When the demand from the inside or the outside becomes overwhelming, the emergency is resolved by dissociating either the inner world or the outer world. For example, the dilemma of trust becomes a perpetual fixation when the internal world is dissociated in favor of a caretaker or false self for the external world. The repressed or dissociated may make a return later, in the form of positive paranoia (Gustafson, 1999, chap. 23, 24), or the delusion that the world is out to be helpful. Momentarily, the patient throws the gate open to complete hopefulness for the internal milieu. Always, it crashes upon disappointment, and negative paranoia takes over, namely, that the external milieu is out to persecute him.

Now, I am not saying that the developmental stage at which the emergency occurs is unimportant. It is very important, in that the therapist has to speak to a so-called adult as if he were speaking to a child at the age of the original trauma. Thus, Balint (1968) argued rightly that the earliest stages of fixation are quite nonverbal and are addressed nonverbally and received nonverbally as a kind of holding environment (Winnicott, 1971).

Take for example the classic Oedipal fixation, or, initiative vs. guilt in Erikson's (1950) terms. Reich (1931) gives a beautifully clear example of a boy with a phobia who is terrified of a violent father. The way he gets temporary resolution is to identify with his uncle, an English lord. This step at once lifts him out of his terror, by dissociating all the claims he is disputing with his father. Instead, he is a perfect little English gentleman, with all of the affectations, and gestures, and attitude of his uncle, and with a phobia which is a residual of the old battle, disguised. The external milieu now has its persona, and he is stuck forever with a dissociation of the internal milieu, unless he gets major help to bring in the opposing current, as we discussed in part III.

So, when you talk with this man/boy, you are talking with a 5-year-old point of view, totally split between great claims and total modesty, between interior milieu and external milieu. If he is at work, you have got a pompous character who seems very generous, but builds up huge resentment. If he is at home, you have got about the same thing with his wife. In other words, the work impasse and marital and family impasse always derive from the developmental impasse, and are merely later variations from the stage of life at which he is having to balance his claims and the claims of the world, or, here, those of intimacy and of generativity. Earlier, this would be played out in terms of industry in elementary school and identity in adolescence, and later in terms of ego integrity at the conclusion of a career and bringing up of a family and having had a long marriage.

My point is that the variations do not need to stick in the mind, nor need they be a complete set, because what matters more profoundly is the balance between the internal milieu and the external milieu, which is always in danger of sacrificing one to the other. The poem of force (Weil, 1937/1993), externally, is the perpetual war for territory, or the extension of niche-holding (Colinvaux, 1983), and what one will sacrifice for it, and this "pressure of reality," as Wallace Stevens (1942/1997, p. 665) put it, is always met by the imagination, "a violence from within pressing back against the violence from without."

The way to last well through all these battles between within and without is built out of a single step, made into a trajectory of a lifetime. That is the step which looks for the available time window and imagines accurately the claim from within and the claim from without. That is the only way to keep from mighty offense to either one, and the resulting retribution which always follows.

The requisite talent is for *crossing* back and forth, as Winnicott (1971) did so well in his transitional space between external and internal milieu. What he did not quite tell us is that the bifurcations between the external life of the group and the internal life of the individual are apt to be entirely different worlds.

For example, if I am delighted in accompanying a patient into a fresh voyage with the opposing current, I am witnessing something like the mounting up of a huge cumulus cloud on a Midwestern afternoon. That is a beautiful crossing inward. But I am going to be tremendously distressed if I cannot cross back to ordinary group life, which is totally a repeating operation, and tedious, and quick to disqualify anything but its routine. My cumulus will dissolve in such dry and arid worlds. Readiness is all.

And so we move into the three chapters 10, 11, and 12, which are the impasses of relationship or marriage, work, and development, respectively. Each pivots on two cases from my Brief Psychotherapy Clinic, for contrast and comparison, and for consideration of the limits of an impasse, and of surmounting it.

CHAPTER 10

The Relationship or Marital Impasse

As Donovan (2003) argues, *marital impasse* is half of the subject matter of individual psychotherapy, if you construe the term broadly as the difficulty of partnership or relationship or being close to another human being. As I suggested in the introduction to part IV, I have come to agree that every such relationship has its single "fight," and that the "fight" is an attempt by each partner to impose his "ideal" on the other and punish any shortcomings.

I do not disagree, either, with Donovan's five stages to resolving the fight, which he borrows from Prochaska et al. (1992; Prochaska & Norcross, 2001) on precontemplation, contemplation, preparation, action, and maintenance. I just prefer to take them as variations on a single step, which is to accept where the claim comes from, while declining to punish for it. It is the identical step described by Balint for overcoming the depressive position (1952), where he describes burying the great claim with full honors and hence being ready for the world as it actually is, and not just as it ought to be, and, thus, surmounting the very mechanism of depression (Bibring, 1953). Of course, such a resolution of the depressive position in the realm of love leaves it to be mastered as well in the realm of work, which is our subject in chapter 11. Chapter 12 is the mastery of love *and* work, as Freud liked to say, the whole business of psychotherapy.

The Marital Impasse in Individual Psychotherapy

It is often not possible to bring in both partners to work on the marital impasse together, because only one partner may be willing to work on it. This leaves the willing one to do what she can with help, and that is often a great deal, namely, to come to terms with her own ideal, and give up punishing for it, and be ready for the same from her partner.

Yesterday, one of our patients in the clinic called me in high anxiety about her marriage because her resident doctor was away and she was being badly punished by her husband. Essentially, she said that he was telling her that the whole problem was hers because she was depressed and had to take Prozac. She wanted me to talk to him and tell him that half the problem was his. I told her I wanted to think about that. Thinking further even then, I said that her entire history was this very difficulty of standing up to harsh punishment, from her mother, her first husband, and now the second husband. I was not so sure that my telling him off and putting him in his place was the strongest move. Wouldn't it be stronger if she held her own ground? Wasn't this an opportunity, after all, for her calmly to declare nonsense for what it was? That was a novel thought for her, and she took to it. This is what I mean about working on a relationship from one side only, in individual psychotherapy.

Whenever I can, however, I invite the partner in, not for couples therapy, but to help the patient and me with her difficulty. The invitation is to tell us his side of the story, so we do not miss it. Usually, such a glad invitation as this is welcomed heartily. He has been waiting a long time for this opportunity.

I recall such a patient vividly from some years ago who took such an invitation to tell me that his wife complained too much of his pleasures. He liked to work, and he liked to come home and watch sports on ESPN television. That was his life, and what was wrong with that? His righteousness was entire. I asked him if he thought there might be anything wrong in this for her? He couldn't think of it. She could think of it, however, and eventually decided that she needed a partner to share some of her pleasures in the arts, and thus she divorced him, and got herself such a partner. Thus, our invitation clarifies both the ideal of the spouse and the righteousness with which it is held. I do not believe that either she or I could have imagined how baldly her husband held his ground. Once it was clear, she could improve her own defense against it. Conversely, he might have indicated some room for her, and that might have led to couples therapy. After all, it takes two to have a conversation, and this is what such an invitation puts to the test. It is a kind of couples therapy in a single step, which opens up a new trajectory or declares it a hopeless impasse for the time being.

The Fate of the Marriage is Embedded in its Social Group

The following two cases brought to me in the Brief Psychotherapy Clinic bring out an aspect of marriage, or any close relationship, which is greater than their own "fight," great as that is in its power over them. Human beings are group animals (Bion, 1959; Canetti, 1968; Gustafson and Cooper, 1992; Colinvaux, 1983), and the groups are run by hierarchies to replicate a culture. From this group dynamic point of view, even the fight is an event between groups. As Carl Whitaker (personal communication) liked to say, "Marriage is when families exchange hostages." As Dicks (1967) portrayed the group dynamics, it is only a little more complicated, namely, that the courtship involves seeking something missing in the family. Thus, our wife selected the husband who was very steady in his work in a very powerful family business. The tendency after the courtship, when the marriage is celebrated, is for the family ideal to reassert its dominance. Thus, she got steadiness as a virtue to add to that of her family, but she also got steadiness as an ideal from the other family that would punish her shortcomings in that department. Thus, each marriage is a merger of two families and their ideals, and "the fight" will negotiate the compromise of these two ideals, or whether one ideal will destroy the other by steady prosecution.

Another aspect of the group dynamics of marriage is the way in which the couple inserts themselves into the available society as a kind of envelope like an extended family. If it is the husband's work group, there is considerable danger for the wife to get lost in it, or vice versa, when the wife is social chairman, and the husband goes under in her social arrangements for the two of them. In Connell's (1965/1986) short story, *The Corset*, both husband and wife are in danger of being good neighbors, and thereby losing their own intimacy. The social envelope can be too powerful for the couple, when they cannot get free of its rules. This will become all too evident in the two cases which follow.

The Case of the Two Ministers

I have seen this couple for a very long time in our clinic, for they have trained a series of residents for over 20 years. Early on, the patient was the wife, because her background was very traumatic and her depressions very dark. Her husband came along as a helper. Recently, the emphasis has fallen on their relationship. Both are ministers in an evangelical church which is the core of their lives. It also tends to swallow them up.

We began our conversation with the wife, who felt pressure from her husband to exercise. She has less energy than he has and tires out. She goes to bed, and he feels depressed about it. This is their "fight." He presses for more good works, and she feels inadequate. The last weekend was typical, and so we spent the entire hour on the fight in that context.

Recently, they have felt assaulted by their parishioners. The entire weekend is apt to be taken over by their needs, our couple not even having time to vacuum or do the laundry. The husband needs to get another part-time job, but he hasn't time on the weekend to do his resume. By the end of the weekend, they are quite depressed. We agreed to go over how this came about.

By Saturday morning, they were already in trouble. The phone was ringing with parishioners needing to come over and talk. They got on the couch together to pray for help. They only felt helpless. There was so much feeding to do, and yet they were not getting fed themselves.

The wife made an apt comment here, saying that she was always tripping over the rug between the living room and the kitchen. Indeed, that was the juncture of feeding others vs. feeding themselves. That was the crossing that tripped them up over and over again.

Back to the details of the weekend, where the battle is lost: Sunday morning, Communion Sunday. He came home from the service expecting her to be up. She wasn't. Her body hurt. A needful lady was on the line, saying she needed to vent for an hour and a half or so. As the wife put it, "We hadn't even eaten yet!" The husband went to bed himself, discouraged. His wife had failed to exercise again. She felt bad too, for this stumbling block of hers. The rest of the weekend blew them away, further. It was lost in taking care of others. Their finances never got reckoned. Their misery was written all over their tired faces, and drooping bodies, just relating the story.

Something was due from me. I simply said there was a limited energy budget, and all of it is given away to the congregation. What did they want to do to provide for themselves? The wife, as always in the feeding metaphor, sadly noted that they were biting off more than they could chew. I agreed that they had a biting off problem. It was a Christian paradox. Doing good is the core of their lives, but there is greed in doing too much good. What is to be given? Where do we rest, eat, and renew ourselves?

Time was up, but, naturally, they enacted the problem of the needy upon *me* as the helper! "One more question, Jim. What if we are resting, and in comes another intrusion? How are we not to feel guilty if we do not answer the phone?" I laughed and said this was the next topic for discussion with their resident. They laughed too, for I was showing them how to hold to a limit (Weiss & Sampson, 1986).

All of these impasses turn on putting the container first. First, the limited energy budget of 1 hour, and then a limited discussion of a single episode of "the fight." My letter to them could not have been simpler:

> Dear _____:
> I'll keep it very simple. Every Saturday and Sunday is a problem of how much to feed others and how much to feed yourselves—which

requires an accurate reading of the actual energy budget. And leads to the next problems of the difficulty of saying no, or later, as you gave me at the end.

The Case of the Beautiful Wife

The fight in some couples is essentially violent. If the patient remains amazed, she cannot quite believe what she needs to believe with all her wits. In this precise sense, Sullivan (1956, chap. 3; Gustafson, 1986/1997, chap. 6) was right about amazement, or disbelief, or shock as the key limiting step in an impasse. So long as it remains in place, the patient is not ready, and will be bowled over again. This is probably why the findings of Prochaska et al. (1992; Prochaska & Norcross, 2001) are vindicated by Donovan (2003) about couples: amazement goes through many stages before it is overcome. I have watched it, and worked at it, for 5 to 10 years with some individuals, before it could be fully admitted, and thus acted upon, and maintained.

Here is such a case where amazement had already kept a woman in place, taking a psychological beating, for about 20 years. Again, the dynamics are group dynamics, and the patient a hostage to them, from her family of origin, and from the family she married into. The history was this. The first 2 years of the marriage, she lived with her parents in the north. She got a teaching degree, which her parents insisted upon. She and her husband then moved far into the south of the country. At that time, her brother got leukemia and needed a bone marrow transplant, for which she was the donor. The couple went back into the crisis for a while. Her husband appeared to resent her involvement back in her own family, and began to be mean to her and to refuse to help her. That was the first time she considered divorce. Because she is from a strong Christian heritage, she decided to stay in place.

Later there was another separation in a similar context of meanness, and she actually left, and felt guilty, and came back. She is still stuck in this dilemma, of staying in a mean situation, or going and being punished for going. She had a dream about her predicament. She was trying to help a girl in a taxi, who was being beaten to death by a man. No one was helping her. She felt helpless herself. This was the report of her resident doctor to me in the Brief Psychotherapy Clinic. She wanted help to help the patient resolve her dilemma of staying or going.

I turned to the patient and asked about what she wanted. There was so much to talk about, she said, in 22 years. She guessed that the guilt feeling was the big thing, over abandoning the children to free herself. Maybe she should just go back and suffer? Already, her amazement put itself forward.

"We were such good friends once, raising the children together. Maybe he was jealous, I don't know. I was quite popular as a teacher." Amazement and undoing. Time and again in the interview, she stated the case, exactly, and was amazed, and undid it with doubts that she could be wrong. At once I knew what held her in place, and what it would take to surmount this impasse. She'd have to admit the truth, and understand how it came to be so, and let it stand. Then she'd do the best she could between being punished for staying and punished for going, for surely these were the horns of her dilemma (Gustafson, 1995a, 1995b, 1999).

I let her take her own course in telling the whole story, confident that every turn would be the same turn, downward. She began with her strict family of origin in the north, under the strictest of Christian mothers, and how painful it was to leave the bosom of this extended family with her husband for the south. The south was depressing in itself, for as a woman, she felt much less respect for herself. This transition was a double loss, an abandonment and an intrusion. I commented that it wasn't just guilt, but loss, and she began to cry.

I felt a need from our limited hour, by a half-hour almost through, to bring her back to her own question about the difficulty leaving. She replied that she got a little apartment, but that it was horribly lonely. She had to leave the children with the husband, who began courting them as the popular dad, in contrast to her strictness. He put her down as sick, and a donkey, which made her cry again to tell me. Her daughter in particular was won over by the father, because he let her out of all her studies, to run around as she liked.

I commented that the lenient parent often wins over the teenage child in a war against the stricter parent (Selvini-Palazzoli et al., 1989). This made her cry again, because she had been such close friends with her two children even in the context of her strictness, and now they were being taken from her by his devious policy. She said, simply, without amazement, without undoing it, "He robbed that." I said, "You've been robbed." She said, "I think I've lost them. I hope it's that. It's nice to know it's 'robbed.' Then it's not my fault." I said, "That is what I think."

But how did she turn being robbed into being to blame? Until she could keep from being blamed, she would allow herself to be punished. If she continued to find herself guilty as charged (and she did by the evidence of Gustafson's sign, of pointing her own finger at her own head; Gustafson, 1992, 1995a, 1995b, 1999), she would allow punishment as wielded by her husband. So how could our findings be turned around? "By blaming myself," she answered. "Yes," I said, "with *lots* of help!" She thought I meant her mother, who was very strict with corporal punishment. That was part of it, the origin of it, no doubt, but the husband carried on where her mother left off. He told her that the children were scared of her. He told her he didn't like her friends. He thought he should have married a different lady. She laughed here, and said, "A *very* different lady with oily hair!" I laughed and said I thought so too. But she was gradually worn down by his running criticism. I could see from her laugh how she was once confident in her appraisals.

"*Where* did I go wrong?" she asked. It seemed essential to find the place and time. It was as if she were bewildered by the contrast between her confident self and her beaten down self. I remarked, "He changed, and that baffled you." She replied, "He said he wasn't going to be my dog!" She thought they were having a good time. Was she spoiled? Why did he say that to her? I volunteered that he meant what he said about feeling vastly inferior to her. She replied that it was a shock he talked like that. Back to amazement, as the sticking point, again, when her brother got sick with leukemia and needed a marrow transplant, the husband got very difficult, telling her he could not be interrupted, and he would not get water for her. So, now, we had a motive for cruelty.

Ten minutes left. Her resident came in here to note that her inclination to get an attorney is stalled. Her husband tells her not to. I knew it was time for my last move. I simply said she got to *prefer*. She was going to feel guilty staying or going. She added that she might be ostracized by her family too. She'd like to put her foot down, anyway, and have a household her children could come to. Only her daughter might not come, seduced as she was by the father. I agreed she was not only seduced but charmed, conned, and paid off. She laughed, with relief, to be confirmed in her judgment. It was time to stop, and for me to get her address for the following letter:

> Dear_____:
>
> Did you notice that every time you volunteered an opinion or I gave my opinion, that you doubted it to pieces? For example, I gave my opinion that your husband felt jealous of your powers, like a poor dog, and began to undercut you, and rob you of your powers, and seduce your daughter against you. I think this is the case, but you are in danger until you can hold onto your own judgment. Leaving or not leaving is less important than being absolutely clear about what is the truth, or you suffer terribly with self-doubts and guilt.
>
> It was an honor to meet with you, and I look forward to consulting with you and Dr._____ again when needed.

As customary in the clinic, we reviewed the videotape the following week. As is not unusual for me (or for Jung, as he related in his autobiography, 1961/1989, and essays on dreams [Jung, 1974b]), I had a nightmare before the discussion, which seemed to map *where* she was stuck with terrifying exactness, so I wrote her the second letter as follows:

Dear_____:

We reviewed the videotape of our consultation in a way that makes me see your question, "Where did I go wrong?" in a different light. I replied in my first letter to the question, "*How* did I go wrong?" My reply was that you allowed your own keen judgment to be undermined, until it has become a habit. But *where* is equally important.

I dreamt the *where* the night after talking with you. I dreamt I was trying to flee across a kind of board game of 16 squares (4 × 4), with a pitiless light overhead, perhaps my imagination of the _____, so there was no shadow and no square on the board to hide from a terrible pursuit. Then I reached the upper left of the board, where I saw some beautiful trees and houses behind them, and, I thought, I shall find cover at last.

At the very second I saw my way out, somebody turned the lights out—and I knew that that pitiless Eye above the Board had watched my every move, and knew exactly when I would find a way out. So *he* threw the switch and it was pitch black. Here, a gap in the dream, and I awake in a kind of total institution like a factory, with only men in one piece coveralls in different colors, and I thought, "We've all been raped."

Now, I've never had any such dream in my life. To make a long reply to the point, I think this dream imagines the *where* in which you lost confidence in your instincts, on a board in which every move is wrong, and where escape is crushed by violence. Either physical at first, and gradually shifting to invalidation, and now, turning you out as the scapegoat, the one excluded from "We three" as he felt himself to be inferior before.

Finally, concerning our clinic discussion. The main thing we discussed was your having a place (as in the houses in the trees of my dream) *where* you could have backing for your good sense, instead of this invalidation which has eroded your confidence. If you give up the place you have worked before, because the board is pitiless cruelty there (the board game), then you must have another place with *backing*—so far, I hear of your son, sisters, Dr. _____, and I see your capacity to win over others as you did singing and teaching—to give up a *place* in traditional _____ culture, and to be ostracized and not to have a home for your children to return to is very dangerous for the spirit, if you do not have an alternative place built for yourself.

Running against Your Own Group

It is so hard to run against your own people. We are built not to. We are built to feel guilty about any departure from where they are going. Both of these cases exemplify the forces pulling us back into belonging as members in good standing (Turquet, 1975). Only an equal counterforce can allow a person to hold her ground, and judgment, and confidence, against a whole group, and that is having a powerful ally alongside (Asch, 1955), either literally in a psychotherapist or friend, or symbolically in terms of a guide figure from the unconscious. The ally is built upon the strength of early upbringing. This can make all the difference, bringing up the interior grid to equal strength with the exterior grid. Like Alice (Carroll, 1865/1965), we all need a Cheshire Cat looking down from the tree to survey the whole situation, interior and exterior, and thus find a step out of the game of Queen's Croquet of a deck of playing cards. A beautiful impartial judgment from the third dimension can surmount the endless circularity of "the fight" in two dimensions of Flatland (Abbott, 1884/1984).

CHAPTER 11
The Work Impasse

I cannot think of a more neglected subject in psychiatry. I cannot recall a single article, let alone a book, in our field that suggests that psychopathology is caused by the daily grind. Studs Terkel (1972) gave enough documentary evidence over 30 years ago to knock over anybody. He minced no words in his opening paragraph:

> This book, being about work, is, by its very nature, about violence—to the spirit as well as to the body. It is about ulcers as well as accidents, about shouting matches as well as fistfights, about nervous breakdowns as well as kicking the dog around. It is, above all (or beneath all), about daily humiliations. To survive the day is triumph enough for the walking wounded among the great many of us. (xiii)

Hardly a soul among the hundreds interviewed and quoted by Terkel is getting farther than his opening paragraph. I open the book at random, and put my finger on three widely dispersed sentences: "Somehow I managed to absorb that when I was quite young" (sex as marketplace transaction in Hooker, p. 93). "You have to be terribly subservient to people: 'Ma'am, can I take your bag'?" (in Supermarket Box Boy, p. 371). "When the diesels came, they cut off the firemen and they gave 'em a little service pay" (in Retired Railroad Engineer, p. 559). What keeps Terkel going is the beautiful exceptions, including himself:

> A further personal note. I find some delight in my job as a radio broadcaster. I'm able to set my own pace, my own standards, and

determine for myself the substance of each program ... but it is, for better or for worse, in my own hands. I'd like to believe I'm the old-time cobbler, making the whole shoe. (p.xix)

Few come out as well as Terkel himself. I recall, vividly, "The Mason" (pp. 17–22) who has had a life like Terkel's in radio, only his is in stone, whose quality and history he dearly loves, and builds, and dreams about, and gets up in the night to design, and passes by in the morning his whole history of building in the Ohio River Valley on the way to the next piece of creation.

I Want to Know Why or Why Not?

Terkel says why it turns out so badly in 1972. It is because you *don't* get to set your own pace and standards, and determine the substance of your own program. Somebody else sets all of these things, and you can consider yourself lucky to have a job, and put up with it. If you can pull it off with skill and style so that you can delight in yourself, that is a coup.

In other words, there is *their* work and there is *your* work. Their work is what is paid for. Your work is what you get in anyhow. This is where the impasse comes about. Thirty years after Terkel's interviews, the pace, standards, and substance are all speeded up, doubled, and tripled in numbers, and specified by manuals. The exterior pressure is simply tremendous, and so the interior of the subject gets sacrificed. The compensations are supposed to come from a rampant materialism such as described by David Brooks (2004) in *On Paradise Drive*. It is a mad rush for houses, and cars, and what-have-you.

Why not different? It can be different for some of us. If you know what to look for, and are lucky enough to get the education for, you can figure a way to surmount this impasse of work. In general, you will need to find a niche in which the exterior pressure is kept at a minimum. Fussell (1983) pointed out that it is not a matter of being in the upper or middle class, as opposed to the lower class. Each of the three classes defined by wealth is subdivided into three classes defined by freedom from supervision. Thus, the upper lower class are workmen who go around repairing things, and the upper middle class are professionals who do things also in their own time. Once you take the step of securing such relatively unsupervised work, you can go about it a great deal more in your own way, like Terkel with his radio programs, or the Mason with his works in stone.

Even these niches are difficult to defend, however. I see plenty of independent workmen pushing their pace. I see countless academics pushing their pace. Why? What is the *fever* that has gotten into this population? What is necessary to get free of this fever?

The Feverish Epidemic

Certainly, there is an epidemic of feverish people, as Brooks (2004) argues: "High-achieving parents are marrying each other and breeding kids who are high-achievement squared, who will in turn make a lot of money and breed their own kids who are high-achievement cubed" (p. 69). This brings about a steep gradient that selects the rich from the poor, and the two get ever farther apart. In the middle is a vast array of people running around with lists of things to do, losing their sense of what is more important than what, or, thus, losing their centers. Attention-deficit disorder (ADD) is essentially this: the lists take over, and jumping from one column to another, and irritability mounts, and concentration is soon gone altogether (Belkin, 2004). These poor souls are supposed to have an illness, which is cured by stimulants, sometimes dramatically, but this syndrome is the tendency of the entire population. I do not doubt its biological origin, described by Canetti (1960/1984) as "the increase pack," a highly contagious frenzy in aboriginal, or modern, societies, when there is a felt need for more buffalo, or more Fords. It is the emergency biology that takes over when human beings are threatened with disappearing as a group, for lack of supplies, or land, or numbers of members.

Three thousand years ago, Homer (1990) depicts this fever getting into the Greeks and Trojans, alternately, and their excitement about taking over their adversaries (Weil, 1937/1993). Little else is played to in our commercials.

The Human Hierarchy

Even when the Homeric heroes were not in a fever, they were highly subject to the hierarchy of their group. The very opening of the *Iliad* presents such a dispute about rank between Agamemnon and Achilles, and this, in turn, mirrors similar disputes of rank among the gods. Aristotle in his *Rhetoric* (336–322 BC/1991) codified the rules for such a dispute very simply. Anyone hoping to persuade the group must follow its procedures exactly. First, state the premise of the group you will contribute to. Second, remove any suspicions against you, which could disqualify you as an outsider or even an enemy. Third, add something to the premise or territory the group always hopes to enlarge. Fourth, stop. Do not attempt anything more, or your argument is upset.

Not a whit has changed in 3,000 thousand years of modern history. The rules of persuasion are the same. You can see them in Shakespeare's plays, or Molière's plays, and you can see them in Borges's parody, *The Congress* (1979). I have traveled around the world to persuade groups from various schools of psychotherapy, and they always behave exactly the same way. There is a hierarchy with a clear rank, and there is a business of adding to the premise, and, thus territory, and nothing else matters. Stick to it, and they will welcome you. Exceed it, and they will turn away.

Young people often have to take many lessons in this iron law, as I took them myself. I did not want so much weight to be put entirely on replication of the premise. When you are young, you think that something else might be interesting. Serious mistake. So many of my patients run straight into this blunder. They are amazed at the results, which seem so unreasonable. They *are* unreasonable. The group is about replication, and the hierarchy enforces it, by exclusion.

The following two cases show the general structure of the work impasse. Either sacrifice yourself to the hierarchy and its fevers and lose your interior world or center, or try to run against it and be put down.

The Case of the Departmental Administrator, Suddenly Suicidal

This man in his 40s was presented to me in the Brief Psychotherapy Clinic for becoming suddenly, and mysteriously, suicidal. The resident was puzzled by his mixup of identifications with Hitler and Napoleon, and yet low worth, self-sabotage, and chronic suicidal ideation suddenly acute in a conflict with his boss who reminded him of his father.

When I turned from this summary to him, he rejoined that he screwed up and deserved it. He got chronic migraines and often felt like shooting the migraine itself where it hurts. I simply commented that a migraine usually means rage (Gustafson, 1986/1997, pp. 183–191, 384–388). He replied that he had a lot of rage as a teenager.

Now I told him that we were right at the center of his suicidal dynamics and that we could take it anywhere he liked. He chose to begin with his childhood, where he was always the new kid moving in, dorky, beat up a lot, until 16, when he got his front teeth knocked out, and has since run away from fights. As he rightly commented, no one ever taught him the social graces.

I asked if he'd like me to teach him? He laughed and said, "Like not to fart and not to wear white socks." I agreed this made you a target. "But why," I asked, "are you wearing them now?" He looked down at his white socks and said, "In defiance!" A quarter of an hour into the interview, we had most of what we needed to demonstrate his vicious cycle (Wachtel,

1993) of self-sabotage. He was the quintessential target, either by not fitting in, or by defiance, or both. Obviously, he had a talent for doing the wrong thing that got him attacked, which is the very mechanism of moral masochism once again (Brenman, 1952), with the rage of moral sadism in shadow in the form of migraine.

Now he was ready to recount the history from the previous job, where he was very successful as the assistant department administrator, to the present job, where he was fired. In the previous job, he said he loved being the second in command. The first in command took all the heat, helped him out, and seemed to know everything.

Now, he was boss. Soon he had dreams of sitting at his desk entirely naked. His stepdad always told him he had to go out there and stand up for himself anyway. Thus, he tried. This is what happened. He did the budget along the same lines as the predecessor, and a big shortfall occurred. He could not have known. He was humorous telling me this, that the professors are always right, and the administrator is always wrong. He knew he had to take the blame, get fired, and go looking for another job.

Being so comical and sensible in my talk with him, how did he end up suicidal in the hospital? It only took seconds. He had resolved to give up fighting with the department *until* his attorney told him to go back in there and negotiate with the department. At once, he felt the rug yanked out from under him and felt like shooting himself. It was like going back to school, sent by his stepdad, to get beat once again. So, here we were at the absolute juncture of life and death for him: Yes means capitulation and suicide; no means refusing to get beat up once again. On the heel of that turn is the whole dilemma (Anthony, 1976; Gustafson, 1995a, 1995b) between two different worlds, the old one of self-sabotage, even when he knows better, and the new one of saving himself, even when he is told to do the wrong thing. He died of deference, nearly, in the last episode.

I felt it was time to drop into a dream (Winnicott, 1971), because we had come to a deep drop off, or bifurcation, between a deference that kept him in serious and recurrent danger and a departure that could save him for another day and a new beginning. He told me a very simple and telling dream. He met his girlfriend from 30 years ago, again, but in the present, and thought, "If you have feeling for me, I'll take you in a baker's minute."

I noted that the dream had a time-marker on it (Gustafson, 1997, 2000; Jung, 1973/1974b) of 30 years ago. What was it like 30 years ago? It was the blissful time of being independent in the summer, of his parents, working, taking out his girlfriend, and staying up until midnight with his pals. I laughed and said, "I think I'll be 17 too."

The meaning of the dream was self-evident, namely, "To hell with negotiating with this department. I want to go back 30 years and suit myself!" He laughed and relaxed his legs. Why hadn't he followed this beautiful opposing current? Now he pointed at his head in self-accusation (Gustafson's sign, Gustafson, 1992, 1995a, 1995b, 1999), and said that he had just been doing what his parents told him to do, and, yet, he feared being too self-absorbed.

Here we have the crux of the work impasse. He sacrifices himself to the exterior grid, to do what he is told. He fears the interior grid, of pleasing himself. My letter to him put it thus:

Dear_____:

Your chief question was this, "In an ideal world how do I get out of being suicidal?" Our inquiry took a series of steps to a clear reply, as follows: (1) You would have to get out the pain and rage that keeps coming around and makes you want out of this unideal world. Thus, terrible migraine gives rise to the fantasy of shooting it! (2) So how is your pain present and chronically recurring? This took us back to high school where the "dork" is an endless target, yet his stepfather tells him just to get out there and take more pain. (3) Next step—so how is that happening now? Paradoxically, you showed a beautiful ability to stay clear of the professors who were blaming their staff member, so why are you suddenly suicidal one night, when you are so clear about its absurdity? Here was a decisive step: because the labor attorney told you, like your stepfather, to go back in there to a hopeless situation of getting hurt, and you deferred to him, against your own sound instinct to decline and say "No!"

Next we took your "ludicrous" dream of taking back _____ "in a baker's minute." Not so ludicrous at all, considering your Monday of talking to the unemployment office and filling out resumes. You simply wanted to go back to the freest and happiest summer of your life with her! A simple wish fulfillment, at one level.

But then your guilt joined the conversation by pointing at your head in self-accusation (Gustafson's sign) and took us to another step in the dynamics of suicide. (4) Opposite to deference is your urge to please yourself and push _____ for sex and take her as "arm candy!" And defy your mother and stepfather not to tell you what to do about anything! So you are guilty, sometimes, of being the 17-year-old self-absorbed young man. (5) Then _____ drops you, and you really hate yourself for driving away the girl you loved most deeply. (6) So we are back to suicidal ideation, not by deference but by self-absorption that also leads to pain, guilt, and destruction. Both are powerful and will suffice.

So finally you asked, "What next?" I replied that you, Dr. _____ and I now have the basis to work together to get you out of the cycles of pain and guilt and self-attack, because we have a pretty good idea of the two ways they operate, and, thus how not to step into them, rather step out of them. Of course, you will repeat them and suffer some more, but you will get quicker at catching the false steps that lead to hell, *which are right alongside* the true steps that will keep you out of pain. I look forward to working with you on this crucial matter.

The Case of the Artist Carried Away with His Own Creations

Now we get to consider the opposite disaster. The interior grid can run away with a person just as badly as the exterior grid can run away with a person. This young man was presented to me in the Brief Psychotherapy Clinic by one of our private practitioners for reconsidering a psychotic break. The young man was recovering from one that occurred in art school in New York, by being back home with his parents.

The story was of a classic manic break. He had been the star of his art school and loved his own work. However, coming to the conclusion of it meant bad things for him. He had to put together a kind of portfolio of his work for graduation, and another for a show in the city, to promote his work into a business, and a third for getting a teaching post in a university.

What he did was to go into a kind of hypomanic phase of sleeping little for months and turning out many works. His girlfriend, a younger art student and a good-natured and down-to-earth person, backed him, but he got depressed and exhausted.

He began to flounder by neglecting his work and hanging out with his friends. He just didn't like his new role as a public figure, promoting his work. His very success put him in a position that could wreck him.

Then his girlfriend stepped in and got him working again. She was a great backer that he needed for his confidence. Here, something strange went wrong. He began to go back to pot with his friends and, feeling bad about this, had a kind of revolution in discovering yoga. He got carried away with it, doing it three times a day for hours at a time. He was in love with it. He felt so good he decided he could stop Zoloft.

His revolution was a kind of revulsion from the ego of the artist. He felt a new commitment to his girlfriend. On the way home from one of his shows he told her about his conversion from ego to her. She was grumpy. Surprisingly, he began sobbing. It felt so terrible to tell her his beautiful new idea and have it virtually ignored. They made up, and he was okay for a few days.

Now came the breaking point. The night before he ended up in the hospital, he was trying to sort a new apartment by cleaning it up and unpacking their trunks. He came upon some old photos of cadavers he had made earlier in art school. He decided to perform a ceremony as a gesture to the dead for helping him and burned a few of the photographs in a little pot on the wood back porch. At 4 in the morning he smelled smoke and went out to find the little fire in the pot had made a hole in it and the fire had made a hole in the porch. He felt as if some strange spiritual force had been aroused by his ceremony.

The next day his girlfriend found him up to his knees in the garden trying to clean it up too. He felt he was involved in some kind of transformative act. The girlfriend didn't understand, so he started a long walk across town. He couldn't sleep. His girlfriend caught up with him and checked him into a hotel. He couldn't sleep until he got between the beds as in a kind of cocoon and drifted off, only to find himself in some kind of terror. His friends finally persuaded him to go to the hospital. He went along with this, thinking someone there would recognize his profound transformation.

The drive to the hospital was terrifying. He felt like he was entering the states of existence after life. At the emergency room he felt the hospital shaking and the lights go out. He felt he had to give in to his own death, closed his eyes, and traveled through the earth. It evaporated and released him. Somehow, he woke up and was greatly relieved.

I responded that this was like a dream that could not stop. He feared slipping back into it. Now he felt quite divided about the "discovery." At first, he felt high about this spiritual journey. Later he felt empty, like it was nothing of worth at all. My letter addressed this dilemma as follows:

> Dear_____:
>
> The key point is that you turned from the difficulties of making it as an artist in New York to falling in love with yoga and meditation as your savior. This opened up too much unconscious material to handle, your declaration of new selfless love to _____, your experiment of meditating on the photographs of the cadavers, which let in the evil burning powers, and hopes of this being a great discovery, and rebirth.
>
> Then you go up the opposite way of thinking that all this daring is an empty and hopeless project. Actually, as I said to you in our conclusion, you do have many virtues of the hero, much courage and clarity to report what you endured. Now it is time to clarify

with Dr. _____ what was right and what was wrong in this project. Essentially, I think the error was to give too much credence to the unconscious. The way forward is to give it equal power with the conscious mind and give each their due. It wasn't entirely right, and it wasn't entirely wrong.

I look forward to seeing you again with Dr. _____, to help you with sorting out this mix-up of good and bad.

Psychic Inflation and Deflation

These two cases show the perils of what Jung (1916/1953) called psychic inflation and deflation. The artist had a kind of revulsion from ego in the exterior world, and as William James (1904/1958) discovered, and as I presented in my thesis (Gustafson,1967), the collapse of an old center to the identity may let in forces that cannot be contained, of huge love, of huge evil. This is the opposite disaster from that of our department administrator who got deflated in the exterior world and just kept himself pinned there in danger of shooting himself.

The way out of these two extremes is in the transitional space (Winnicott, 1971) between an old world that is deflating and a new world with inflating powers. Letting either run away with you is the catastrophe.

As Terkel (1972) showed in his interviews, the commonplace disaster is the mundane one like that of the department administrator. So many are blamed unfairly, pushed too far, and robbed of credit. Yet, as Arthur Miller shows in *Death of a Salesman* (1949), the fantasy of being a hero often gets the person set up. As Willy Loman's wife put it, "Attention must be paid. He's not to be allowed to fall into his grave like an old dog" (p. 57).

CHAPTER **12**

The Developmental Impasse

There is a consensus in the field of psychodynamic and interpersonal psychotherapy that a patient who is stuck goes around the same circle endlessly (Binder, 2004; Coren, 2001; Genova, 2004; Goldfried, 2003; Levenson, 2003; Wachtel, 1993). This is a very ancient formulation, actually, which Dante Alighieri (1300/1994) made the very structure of Hell, or *The Inferno*. Sartre (1943/1989) described it as *No Exit*. Thus, it is a kind of space, with a circular motion within it.

How does this come about? Freud called it a fixation and argued its mechanism was repression: "*the essence of repression lies simply in turning something away, and keeping it at a distance, from the conscious*" (Freud, 1915/1975f). The condemnation of an instinct as dangerous is what drives it away and keeps it away. Thus, the conscious mind is left with the acceptable part, while the unconscious mind is driven away with the unacceptable part. The acceptable part repeats, or goes around in circles.

Jung's (1916/1953) formulation is closely related, if a little more complex. The acceptable part is called the persona, or social mask. It is a static thing. Another way to get a static thing is to identify with a god; for example, as a follower. Either way, development comes to a halt, in a kind of one-sidedness which goes around in circles.

Reich (1931, 1949) combined the two aspects of a developmental arrest in the identification with an admired figure, like the little boy with his uncle the English lord (Reich, 1931), or the identification with an aggressor toward oneself (A. Freud, 1943/1966; Reich, 1949). This attitude of the other is made one's own constant attitude and regulates what is in and what is out, what is acceptable and what is unacceptable.

This organizes the entire trajectory of one's life by fitting one into a role, in marriage and in work. This security is the good news (Sullivan, 1956). The bad news is the sacrifice of the whole personality, and it is very central. As described in part I of this book, the signals of anxiety and depression announce the emergency of going too far in fulfilling the claims of others, or of going too far in compensation in making claims for oneself. The general strategy for this emergency is to contain the signals and the compensations, to allow the functioning in role to go on as before. As described in part II of this book, the continuation of walking into bad deals is continued by selective inattention and especially rushing forward. Such selective inattention can be ignored or revised with help.

As described in part III of this book, a fundamental change is possible when the opposing current to the usual role taking is allowed in, whether of one-sided receptiveness or of one-sided pushing forward, of binding to the role by guilt. The great trouble with letting in the opposite and shadow side of being is that it calls into question one's niche in the old roles. Thus, it is commonplace for a development to begin, letting in the forbidden instinct once put at a distance, and then to find that it threatens the spouse or the career. The promising beginning has its own dangers such as these, and may be sacrificed in the interests of resuming security.

Thus, the key step in surmounting this impasse is to recognize how to satisfy oneself, while good enough (Winnicott, 1971) in satisfying others who are important in one's niche. This was discussed in Chapter 10 on marital impasse, and in chapter 11 on work impasse. Again in this chapter we will consider it in terms of love and work, but with careful reference to the past and childhood history where a sacrifice of the interior world was made in order to fit into the niche of the family in the exterior world. This sacrifice is what is continued in adult life in the roles of marriage and work. Therefore, a fundamental change in the personality (Malan, 1976) will involve a change in the developmental arrest and in love and in work.

The Case of the Sacrificed Daughter

I have known this patient for a little over 2 years since she was presented to me in the Brief Psychotherapy Clinic for depression. I described her dramatic opening dreams from that first consultation in my review (2003) of Coren's book (2001), and will go over it again here. Already from the outset she was oriented to the sacrifice of her own center, and to getting back to herself by closing her eyes and finding out what mattered to her. She was quick to see how she walked forward into putting herself last, and she was quick in getting under way with the opposing current of her own imagination.

The trajectory of the next 2 years followed from this key step in the first consultation. I saw her for about 25 minutes of her full 50 minutes with the resident. We had 36 meetings in the first year, and 18 meetings in the second year. Then we had a second consultation for a second full hour in the Brief Psychotherapy Clinic to summarize what had been accomplished and see what needed further work at the time of the graduation of the resident. I became her doctor soon after the consultation and have seen her another 6 hours at the rate of about twice a month.

I will summarize this extensive work from three reference points: the first consultation, the second consultation, and the sixth meeting thereafter. All three of these reference points are conveyed most dramatically by key dreams. All along, however, the same was true of nearly every session. Typically, she would discuss her present distress and response in a dream with the resident, and I would come along and help them get to what was difficult to face in the dream material. In this specific way, every session is the same as the first session, repeated on demand with slightly different examples (Winnicott, 1971).

The First Consultation

I can do no better in describing the first consultation than I did in my review of Coren's (2001) book (Gustafson, 2003, pp. 585–586). My argument was that the traditional psychodynamic brief psychotherapy, such as espoused by Coren, could be beautifully augmented by the use of the dream, because it makes the *diagnosis* of the *motion* into the patient's absurd predicament, and it makes the treatment out of a *motion* into the opposing current:

The patient came eagerly with two dreams to work on. The first made the diagnosis of her absurd direction with a powerful metaphor, and the second repeated the diagnosis with the surprising second metaphor, and showed the opposite motion of the treatment.

In the first dream she drove to her mother's funeral service at the top of a hill where she crashed the car into the guardrail. Then, she frantically ran up and down the hill looking for her husband, who was off doing good for someone else. The dream took her back to her terrible predicament a year ago, when her husband could not bring himself to be with her. Now, she could rely on me to feel the intensity of her hurt and anger. Her absurd idiom is painfully evident to her: Here she is running after her husband, and his needs, when she is deeply needful herself.

The second dream is a similarly desperate metaphor, of surprising force for her. She is taking an express elevator up 76 floors, but on arrival finds she has left behind her three bags. The people at the top are not helpful, because they blame her for her error, and they put her on a different elevator going down. At the bottom, she goes to the information desk, where she waits patiently in line behind other customers until she can make her claim. Two of her bags she can describe and identify, and the third is more difficult. The lady behind the desk says that she will open the available bags and see if they contain what our patient knows to be inside. Our patient finally puts her foot down, and says, no, she will not have the lady looking through her bag.

The second dream occurred on Friday, when she had been following her husband around on one of his presentations and then began to think about being behind in her own work. So, here she was on a Friday night zooming up 76 stories to work! Again, she was losing herself, and she felt the absurdity of *this idiom of rush for others and leaving behind her own things*. Actually she didn't want to work on weekends, and she had beautiful things of her own she wanted to get into! Thus, the *diagnosis* is of the usual one-sided idiom of receptiveness to the needs of everyone else, and the *treatment* is of finding a surprising readiness in herself to put her foot down on her own behalf and say no.

Thus, the dream is the method par excellence for conveying the *experience* of the disaster of the usual idiom, and the *experience* of the relief of going in the opposite direction, quite as Winnicott (1971) demonstrated (Gustafson, 1986/1997). Of course, the treatment is not completed with these two striking experiences. For the working through is to find a *balance* between these two opposing currents of receptiveness and of putting her foot down or *between* yes and no (Anthony 1976).

As Jung (1974b) argued, the unconscious is a beautiful balancing instrument for righting the one-sidedness of the conscious mind. Why not use it precisely to carry the work that Coren outlines so beautifully in his idiom? The royal road is essential, not to psychoanalysis alone as Freud argued, but to brief dynamic psychotherapy, as Coren would have it.

My follow-up letter to the patient ran simply as follows:

Dear_____:

Your dreams go straight to the pain that has gotten you down: to your mother's funeral service, which you are full of, because she died just when she had begun to acknowledge you, and this chance was cut off, leaving you with all the pain of your childhood from her, and anger, and with not being able to get to your own needs, for following _____ into his needs.

Your second dream shows you on Friday night rushing off to an express elevator that makes you sick, and losing your own things. Fortunately, this dream also shows that you begin to put your foot down, and hold onto your own, for this is the way to back out of being robbed.

Your emotional honesty and directness in your dreams show a great deal of potential strength, which it is time to bring forward. It was an honor to work with you on this.

The next 2 years continued the first step in all the domains of her life: in relation to her family of origin, husband, sons, and job. This is what Freud (1914/1975e) meant by working through. She repeated sticking up for herself in the face of the demands and criticisms of others. It was a matter of practicing her own claim on the world, losing it, and getting it back.

The Second Consultation

Two years later, she was not finished. Her resident, leaving, essentially asked me what next was to be done? I turned to the patient, and she made her new characteristic move of closing her eyes to see how things stood with her. She felt guilty as if she had used up her share of our time. I just replied that the struggle of the last 2 years was about whether she could be as she was and not as someone else thought she ought to be. She noted that she had just written a draft of a policy manual at work and let it go. I said she was herself a draft in progress. She credited herself with being more vocal with her family and at work. I commented that she had taken recognition into her own hands. As Malan (1976) found in his study, this progress was accomplished sooner in the work world than at home. It is generally easier to challenge colleagues than it is your own family.

Now she was ready, as was her habit upon stating the situation, to drop into a dream. It was a triptych, or dream in three panels, so typical of an epic struggle (Gustafson, 1997b, 2000; Jung, 1974b). In the first panel of this night painting, she was moving back with her husband and sons to their college town. She felt helpless, because it was not her choice. A daughter ran up naked. She rummaged for something to put on her, and only could find underwear. She felt like a bad mother.

In the second panel or scene, she realized that the Halliburton Company owned the house they were renting. Their car was back and had been used for a murder. There were cracks on the hood on the passenger's side. She wanted to call the police, but her husband insisted they should wait and not call. Very upset with him, she walked off, feeling controlled and helpless once again.

In the third panel or scene, a female attorney was moving out of the house and wanted them to buy it. This person was standing on the stairs to the basement, while the patient stood at the top on the landing.

I was curious at once about the cracks on the hood and asked her to draw them for me. She noted they looked like the number four, and they also looked like Chinese characters (see her drawing in chapter 14). This was the strangest element in the dream text, and thus, I thought, the most important. I turned the analysis over to her first, however, to translate what she could on her own. This is always my procedure with experienced patients, because it throws into relief the elements that are most troubling and need my assistance.

The first panel was painful for her but manageable. It took her back to the early days of her marriage and how alone she had felt. She cried remembering it. Her husband had friends in school, while she had no one waiting for her. She felt trapped. The daughter in the dream, about 4, felt like herself, neglected. Maybe this is how her own mother felt, alone with five kids. She pointed unconsciously to her head with one finger (Gustafson's sign, of self-accusation, described in Gustafson, 1992, 1995a, 1995b, 1999). She didn't take very good care of herself, with a messy office, too little exercise, and too much eating. I noted she felt guilty as charged.

As for the second scene, the house owned by Halliburton referred to Iraq. Her husband is a kind of running expert on the subject, and she feels judged a little for her lack of knowledge on the war. She is getting more vocal about it, she noted, and smiled. As for the murder, her husband himself seemed suspect, but she was afraid to say it. She had never had a murder in a dream before. I laughed and said it was about time!

The woman in the final scene was a fellow student of her husband's with whom he studied a great deal. She felt very pained by their close connection, but her husband told her she was crazy to be upset about it. She was most upset when the woman and her husband were away 4 days together at an exam, and didn't call. The woman in the dream is trying to convince her to buy the house, and thus stay in it.

With a quarter of an hour left, I asked her what the dream told her that she didn't know? Just that there was unresolved pain from that time, and that they never talked about such matters. What upset her the most was not the closeness with the woman, but how she was handled in being upset about. Yet she deferred to her husband, and never brought it up again.

It was time to deal with the neglected murder. Something was due from me. I asked about it, and noted the crack on the hood on the passenger's side. She answered that the mark was made by her own head cracked under the hood. So that's how she felt about being shut up. She laughed and commented that it was hard to fight back with a hood over your head. She was trying to get more clout in the marriage, but was still feeling helpless lately.

We were about out of time, and I noted we had not yet translated the Chinese characters of the pattern made by her head on the hood. I suggested we work more on that, later. It seemed as if she felt about her husband as she had felt about her mother, namely, reduced to silence. She replied that she went directly from her mother to her husband at a young age. She seemed elated at the end of the interview and said, "I'm going to pick up my husband now after work. Won't he be surprised?"

My letter in summary to her went as follows:

Dear_____:

    I believe Dr. _____'s question is: What next? and yours is about your relationship with _____. You caught on very quickly with us that you can turn your eyes inward and center and find yourself. But why, then, do you keep losing that center, after a year and a half's work? Each defeat is actually a chance to catch on to the force that drags you away from yourself.

    So we returned in this triptych dream of "The Murder of _____": (1) Losing yourself once again in _____, like the 4-year-old daughter neglected. (2) The mysterious murder in your car for which there is an X-ray of curious cracks in the hood, from the head smashed down inside the hood. (3) The female attorney trying to convince you to buy the house owned by Halliburton.

    A very condensed X-ray of what happened to you between1985 and1990: It seems your most important realization about this is: it isn't what he did with _____ that was so bad, as telling me I was crazy to have feelings about it. That is how one loses one's center within, by having it disqualified.

    P.S. Some of my colleagues thought the pattern of cracks looked like an array of 4s. Is that possible?

We did discuss the fours in the pattern later. They were indeed clues to the "murder," for, like the girl in the dream, she had felt suppressed by her mother about age 4 and she felt particularly suppressed by her husband about the trip away with the woman for 4 days. Thus, the developmental impasse at age 4 was condensed in the key symbol of the dream with the marital impasse.

A Final Dream on Work in Progress

Six sessions later, with me, the resident now graduated, she had another dream image about her developmental impasse, this time connected to her work impasse. She was away at a conference feeling quite vocal and pleased with herself, when she had the following dream.

She was washing chicken according to her mother's directions and putting the pieces into little packets. This used to be one of her punishments for "talking back!" She sees a spine in the remnants which looks just like a human spine, only it is the size of the chicken. She says to her mother, "Are you going to take that too?" and walks out of the door of the kitchen, to discover that the house has been beautifully redecorated!

This dream delighted her and needed little assistance from me. She laughed at its diagnosis, namely, that she had the spine of a chicken. We were at the very scene where she had been taught not to "talk back!" This was the kind of miserable punishment, of washing raw chicken, that had gotten her to give up her own voice, or, as Breuer and Freud (1893–1895/1975) put it, to be self-strangulated. We were at the scene of her *treatment*, for she was "talking back" once again after all, in challenging her mother, and it changed the whole house at that very moment!

Saved in a Moment, Lost in a Moment

I am quite aware that there will be objections to my concept of Very Brief Psychotherapy as a single step, iterated. After all, the Case of the Sacrificed Daughter has taken over 2 years and is still in progress. This would generally be considered long term in duration. It is very brief, but a moment, in *change*, however. The world symbolically is new when our patient "talks back" to her mother and goes out the kitchen door. She has made the key move that will save her over and over again from that kitchen of hell, and from putting her head under the hood in her marriage, and from riding up 76 stories in an express elevator. Certain spaces arrange hell, and the key step is to say no, and leave.

The working through is long in duration, however, whenever there is slipping back into the old step of walking right back into being punished, and silenced, and, as it were, murdered by self-strangulation. The patient's blunders are the opportunity to wake up, and be entirely clear about what is what in exchanges with other human beings.

Such moments are epiphanies. An epiphany is a sudden enlightenment. It is an enlightenment about something of divine importance, such as the difference between being saved and being lost.

I am not saying that a single epiphany will suffice, necessarily. This patient needed a series of them from her remarkable capacity to imagine them in dreams. In between, she slipped back into her old subservience. A new epiphany got her out again. Often, such a series of crossings between heaven and hell is necessary for the patient to jump to another level beyond the single incidents or episodes. Bateson (1972) used the term *Learning 0* for learning nothing about walking into hell, *Learning I* for grasping the single episode of stepping back out of it, and *Learning II* for getting the entire series as a pattern that connects the episodes and makes them entirely clear and allows the patient to remain oriented to the absolute boundary between inferno and not inferno, as Calvino (1972, pp. 164–165) described it. This is what Malan (1976) called "dynamic change." It is the capacity to be subject to the forces that would drag one down once again, but to be able to fight them off, and do something different.

Occasionally, a single conversation can operate as a dynamic change. Freud reported a beautiful one with Lucy in *Studies on Hysteria* (Breuer & Freud, 1893–1895/1975), in which Lucy realized that her being in love with her boss was destroying her, and that giving it up got her out of such a hell. Malan, Heath, Bacal, and Balfour (1975) documented a series of conversations from intake evaluations at the Tavistock Clinic, which concluded the treatment for lack of openings, and which were followed up 5 to 10 years later.

Most recently, Talmon (1990) and Hoyt, Rosenbaum and Talmon (1992) coined the term *single session psychotherapy* for this phenomenon and argued some of the conditions for this possibility. In discussing Very Brief Psychotherapy as a single step, I am trying to draw attention to the moment of change and the infinitesimal step that is its defining mark. It can be prepared for a long time as Prochaska et al. (1992; Prochaska & Norcross, 2001) and Donovan (2003) showed in relatively long-term therapy. It can happen in a single session, if the patient has already completed the preparation herself (Malan et al., 1975). It can take 6 to 30 sessions, if the patient is relatively prepared (Malan, 1976). Finally, it can be a single interview session, with some preparatory sessions and some follow-up sessions such as in the case that follows.

The Case of the North Woods Girl

The following case is of great interest because the patient made a remarkable change from a single consultation with me in the Brief Psychotherapy Clinic, so it shows the kind of preparation a patient may bring with her to a single visit. Yet she slipped back 5 months later and required 14 more sessions to get her footing back again over the next year. Thus, it also illustrates how the forces can shift and bring a well patient back for more crucial work.

This young married woman and mother of two girls was brought to me for consultation by a colleague after a few visits with her, particularly because of dreams of violence in the postpartum period. She was now 2 years postpartum, and still not sleeping in the middle phase of sleep after frightening dreams. Usually, she was awake 5 or 6 hours.

The other striking feature presented to me was the loss of her brother 15 years previously by suicide, and a sexual advance made by him upon our patient some weeks prior to his death by his own hand. This history came up a little into this first consultation, but came up later in full force.

In any event, the patient wanted to go back to sleeping like a rock, and was eager to deal with the evil beings in her dreams. One was a horrible cat holding up its claw. She showed me this gesture, dramatically, complete with an ominous hiss. For fear of such a being, she kept waking up and not going back to sleep. That was the only exit that had been available to her for 2 years.

I told her that evil could not be defeated in the abstract, but only in particular, so we might as well pay it a visit in one of her dreams. She agreed and told me one about the evil cat. She was visiting someone else's house and going from room to room. Each one was decorated in the most up-to-date and fancy way, like Ethan Allan. Suddenly, she looked out the window toward the garden and saw this black cat hanging from a spindle. It hissed at her, and said, "F____ you." She woke up at once and could not go back to sleep, for that would mean re-entering the inferno of the dream. For that she would need a guide to help her face it, which she now got in me. To make the next half-hour relatively short, we began with her day that preceded this, and she told me about taking her oldest girl to preschool. There were two classes, for the advanced kids and for the newcomers. What upset her is that the mothers of the advanced didn't even say hello to the mothers of the newcomers. She was totally amazed. As a girl from up north in Wisconsin, this big city behavior seemed totally wrong and totally shocking. I said, "The bitches!" and she laughed, almost shocked by my boldness. Actually, the same scene had been going on for weeks, and she felt pent up and ready to punch somebody. She felt like they were treating her as "crap."

I remarked, "So you've been knocked down by the bitches!" She replied, "All my life!" We were right in the middle of what Mann (1973) would call "the present and chronically recurring pain," of inferno for her. She volunteered that she wrote a short story about it just recently, which was quite autobiographical. She was in church in the story where her mother played the organ every Sunday. In front of her was an old couple, and the old man was having trouble finding the right hymn. Our protagonist leaned forward to show him, and the old lady criticized her, sneering, "I suppose *you* are going to say his prayers for him next!" My patient sobbed after mass at the injustice of the scene, but in retelling the story to me, imagined what she could have said to the crass old lady in reply. "It was awesome and liberating," as she put it.

Back we went now to her antagonists at preschool. She felt they were snide. They crushed her when she broke her leg, by joking about the lack of sex for her husband. Actually, her husband, himself, had a terribly hard time, and she would have liked to say to them, "How would you like to have your husband fall apart in front of you?" Also, in this same 2-year period, her older sister rejected her for life for bringing over her children when they had colds.

That was background, and now for entering the space of the dream. The fancy rooms were those of the mothers from preschool. The cat on the spindle? She pondered this one a moment, and exclaimed that the spindle was a clothes-drying thing in the back yard of one of these fancy ladies. So the cat was one of these bitches giving her hell. She imitated the cat, "Grr. ..." and seemed greatly to be enjoying herself. My letter summarized the situation as follows:

Dear_____:

Your dream is as precise as possible: It says, "You get trapped with these fancy, and rather mean, and snide ladies, and it upsets you terribly." The "North Woods Girl" walks right into these drawing rooms and is as open and honest and forthright as she is, and gets screeched at! Of course, you are full of rage back and that is scary to feel full of the devil yourself at such so-called nice people! Hence, no sleeping from 2 to 7 a.m.

The way out of this is simple but difficult: to enter relating to these bitches so you don't get hurt, and so you don't end up in rage and fear of your own outrage. Could you be a little more discrete?

I loved seeing you. You are a wonderfully capable patient. Perhaps I will get to see you at a later date for a follow-up with

_____.

She felt pretty well after this single consultation and did not return to my colleague. The next 4 months went quite well. Five months later, I got a call from her ob/gyn doctor saying that the patient was crying in his office and could not stop and was asking for me to see her. I agreed and cleared it with my colleague, and we met on and off for the next year for 14 visits.

I am going to be quite brief about the material of the last year, because it is relatively simple in its content, but devastating in its force. That call from the ob/gyn about her crying concerned the continuing rejection from her older sister over the episode of her own children having colds, and possibly contaminating her sister's kids with the flu. She couldn't believe the older sister would be so cruel about nothing. But the graver trouble was that she got a life-threatening illness and had diarrhea that could not be stopped for a half a year. She went into despair, and seriously thought of killing herself.

Of course, I thought of her brother killing himself, and I felt pretty sure she was still identified with him. Thus, I asked her to tell me more about him and in relation to herself. What this came down to was that her brother was the most rebellious of the children and that her father never was willing to reconcile with the brother. She herself could forgive her brother, even for his strange approach to her and for his cruel teasing of her as a child. She believed in mercy for those who have faults. What upset her the most was her father's lack of mercy. After this conversation, she felt greatly relieved.

This summarized a number of conversations which turned out to have the same subject, after all. Her struggle with the rival mothers, with her sister, with her brother, with her father, all turned on this pivot. It was hell when people were harsh in their judgments, and it was heaven for her when there was mercy for faults, whether her own or her husband's or her brother's or the poor old man in church. She was determined to keep to her own belief in merciful judgments, and let other people go who were cruel. She wasn't going to petition her older sister any more for acceptance, and she wasn't going to tackle her father.

She has taken off time from seeing me now, but we will surely talk again, with new variants of her main theme, which might cause her to slip up.

Preparation for the Moment of Change

A comparison of these two patients may clarify the moment of change and its preparation, in terms of all the steps of this book. The North Woods Girl differs from the Sacrificed Daughter chiefly in having a strong opposing current from the outset of our work, personified in the clawing cat which she enjoyed showing me right away and humorously. The Sacrificed Daughter took a long time to let such a fierce current back in, because it had been cut off when she was 4 by her mother's harsh punishments for talking back. Thus, her developmental impasse took much longer to find an adequate reply in her own voice (Gilligan, 1970).

The North Woods Girl principally was stuck in her amazement at what she kept walking into, with the other mothers, with her sister, and with her father. As long as she was amazed by merciless judgment, she was going to get knocked down, and she was going to have a great deal of difficulty with anxiety and depression which could hardly be contained by day and even worse by night. She had the vigor to oppose it, but such vigor could not come into play when she was continually caught off guard.

Actually, the North Woods Girl turned out to be in more danger, because of her identification with her suicidal brother in his opposition to the stern father. This pathological grief reaction (Freud, 1917/1975g) can finish a person off without help.

The Sacrificed Daughter needed help with all of the key steps. Her depression was relatively uncontained, and was managed with 250 mg of Serzone twice a day. Her selective inattention to walking into being neglected and silenced was powerful in her marriage, and also in her work where she rushed to meet everyone's needs but her own. She never was in mortal danger like the North Woods Girl, but she needed long steady work to get fully oriented to her own center when she began so beautifully by closing her eyes and coming to herself.

Sovereignty

Having given my explanation for the length of working through on a single step, I want to close this chapter with two very brief examples of moments in the clinic for significant interactions. I am reminded of a book from the tradition of English general practice called *Six Minutes for the Patient* (E. Balint & Norell, 1973) because 6 minutes was the average time a patient got with the doctor, and because the doctors were bent on doing something meaningful with it.

The two patients, female and male, were typical of our patients, and just happen to come to mind because I saw them in the last clinic afternoon. The female patient was a schoolteacher who complained of being overwhelmed at the end of summer. She had used her summer vacation to be free of responsibilities, and now she had so many responsibilities she did not know what to do. Having only 5 more minutes of our 10, I proposed to ask her a single question, and she agreed. I said, "Rather than focus on all of your lists, which is overwhelming, why not focus on the window of time you have and consider what you want to put into it?" Well, she had 2 weeks until school starts. Into that, she wanted to put her preparations for her own classes, her preparation of her own daughter for going back to school, and the house being torn up by workmen for the new bathroom. She laughed at the absurdity of her proposal, for 1 of the 3 jobs would have been quite enough. For now, she was stuck with it, already in it, but at least she could laugh. Instead of being driven by her figures, she was standing back to get perspective on the ground or container, and its actual capacity. This was a start.

The male patient complained bitterly to the resident about being mistreated by his boss. Having been delegated the management of the retail store by the owner, he faithfully reported to the owner on a Friday afternoon that he figured out which of the teenage employees was pilfering the store. The owner replied, "Thanks for ruining my weekend," and our patient was amazed and hurt and enraged. He ran on to the resident in bitterness about this exchange, because he had been the faithful steward of the store, and only gotten back blame.

Having listened to this for 5 minutes, and only having 5 more, I asked if I might ask him one question and he agreed. I said, "How do you want to approach him differently, next time, when you have bad news?" He replied with a diatribe, about handing in his keys, and refusing to work for such a guy. I could see he was unstoppable in his righteousness and left him to it for the time being. I had heard him before.

I was giving him, like the female patient, a chance at a perspective, instead of being driven forward willy-nilly by his claims. Essentially, I was implying that the ownership was a given, and that bosses do shoot messengers of bad news all too often. If he stood back far enough, he might consider what *he* wanted to put into that situation? Did he want to hold the phone away from his ear? Did he want to ask the boss if he wanted any news, or wanted to wait until Monday?

This, I find, is the great divide (the difference between the small world and the great world; Adams, 1966; Ibsen, 1879/1961; Lebowitz, 1990) between patients we can only contain in their anxiety and depression and compensations, because they are entirely caught up in being driven forward by their righteousness, and lists, and notions, and so forth, and patients who can stop for 5 minutes, and stand back, and look at the world afresh.

Walker Percy (1975) called this latter capacity a kind of sovereignty. It is the opposite of drivenness. While drivenness is captured by its agenda, it cannot see the field it is rushing into, and it cannot even consider going another way. It is alienated from itself.

The step into sovereignty is granted to us all if we can suspend the agenda, and ask ourselves what interval we now have in front of us, and what we would like to put into it? Often something fresh will come up from the unconscious into this well, and often it will be humorous. We have a moment at the center of ourselves.

PART V

Background

I could not have explained the background to how I work, without the figures of the foreground presented in Parts I to IV, Chapters 1 to 12, which are single steps. Orthodoxy can only tolerate single steps, as Aristotle argued (336–322 BC/1991). My book is an argument for an addition to orthodoxy, which anyone in the field can lay hands on for their own use. Nothing else would justify the book.

If the reader has come this far he or she might want to understand the point of view of the author that generated the book. This is the scaffolding that was necessary to build it, left in shadow until now.

Chapter 13, "Scientific Evidence and Very Brief Psychotherapy," considers outcome in psychotherapy sprung from a single step, from a surprisingly long perspective. Chapter 14, "Follow-up Judgments by Patients Described in the Text," shows the results of inviting the patients I described to describe themselves. Chapter 15, "Drawings and Letters," is about my mapping interviews as I go along, onto a field into which the patient plays his/her motion, and afterwords, summarized in a terse letter. Chapter 16, "The Defense of the Doctor/Psychotherapist," is concerned with how we enter the world of the patient, but also prepare to spring *ourselves* free of its perils. Chapter 17, "Dreaming the Theory," tells of four dreams that preceded my writing the first four parts of this book, beautiful calm containers for the violent bifurcations we must cross over. Finally, Chapter 18, "A Theoretical Note on the Scaffolding of This Book," folds into single paragraphs, mostly, a vast array of theoretical problems I have found necessary to figure out in the last twenty years since I posed them in *The Complex Secret of Brief Psychotherapy* (1986/1997).

CHAPTER 13

Scientific Evidence and Very Brief Psychotherapy

As Popper (1965) argued, there is no such thing as evidence *for* a theory, because many explanations can encompass any particular evidence. Rather, a theory is only so good as the attempts, via evidence, to disprove it. It survives only so long as it remains consistent with the findings of many investigators.

I am not going to be encyclopedic about the studies of evidence in psychotherapy, because they are remarkably consistent. I am only going to take up a number of them which I think are particularly astute.

Malan (1976) really founded the study of psychodynamic outcome. His chief distinction was between symptomatic improvement and dynamic improvement. By this he meant that symptoms like anxiety and depression might get better by the patient avoiding the disturbing situations which made him ill, while a dynamic improvement would be tested only by handling such situations in a new way without symptoms. From his point of view, containment as described in part I of this book is symptomatic improvement, whereas revising selective inattention, riding the opposing current, and surmounting the impasse as described in parts II, III, and IV is dynamic improvement.

The only way to fulfill his criteria for dynamic change by my therapeutic methods would be to have a team of researchers specify the necessary findings for it case by case, and to have an entirely independent team of researchers judge whether the outcomes met the necessary findings of dynamic change case by case. In my first book (Gustafson, 1986/1997), I specified the criteria for dynamic change for all the cases discussed, and

I specified my judgments on the outcomes. This was a move in the right direction, as a kind of thought experiment, but lacked the independent rigor needed from two wholly separate teams of researchers.

I would really like to provide this kind of evidence myself, but I do not have the resources to mount it. The least I can do is ask the patients described in this book 6 to 24 months later for their comments on what I have written. Granted, they may feel obliged to agree. Yet, I am inviting them to disagree insofar as they do. That is the very stance I take in the interviews themselves as we go along: Maybe this is the case, and maybe something else is the case? Such an attitude from the doctor invites the opposing current to make its statement. The replies of the patients are provided in chapter 14, "Follow-Up Judgments by the Patients Described in the Text."

The next best thing I can also do is consider to what extent my methods have *already* undergone rigorous tests by other investigators. By this, I do not mean that previous writers have put things as I have in terms of "sensitive dependence on initial conditions" and thus the trajectories generated by different initial and single steps. They have sought to test other hypotheses, but in doing so, they test mine as well. At least, my claims would need to be consistent with their findings.

Long-Term Effects of Single Interviews

Malan et al. (1975) provided very long follow-up on single intake evaluations at the Tavistock Clinic. These findings suggest that about a quarter of the patients changed direction markedly following the single interview, and they remembered what was said to them that made such a great or opposite difference in trajectory. For example, a patient who was wasting her life in doing nothing took responsibility to make something of it from the moment it was made clear to her in the interview and kept right on going for 10 years. On this new path. Talmon (1990) and Hoyt (1995) report similar results.

Working through the Single New Step

Prochaska et al. (1993; Prochaska & Norcross, 2001) supply another key empirical finding, which is that a single step of action often has a long preparation, in what they call precontemplation, contemplation, and preparation, and it also has a long aftermath of maintenance, despite slippage. In other words, working through (Freud, 1914/1975e) is profoundly important for single steps that lead to dynamic change. My argument of iteration of single and different steps is consistent with this evidence.

Revising Selective Inattention and Riding the Opposing Current

McCullogh Vaillant (1994) provides an argument as well for the revising of defenses, which have led into the same vicious cycle, vs. affective support for new developments in the opposite direction. She described these two steps, which are closely related to those in parts II and III of my book concerning selective inattention and the opposing current. In her language, the first is defense restructuring by defense recognition and defense relinquishing, and the second is affect restructuring by affect experiencing and affect expression. This is also in the context of relatively brief dynamic psychotherapy of 40 sessions or less, studied for over 10 years at the Beth Israel Medical Center in New York City (McCullogh & Winston, 1991).

Very Long Follow-Up Prospectively from Prenatal Care for over 40 Years

For me the most remarkable study consistent with my theory is from the University of California study of over 600 children from prenatal care to over 40 years of age. Specifically, a third of these children were from disturbed families with alcoholic, psychotic, and violent parents. Those who *acquiesced* and stayed in the middle of such families had disastrous outcomes, while those who *went out the back door* to find backing from extended and neighboring families and school and so forth had remarkably good outcomes, with a middle group in between, half in and half out of their pathological origins (Werner, 1989; Werner & Smith, 1992, 1998). The authors of this study see what makes a difference in terms of a constitution that seeks out a different niche and refuses to acquiesce and be destroyed. In terms of my language, the difference is to see what you are walking into, and to go the other way. The decisive step is in providing this orientation. Some children seem to insist on finding it, but the social envelope has to be capable of providing it. Repeat this difference for 40 to 50 years and you are in a different world from that of your unhappy origins.

The Monomyth

Finally, the longest line of evidence is about 3,000 years old, or more, and exists in all of the major religious traditions of the modern world, and farther back, into the mythology of virtually all aboriginal peoples studied, which is virtually to say throughout human history. The way out of disaster and into being saved is always the same, whether in the *Tao Te Ching*, or the *Bhagavad Gita,* or in the very building of Chartres, or way back into the mythology of South American Indians described by Lévi-Strauss (1964/1983). The unity of this evidence began to be apparent starting about 1920 when there was a remarkable movement to consider the parallel structures of all the great religions of the world. This movement eventually gave rise to the work of such writers as Burckhardt (1962/1996), Joseph Campbell in his book, *The Hero with a Thousand Faces* (1949), Coomaraswamy (1997), Eliade (1949/1954), Pallis (1960), and Suzuki (1939/1970). To paraphrase Campbell, this monomyth which comprises all the variations of the hero mythology, is in three acts: Act I involves leaving the deathly situation, as in Werner's study; act II involves riding a deep opposing current to meet the monster in the depths and take its treasure in battle; and act III involves returning to the hero's origins to renew them with this great gift.

These three acts are parts II, III, and IV of my book. I did not consciously set out to verify Campbell's schema of the monomyth, but found it anyway on my own. That is his argument in a nutshell. We have within us this profound path of rebirth from death. Over millennia it has been selected for its saving power. Every culture that lasts well comes upon the same discovery, and thus, so did I.

CHAPTER **14**
Follow-Up Judgments by Patients Described in the Text

I have reprinted the responses of all of the patients available by mail who were described in the case reports of this book, and who wanted to reply with their own points of view. My letter to each of them ran as follows:

Dear _____:

    I enclose my draft of a description of our work together for my forthcoming book, *Very Brief Psychotherapy,* to be published by Brunner-Routledge in the spring of 2005. Please correct any errors and supply any improvements with a red pen and make any suggestions for further disguise of your identity if needed. If this is satisfactory as is, or with your suggestions in red, please sign and date this letter below. I would also like you to write a few paragraphs on your own point of view of this work if it differs from or augments the text as written. I will include your addition in a chapter titled "Follow-Up Judgments by Patients Described in the Text."

    I hope this finds you very well, and I look forward to your reply as early in September as possible.

Yours sincerely,

James P. Gustafson, M.D.
Professor of Psychiatry

_____   _____
      Signature of Patient   Date
Enclosure: Your Case Description

I have also included the DSM-IV-R diagnosis given and psychotropic medications taken, because they have important bearings for the judgment of the outcome of the psychotherapy (American Psychiatric Association, 1994).

Chapter 1: The Case of the Potlatch Grandma
DSM-IV-R Diagnosis: Major Depression, Recurrent, Moderate
Psychotropic Medications: Paxil 40 mg and Ambien 10 mg
Number of Visits: 17
Patient Reply: No further comment

Chapter 2: The Case of the Sister of the Dead Pilot
DSM-IV-R Diagnosis: Major Depression, Severe
Psychotropic Medications: Records not available
Number of Visits: Records not available
Patient Reply: No further comment

Chapter 4: The Case of a Doll's House
DSM-IV-R Diagnosis: Anxiety Disorder Not Otherwise Specified, MJ
    Abuse
Psychotropic Medications: Lorazepam 0.5 mg, Paxil 30 mg
Number of Visits: 14 visits
Patient Reply: No further comment

Chapter 5: The Case of the Antihero in a Vacuum
DSM-IV-R Diagnosis: Major Depressive Disorder, Recurrent, Moderate
Psychotropic Medications: Ritalin ER, 20 mg, 2 times daily; Effexor XR,
    75 mg twice daily; Clonazepam, 0.5 mg, 1–2 at bedtime
Number of Visits: 68
Patient Reply:

As described, I had a period in which I was highly productive in graduate school, so much so that I was highly sought after when I went looking for a faculty position. Then, since starting in the position of my choosing, I have been completely, thoroughly floundering. When I have discussed this with therapists, a common presumption has been that this had to be some kind of negative "cognitive distortion" on my part and that the contrast between then and now could not be so great. I am glad that I did have the period of high productivity, as otherwise I am sure I would just presume that I am dispositionally hopelessly suited for an academic (or maybe any kind of professional) career. I have wondered how many failed graduate students have reached such a conclusion about themselves when, in a different environment, things would have indeed, been different. In any event, I have regularly wondered whether what I needed was more a coach than a therapist, and I am eager to meet the behavioral coach mentioned in the case study.

As noted, during my productive period in graduate school, I met with my advisor practically every day. I don't know if I would characterize our meetings as "agenda-setting," which I noted only because I don't think that level of detailed structure was required. Just having someone to regularly check in with, day after day, makes a big difference for large academic projects that basically involve one plugging away at the same thing, day after day. Missing in the account is also that during this period I also had a high level of stability in my personal life. After I started my job, my personal life also became highly unstable, and I have wondered the extent to which this has contributed to my failure to get any kind of traction in my work. If I were going to sketch out my own casual theory of My Problem, it would be a circular diagram with arrows connecting No structure Low productivity High depression Withdrawal from social/professional ties Low structure.

Chapter 5: A Case of Service
DSM-IV-R Diagnosis: Bipolar Disorder Type 2, General Anxiety Disorder, Cocaine and Marijuana Abuse, fully sustained remission
Psychotropic Medications: Lexapro 15 mg a day and Lamictal 250 mg a day
Number of Visits: 57
Patient Reply:

I don't disagree with anything Dr. Gustafson writes, but I should [like to] present an alternate (complementary?) argument.

There seems to be an implication that if I could only change my way of thinking, I would be back to the land of the normal. It's hard to express how disheartening it is to constantly struggle between the argument that mental illness is a physical disease and the argument that one can think their way out of it. Especially disheartening coming from someone that I know knows better. I'm bipolar II. I've invested a lot of time in that diagnosis and, while trying not to get too hung up on the labels, it matters to me that it be understood as a physical as well as mental ailment. It has to be something REAL, not just something in my head. We already feel that way.

There seem to be elusive truths that can't be explained by faulty thought patterns. Maybe I'm burning off sins of a past life, maybe this is a test, maybe I'm just nuts. On some level, "correcting" those thoughts may cause more harm than good in the long run. Or maybe the implications are the same either way. No way to know for sure, but there's definitely a desire on some level not to swallow everything they want you to do. This partly explains my reluctance concerning hospitalization. Besides, who knows what happens once you're in there? I usually don't mind sharing when things are perilous, but can't risk losing control of my fate. The danger is that I won't be sufficiently aware when the next external attack comes. The wrong combination of events could be bad. This is where I need the help.

I think that I can be more skillful than I am now, but I'm never going to be all-the-way better. These forces will always be following me. All I can do is figure out better ways to keep them quiet and at bay and to slow any deterioration. If they do leave, I'll know to be extra cautious, because that's when I'm going to get blindsided. [Please don't edit this. It says what I want it to say. Changes would alter my meaning.]

Chapter 5: The Case of the Missing Kangaroo
DSM-IV-R Diagnosis: Generalized Anxiety Disorder and Dysthymia
Psychotropic Medications: Trazodone 50 mg 1–2 at bedtime as needed
Number of Visits: 4
Patient Reply: No further comment.

Chapter 6: Your Partner's Troubles Are Your Own
DSM-IV-R Diagnosis: Adjustment Disorder
Psychotropic Medications: None
Number of Visits: 14
Patient Reply: No further comment.

Chapter 7: The Case of a Reasonable Woman
DSM-IV-R Diagnosis: Not available
Psychotropic Medications: Wellbutrin SR 200 mg bid and Amitriptyline 10 mg qhs
Number of Visits: 86 (group therapy)
Patient Reply: No further comment

Chapter 7: The Case of the Woman Who Could Help Everyone
DSM-IV-R Diagnosis: Major Depression, Recurrent, Moderate
Psychotropic Medications: Clonazepam 1 mg 1 ½ tabs 2 x daily and Lexapro 10 mg
Number of Visits: 19
Patient Reply:

As I reflect on the Very Brief Psychotherapy session, it is colored by many months of additional therapy (for me) and medication (also for me). What I took away from the brief session alone was the beginning of an understanding of *separation*—that if I didn't separate from my son,

I would stay/become sick (mentally and physically) and would be of no help to anyone. I found myself at the time of the initial session to be very depressed, unable to concentrate at my demanding job, and crying while alone, especially while driving home from my mother's house (who was, and remains, very ill, with me as her primary advocate and secondary caregiver). So I knew enough to ask for help, and I received it for the first time in my life. I had tried counseling (with my husband) earlier with no success. And I read lots of books and websites, but they didn't cure me.

What happened to my family and to my son especially can only be described as heartbreaking. Suicide can affect families for generations. Watching him (my son) lose his life, relationships, and jobs piece by piece through psychotic and/or bipolar depression is more heartbreaking, *much more* heartbreaking, than the suicide of my first husband. It is the worst thing in my life.

It doesn't seem fair that I should have to go through this twice, and I agree there is a lot of anger and grief to be dealt with on my son's part and on my part. I am not sure exactly how to do this, since I am not by nature an angry and grieving person. Anyone who knows me would say I am optimistic, full of energy, and that I can "do anything" or "make anything better." I feel I am tapped out, and I need to stop it—STOP IT—and focus on myself. I think I keep so busy so that I don't have to think about things too deeply.

That said, I can tell you now that I have gained a great deal of insight into how to handle my feelings—how to do *what I can* for my son, and how to *NOT do* what I cannot do. How to set boundaries. We talk much more and I am much more honest. I don't try to spare his feelings as much. I can't cure his illness, I can't live his life, and I can't feel his feelings. If I keep trying to do this (for him, and for many others to a lesser degree) I myself will have an unhappy life. And so what is gained? Nothing but more heartache. So I am working very hard to be supportive without being consumed. I am getting better every day at doing it. I have a good husband and in most ways a very good life. The brief therapy set me on the path to separation and I intend to work on it until I am done, which could take forever with the aid of good doctors and a little medication thrown in for good measure.

It is now about 2 months before my son's 27th birthday. He never thought he would, or should, live longer than his father did, so I am terrified about this but also know I can't control what happens. I can be supportive (which I am) and tell him how many people love him, and have him over for dinner, and give him a sort of safety net of family. But that's all I can do.

Thank you. Therapy has helped a lot. I didn't realize how much until I gave myself permission and time to think about it.

Chapter 7: The Case of the Vortex
DSM-IV-R Diagnosis: Major Depression, Severe; Narcissistic Personality Disorder
Psychotropic Medications: None
Number of Visits: 15
Patient Reply: No further comment

Chapter 8: The Case of the Robber Robbed
DSM-IV-R Diagnosis: Major Depression, Severe
Psychotropic Medications: Trazodone 50 mg qhs and Celexa 40 mg q day discontinued after 2 months
Number of Visits: 10
Patient Reply: No further comment.

Chapter 9: A Case of Seeking Justice from a Violent Family
DSM-IV-R Diagnosis: Major Depression, Moderate
Psychotropic Medications: Lorazepam 0.5 mg and Paxil 60 mg q day
Number of Visits: 11
Patient Reply: No further comment

Chapter 9: A Case of Jumping 40 Years in One Second
DSM-IV-R Diagnosis: Adjustment Disorder with Anxious and Depressed Mood
Psychotropic Medications: None
Sessions: One
Patient Reply: No further comment

Chapter 10: The Case of the Two Ministers
DSM-IV-R Diagnosis: (wife) Major Depression, Severe, with Psychotic Features
Psychotropic Medications: Not available
Number of Visits: 15 (since 8/11/03)
Patient Reply: No further comment

Chapter 10: The Case of the Beautiful Wife
DSM-IV-R Diagnosis: Adjustment Disorder with Anxious and Depressed Mood
Psychotropic Medications: None
Number of Visits: Two
Patient Reply: After the therapy session with you, I must tell you that it brought me such healing and inner strength that I began to regain

my self-confidence and put my foot down! My husband moved out of the house, for a change (a month ago) and I remodeled the ranch house, cleaned up the mess and the psychological dust from his office he occupied (and rotted) down in the basement of our home. Everything looks different including my children!

My children respect me more and hug me and kiss me before they leave home. I have given my daughter especially, a deadline to move out of the house so that I may live my life in full, without worrying about how and when she returns home or about her studies.

They had visited _____ last month and finally realized that their father was foolish to sell the three condos (luxurious) without discussing with me, especially the one overlooking the lakes. My daughter told my sister in _____ that she was proud of me and that most of the values they have were from being around me. She would call me almost every day to hear my voice and to say that their father's brother was not as pleasant as they thought. They both stated that I may have suffered under my in-laws.

I cannot see myself with him anymore although I must confess that I dream of being alone and not having him around to help me when I'm sick. This feeling is from being around the geriatric population I work with.

My mind is so much clearer that I see my past in other women whose husbands play mind games with them. I realize I have no direction and I'm not afraid of suffering from the first stages of the dreadful Alzheimer's disease!

Thank you for your healing spirit, you are a blessing, and what you do is wonderful.

Two Additional Items:
The first 2 years I was with my parents in the North completing my teaching degree my parents insisted that I had to have a qualification that I could make use of. They paid for everything and I lived in their house.

I was the only donor among eight siblings that matched my brother's (HLA). We went to _____ to have the bone marrow transplant. My father paid for my husband's ticket and expenses because he was needed to take care of our son who was only a year old. I could not leave him behind. I was pregnant with my daughter who was born in _____. My husband was horrible and had the worst attitude ever. I began to see his true colors then. He knew my brother was dying and we were disappointed since he could not have the transplant—he was dying. My mother, my younger little sister, and my elder brother were all there taking turns to sit with my sick brother. I used to be a good singer, when I would hum or sing tunes of my favorite spirituals in the bathroom. My husband would work and ask why I was singing when everything was so sad and my brother is sick. That's how he was! I had a C-section for my daughter and I was in pain and breastfeeding all the time. My husband would refuse to help me and bring me a glass of water when I asked him. He lived with a close European family friends for a few weeks after my baby was born. My husband said that it seems the man stated that they do not bring water to their wives "like you are doing." I know he would not say that because he sees me feeding the baby all the time and I was in pain. I believed him for some reason and this is the beginning of the problems that came after. Yes, I considered divorce and even moving out and living in the North with my children.

> Chapter 11: The Case of the Departmental Administrator, Suddenly Suicidal
> DSM-IV-R Diagnosis: Major Depression, Recurrent, Severe
> Psychotropic Medications: Lexapro 20 mg and Trazodone 100 mg
> Number of Visits: 16
> Patient Reply:

Let me begin by saying that I am honored that you found my case so interesting as to be worthy to be included in one of your books. I would very much like to receive a signed copy when it is published. That being said, I feel that there is little or nothing that needs changing in your chapter as it currently stands. If memory serves, it quite aptly characterizes our work together. However, I did want to provide you with a brief update on what has been going on with me since our last visit.

As you know, I moved down to _____ and in with my mom and stepdad. My girlfriend and I decided to get back together (again!) and give it another try. So she moved down here, too, and we have since moved into an apartment of our own. I don't think my mom was entirely happy about that. I think she enjoyed taking care of me for a while. At any rate, while I was still living at mom's I applied to the Ph.D. program in arts and humanities at the University of _____ at _____. I was later accepted and I have started my coursework. It's a lot of hard work (more than I expected, actually), but this is quite literally a dream come true for me and it's been a long time since I've been this happy about anything. I have still been unable to secure a professional level position. This is just as well because I'm not sure I want one for the reasons that we've talked about. Instead, I'm working as a cashier at a Barnes & Noble Bookstore. I love it! First of all, I'm around books all day. Second, I have a few very clearly defined responsibilities. Finally, I only have one boss to answer to. Frankly, the pay is not great, but that is way down on my list of priorities right now.

Nevertheless, I am acutely aware of how much work I still have to do. For example, I still get migraines and I will have to be able to function at a higher-level job someday. I was wondering if you could recommend someone in the _____ area to continue to work with. I would definitely like someone who takes a broad view of things and is bright enough to keep up with me. If they're half as smart as you are, that shouldn't be hard.

> Chapter 11: The Case of the Artist Carried Away with His Own Creations
> DSM-IV-R Diagnosis: Bipolar Depression
> Psychotropic Medications: Lamictal 150 mg 2 x daily, Trileptal 600 mg 2 x daily,
> Lorazepam 0.5 mg as needed, Bupropion 75 mg 2 x daily
> Number of Visits: 8
> Patient Reply:

The account of my acute manic episode and resulting psychosis appears to align itself squarely with the facts of my case as recounted by myself. The consultation session provided an opportunity to testify to the events which took place at a time when perspective was much needed. In regard to my point of view, now 3 years after the fact, something seems altogether missing and perhaps ultimately unaccountable in this transcription. This may simply be a discrepancy between rational and irrational discourse or more pointedly the opposing perspectives of the psychotic vs. the analyst. I do not mean to suggest that a diagnosis of a psychotic break is impossible, but rather that a fundamental lack appears between a language explanatory in nature and one which is closer to the poetic, the spiritual, the recounting of a dream, the importance is not the factual account but the experience itself. Perhaps this is a bedrock problem for the analyst. For psychosis is not a dream, and the analogy does not serve it justice.

> Chapter 12: The Case of the Sacrificed Daughter
> DSM-IV-R Diagnosis: Major Depression, Moderate
> Psychotropic Medications: Nefazodone 250 mg. bid
> Number of Visits: 54
> Patient Reply:

The day before I received your correspondence, I came upon a shop window filled with tiles that were engraved with Chinese characters. A beautiful purple tile carried a symbol that looked like an upside-down four. Upon closer inspection, a tiny sticker told me the name of the character was *strength*. I will now explain how finding this tile has helped me to look differently at my dream's "murders."

I can appreciate that some may see multiple fours in the pattern of cracks on the car hood. However, I have always seen a single four. Below I have traced the outline from the drawing I made when I first awoke from my dream. (It is slightly different from the one I made for you and Dr. ____ during the consultation). When I tilt the page to view the car from the front headlights, the cracks look like a *four* with a line over the top and underneath—the hood on top and the car's body below. When I tilt the page to view from my seat on the passenger's side, they look like an upside down four, *strength*, between the hood and the car.

From the outside view at the headlights, I see a 4-year-old daughter's questions smashed and a wife's 4-day worry disqualified. From the inside view of the passenger seat, I see my strength (my power) feared and challenged. The wonder here is that neither the *four* nor the *strength* is smashed. Both hold their shape perfectly under the force of the hood.

Chapter 12: The Case of the North Woods Girl
DSM-IV-R Diagnosis: Adjustment Disorder to Family Tragedy
Psychotropic Medications: Paroxetine, 20 mg
Number of Visits: 23
Patient Reply:

My introduction to Doctor Gustafson was one of those moments where I just knew I was in good hands … like great things are going to happen. I came to him with what I referred to as a "mixed bag." There was my dad's abusive relationship with my brother that left devastating effects on me, the star witness. Then came my brother's suicide. Depression followed for me and remained over the past 15 years. Then severe anxiety and nightmares took hold after the births of my two daughters. I couldn't shake my obsession with death, dying, and the devil. In recent years, my eldest sister cut ties with me and my family over a trivial incident. There was a lot of pain and anguish there, and I felt like I was a big open wound walking around in the daytime and bleeding in the wee hours of the morning. I needed some sort of comfort, some sort of peace, or life was just too hard for me to want to continue living.

Doctor Gustafson helped illuminate my patterns of hopelessness and despair when confronted with the judgmental, the mean, and the insensitivities of the world. I came to realize as each session built upon the last that I was allowing other people's poor judgments of me to wipe out any self-worth I had. In mantra, and just as my dad had used it toward my brother, and my sister toward me, I was adopting it against myself too.

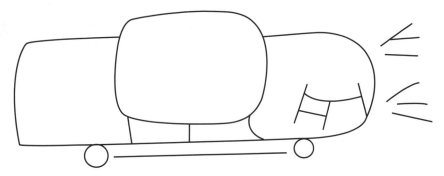

Fig. 14.1 Drawing from the case of the sacrificed daughter.

This, coupled with a newly diagnosed digestive disease was leaving me seriously considering suicide this past year.

The timely intervention of a gastroenterologist and the continued support of Dr. Gustafson helped me to regain perspective and reason. I want to live now. I want to give myself the love I deserve and others the same. It is not the aggressive or stubborn or hard-nosed in life that I admire. I see now that there is no glory in that. It is those who embrace, who forgive, who show mercy that I want to emulate. I want to live life with compassion toward others, and most of all, toward myself. Dr. Gustafson helped me to realize how crucial that compassion and forgiveness is to my life, and my desire to live it.

CHAPTER 15
Drawings and Letters

It is not usual for a psychotherapist to draw (Winnicott, 1971) while he listens to the patient nor to send the patient a letter afterward (White & Epston, 1990). It is not essential to the method advocated in this text, yet I find it helpful, and I will explain why in this brief chapter. As with Winnicott (1971), I find it a natural extension of psychodynamic thinking.

If history is essential to this method, it is because it has generated a vicious cycle which repeats endlessly. A reader wrote to ask me for my history form. I wrote back:

> Dear Dr. _____:
> Here is my history form. You can map the circularity of the history in this space: start anywhere and it travels around this.
>
> Sincerely, Jim Gustafson
>
> PS: The outer triangle to the right is the perversity of society for the body, and the inner triangle to the left is the opposite perversity of the body for society. Thus, it begets Dr. Jekyll and Mr. Hyde in the male, the exploding doormat in the female. The entire common dynamics (Gustafson, 1999) are variants thereof: of the theme of perversity in all its variations, a music, or musical score.

The history will go around this circle while slowly descending to the lower right. Of course, I am equally interested in departures from this

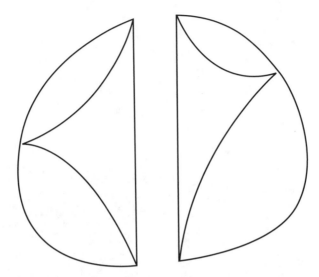

Fig. 15.1 A grid on which to take the history and follow the patient.

psychopathology, which always move in an opposing current to the left. Therefore, I revised this grid to include the trajectory to the right of a downhill course and a trajectory to the left of an opposing current. Of course, the trajectory to the left always has to re-enter the one to the right of the social group.

I literally map the interview onto this grid as onto the staff markings of a musical score. I follow every episode around its vicious cycle. I draw body language which calls attention to the situation (such as Gustafson's sign, of one or more fingers pointing to the head in self-accusation, Gustafson, 1992, 1995a, 1995b, 1999). I generally use black and red pens (color gives a third dimension in the two-dimensional score of the page in black and white) for the circularity, green and blue pens for departures to the left, and for their return.

As for Winnicott (1971), I find the space of the patient of absolute importance for his or her trajectory. That is why I am always looking into it and always drawing it. If you look merely into a one- or two-dimensional space, you cannot escape going around in vicious cycles. If you can look at it from above in the third dimension, like the Cheshire Cat in Alice (Carroll, 1865/1985), you can see the limits of the space in the Game, as of Queen's Croquet, and of the difficulties of leaving the Game, and consider departures that will actually get free of it, if they must continue to revisit it!

Finally, I reply to every visit of the patient with a letter, usually in one or two lines, in contrast to the full-page letters of one-time consultations in

Fig. 15.2 The grid revised for the two trajectories.

the Brief Psychotherapy Clinic. In these briefer letters, I point to the key step or steps taken by the patient in the interview, that is, to repeat the circularity of a downhill course, or to depart from it (see Introduction to Part I). In other words, a letter of this kind follows naturally from a theory which says that everything depends on the single step for its trajectory. Actually, I began writing letters around 1990, and through doing so I discovered that my subject was the single step! I began to see that a sentence or two captured the entire motion of the hour and of the entire history in microcosm.

CHAPTER 16
The Defense of the Doctor/ Psychotherapist

I was asked the other day by a group of our secretaries and administrative assistants what is the "brief therapy" of my Brief Psychotherapy Clinic. They understood my answer at once by reference to the cartoon on my office door. It is a picture of two mechanics sitting on their chairs in the doorway of their service garage, watching a person driving a convertible go around in circles waving to them (counterclockwise). One of the mechanics (on the right) is speaking to the other in the caption of the cartoon: "At what point does this become our problem?" (*New Yorker,* February 18 and 25, 2002, p. 202).

I explained that the trainees and staff bring to me cases going around in such endless circles (as of hell!), and it becomes my responsibility in a consultation in the Brief Psychotherapy Clinic to point out what setting of the steering wheel will repeat this cycle forever, and what setting of the steering wheel will get the patient out of it and on another course (purgatorial or circles up a mountain).

Such a point of view as of the two mechanics is also essential for their own protection. They see the comedy of the patient's history, which is *not* their responsibility. Their light-heartedness comes from keeping apart from what a mess people make of things for themselves. They will take *some* responsibility at the point they are asked for their opinion.

Even with such a perspective, however, the two mechanics are in danger of getting dragged into the patient's misery. Every car mechanic knows how to keep a distance from complaining customers, who will try to put their helpless rage into him. It is harder in the mechanics that we deal in.

Defense by the Hour

In my own private practice, I see patients for three-quarters of an hour. In the first quarter, I get a reckoning of what the patient is trying but failing to do. In the second quarter, I tell him something about the step that continues his misery and the step that gets him or her out of it. In the third quarter, I watch the patient deal with what I've told him or her, and especially, watch the patient trying to load me up with too much to do before the end of the session. This third quarter is especially dangerous to the well-being of the doctor or psychotherapist. The patient will often, or even usually, give you a load that was put onto *him or her* to see how you cope with it. This is called projective identification or turning passive into active (Weiss & Sampson, 1986). In other words, what the patient suffered passively at the hands of someone else, he or she actively makes you suffer by giving it to you. If the patient is a kind of Dr. Jekyll, for example, he will have taken too much responsibility for every patient he saw all day and then come in to give you too much responsibility for him! For example, if the hour has dealt with one big thing, the patient will give you a second big thing near the conclusion with much too little time to deal with it, raise a big doubt about your reply to the first big thing, or mention a favor, or a report or a prescription for you to take care of. You need to be ready to tell him or her you will discuss it next time or, at the very least, another time in which it can be accomplished.

This is why I routinely draw a little window in my grid (Figure 15.2) as I turn into the third quarter of the hour, simply to remind myself to look into it carefully for a trap.

This amended grid has several other advantages, which also keep me from getting weighed down. The first quarter of a very tedious patient is much more bearable knowing the second only needs a brief reply, and the third quarter needs nothing but to decline a further load. The fourth quarter always belongs to me. It reminds me to do nothing but lie on my couch and get back to myself.

Defense by the Case

As well prepared as I am in this way, certain patients still get to me. This occurs when I underestimate them. They may have an unusual talent for projecting their misery into those around them, and I am going to be a prime object for such efforts (Winnicott, 1958). This also occurs when I have worked as well as I could and yet missed something big. As Jung used to say (Jung, 1944/1974a), the unconscious gets "constellated" when the conscious has done all it can do on its own. This happened to me in the Case of the Beautiful Wife in chapter 10, where I consciously reckoned

Fig. 16.1 The window of the third quarter of the hour.

her perpetuation of allowing herself to be put down by her husband, and which I explained to her in my first letter given in that case report. A week later when we reviewed the videotape in the clinic, I was more alarmed by what I saw, and dreamt of it that very night, and wrote to her of the map my dream provided of the danger of trying to leave this man, and of what to watch for.

In general, I find that my conscious mind is only able to reckon this *weighing down* to a certain point. I can make note of feeling that a certain case is getting to me, and I can write down what sense of it I can make. My dream always responds to this account with a full picture of the situation, both the diagnosis of what has dragged me down with the patient, and the treatment for getting out of it, as in the Case of the Beautiful Wife.

Defense from the Entire Field and Culture

Even when I can free myself by the hour and by the case, I end up in a third quandary, weightier by far than the other two. This is because the troubles of the patients, and myself, are the troubles of an entire discipline, psychiatry, and an entire culture, that of the West for the last 3,000 years. This is explained most readily by reference to the monomyth (Campbell, 1949) as described in chapter 13.

Invariably a patient caught up in being a cog in the megamachine will be exhausted by it and will seek compensation in one privilege or another. If I think and believe I can save a person from this, without the person departing from it, I am acquiescing in his misery and will feel the weight of his fate.

If I can decline this identification with his fateful steps, I can stand apart and go elsewhere out the back door he cannot take himself. Yet, that always puts me into some kind of danger, because it is hard to run against your own group. We are made to do it, in general, and the path we have for getting out of it is the monomyth which has suffering built into it. I am going to have to feel alone, outside the group, and I am going to have to make a journey in a dream to wrestle with it, and then I am going to have to come back with my finding in such a way that I am not dismissed or punished and get some good exchange for my contribution.

By and large, this means running against an entire profession which is a microcosm of Western culture in its present state. This is a culture which privileges functioning and dissociates everything that interferes with function. Thus, anxiety and depression are not signals, but illnesses! This dissociation of the exterior from the interior reduces the interior to a compensatory fantasy. The net result is sterility, when you have a cog role in behavior and a fantasy life in feeling.

Chapter 17, "Dreaming the Theory," will show the kind of dream journeys I have had to take to get out of such a deathly culture, like the sepulchral City in *The Heart of Darkness* (Conrad, 1902/1992) and risk myself in the dark and primitive, and then return alert to what reception is possible and not possible.

The Particular Burden of Practice with the Chronically Mentally Ill

A friend and colleague (Michael Moran, personal communication), who has 20 years experience in community mental health center work, asked me to say more about a stance to take with chronically disturbed patients. Dr. Moran is much more qualified than I am to write such a book, and I hope he will write it. In the meanwhile, I will say a few things I find key to this work, which I have discovered in our own HMO, and which is virtually the same population as a community mental health center.

As Dr. Moran and I have discussed for a long time, concerning his staff and my residents, there is a considerable danger of becoming disheartened by downward-going patients or by patients who are always the same. On the other hand, it is not good to give up on them. There are some remarkable surprises from patients we have stood by for a long time. Furthermore, many are grateful just to keep going at all. Thus, this work is quite a bit like that of a pastor of a church.

Of course, pastors are well known for getting worn out. Malan (1979) called it "the helping profession syndrome." It is essentially a matter of giving out too much, such as working long hours, and being burdened by identification with miserable souls. This builds up rage, for compensation, and then guilt for this dark side of the pastor.

Therefore, I think it is essential for the doctor or psychotherapist with such a load to *arrange a good exchange* for him- or herself with every patient, every hour, and every day. *It is not to be put off for some final reward* (Brooks, 2004). Such a delay steps right into the helping profession syndrome, and ends up with the trajectory of Dr. Jekyll.

I often have to see four to eight chronically mentally ill patients in 1 hour with their resident doctors. Four hours of this could exhaust me, and 8 hours put me into a rage. Here is how I arrange a good exchange. First of all, I set the time available strictly before the patient and the resident. If it is 5 minutes, I tell them it is 5 minutes, and time to ask me 1 question right away. If the patient is very troubled that day, I will have left another 5 minutes in reserve. He or she gets 10 minutes, and is usually grateful that I am paying attention.

My entire point of view about sensitive dependence on initial conditions, and the geometry of the patient's space, helps me to *conserve* myself for what makes a difference. I think of it as sketching in a line, which alters the geometry of the space. Thus, I sketch in a line under the space, to make sure what kind of bottom there is to the treatment. Or, I sketch a line over the space, to make sure there is some kind of limit to the patient's acting out as of violence. Finally, I sketch in a line going backwards, because most of what these patients can do, once contained from disaster, is back out of bad arrangements (exchanges in favor of others, at the expense of the patient).

A few days ago, we had a patient who had agreed to some work, unwittingly, that took three times as much time as the owner had offered to pay for. She was exhausted, yet she felt she could not quit for fear of not being hired again. Even worse, she could not stop thinking about it, day and night, worrying. I asked her how she got away from it, and she remembered playing with her cat. A weekend trip helped her forget it also. It was hard to forget it in her own house, because it was take-home work on the home computer. I asked her if she took walks, and then she remembered she could forget it that way too! So, in 5 minutes, I helped her a little to go out the back door.

Then she brought up the difficulty of forgetting it at night, and waking up worrying, and not being able to go back to sleep. I smiled and said we could talk about that next time. She smiled back in understanding, intuitively, that I was showing her how to give something, and then limit it, in the face of pressure for more giving. This is called learning by turning passive into active (Weiss & Sampson, 1986); namely, the patient gives you the problem she or he has to see how you handle it!

Dreaming the Theory

I could not have written this book without dreaming the theory that constructed it. Why has my dream instrument been so essential? I believe it is because my motion as a dreamer is disturbed when I cannot read the surfaces on which I am moving. These surfaces have huge bifurcations where the forces run in opposite directions, like the steep gradients between cold and warm fronts that let loose tornadoes. As Riemann (cited in Kaku, 1994, p. 36) put it, we are like bookworms moving across a sheet of paper, and suddenly come to where it is crumpled up into a high ridge. On that high ridge we will be subject to enormous forces. If we are not ready for such forces, we will be very disturbed by their sudden arrival, or, more exactly, by *our* sudden arrival to where they are placed.

I have depended upon my dreams nightly for nearly 20 years to read where I am on these surfaces, and I depended upon them the most during the summer of 2004 to imagine the surfaces described in this book. It would be an entire book, as Jung showed for Wolfgang Pauli (Jung, 1944/1974a) regarding his physics and personal analysis. I will only choose four of them, which appeared as I was writing the first four sections of this book. I will only give a single image from each of these four dreams, because I have come to think that a single image acts as a kind of condensation of the whole dream text folded into it. I can explain that fully in my next book, *The Dream As a Single Image*.

A Single Dream Image of Part I: The Military Trunks on the Tide

The dream image which appeared as I was composing part I of this book was as follows. My wife and I and an old friend from 20 years ago are wading toward a tropical shore in beautiful blue water, each of us with his or her military trunk of belongings floating alongside with a strap around it which we hold onto. My wife and I show this old friend how to cinch up her trunk so it is watertight, and show her also how to hold the strap loosely as we make our way to shore.

The surface of this dream is so pacific, so to speak, you would have no idea of the forces pent up in it. This friend was a person who could never contain her own disturbances. Every meeting with her was a trial of her spilling them all over us.

Now, 20 years later, I understand the absolute necessity of containment as the first step of this book. Also, I understand the loose holding of the strap so that I am not buffeted by my own trunk.

Finally, the military trunk refers to that of the famous Chamberlin family who invented the forceps and kept it secret in their trunk, which they brought into the delivery room (Hibbard, 1994). The patient never saw the forceps because a sheet was put over her head while the Chamberlins performed the delivery. So, the dream dreams of my forceps of the single step brought in from the unconscious.

A Single Dream Image of Part II: The Goddess Standing on My Shoulders

The dream image which appeared as I was composing part II of this book was as follows. A young woman stands on my shoulders while I have one finger lifted up to touch each of her nipples so that I can feel the pulse of whatever she sees while she looks ahead to where we are going in the next step. Her head is touching a roof cloud (roof clouds generate tornadoes!), and her appearance reminds me of the Egyptian statues of the immortals, especially Isis.

The mood of the dream is absolutely calm, as in the first dream image of part I, while, like that dream, alluding to tremendous pent-up forces, like tornadoes. Obviously, I am calling upon the receptivity of the female to assist me in reading what I am walking into, and together we are a kind of divine marriage, or syzygy, which balances male forcing, and female receptiveness.

A Single Dream Image of Part III: Renting Shells of Old Cars for Boating on the River

The dream image which appeared as I was composing part III of this book was as follows. At a kind of headland under a bridge (like the famous Hiroshige painting), Ted Hughes, the late poet laureate of England, is showing me a game with shells of old cars. He rents them out to all takers. At first, they float on the surface in the sunlight, and suddenly, after a few turns on the river, they sink of their own cast iron weight. Under the surface, the renters see a panther coming at them from up the river!

The mood of this dream is also deceptively calm and sunny, as in those heralding parts I and II of this book, as this heralds part III. Of course, the violence of the sinking is sudden and its coming face to face with the panther or mountain lion in the unconscious. This is my mapping of what it takes to be ready for the opposing current of the unconscious.

Ted Hughes is the guide in the dream, because of our correspondence before his death about such matters. The rusted shells of cars are from his children's story *The Iron Man* (Hughes, 1968) and the panther or mountain lion is a huger version of his poem, "The Thought Fox" (Hughes, 1957/1988).

A Single Dream Image of Part IV: A Design for a Sovereign Human Being

The dream image which appeared as I was composing part IV of this book was as follows. All night, I wrestled with straight lines which are never ready for what they run into. Toward morning I had a beautiful image of a design for a human being who was ready for the force she would run into. The image was a set of four bows, or arches, connected into a kind of square (thus, a mandala in three dimensions).

The idea was that you could move either way on any of the four arches, freely, for a kind of free passage (Gustafson & Cooper, 1990, chap. 7) toward any line of force or away from it. Because you approached or departed in an arch, you descended to the force from the third dimension above it, and so you could see before you got to it. This made for a suppleness in your response which you could never get head on in a straight line in the same plane. This also made for a suppleness when you moved away from the force in the opposing current so you could see where that was leading as well.

A friend and colleague reading this book as I wrote it (Gary Simoneau, personal communication) told me this book struck him as "the poem of readiness." That has seemed entirely apt to me, and so this is a single image of the book as a whole. Again, it is entirely calm, as in the heralds to parts I, II, and III, so it is for the herald to part IV. For enormous forces, one must have complete calm to compose oneself for them. Much turmoil followed this last dream and this image helped me bear it. The turmoil was about being dragged down by patients in hell. The problem was settled by chapters 15 and 16, where I design a protected *space* for receiving those in hell, and then a protected *time* for receiving those in hell.

This is the key problem of re-entry in act III of the monomyth: how to bring heaven or non-Inferno with you into the Inferno or Wasteland (Calvino, 1972). It is the problem Dante (Dante Alighieri, 1300/1994) solved in his own *Inferno* where he and Virgil met one soul after another in a circular hell. They had to bring heaven with them, in order to bear witness to this suffering. The idea, as John Freccero (1994) writes in his Foreword to the Pinsky translation of *The Inferno of Dante* (1300/1994) came from Saint Augustine, namely, "Descend so that you may ascend" (xiv). In other words, you get what ascends only if you also get what descends. This is the difference that makes all the difference, between death and rebirth.

CHAPTER 18

A Theoretical Note on the Scaffolding of This Book

Riemann imagined a race of two-dimensional creatures living on a sheet of paper. But the decisive break he made was to put these bookworms on a *crumpled* sheet of paper (Michio Kaku, 1994, p. 36; emphasis added).

For those not versed in the psychodynamic field, the theoretical scaffolding of this book is unimportant. For those who have struggled with its problems, the theoretical advance made by this book is very considerable. Therefore, I am putting the theoretical discussion at the end as an afterword for insiders.

The Dilemma of Simplicity and Comprehensiveness

As I see it, the psychodynamic field has been troubled all along by the dilemma of having to make treatment simple, as a sequence of things to do with the patient, while still being comprehensive in its view of the relevant forces for staying the same or making a dynamic change with the patient. The leading writers in the 1980s, Malan, Mann, Sifneos, and Davanloo, knew how to make it linear as a program to teach. The treatment addressed the core conflict of the patient. This simplicity would take care of everything necessary, because everything was a version of the patient's core conflict. In other words, everything was derivative from the intrapsychic core situation.

The Surrounding Force Fields of Interpersonal Relations and of the Systemic Machine of Society

I opened my Brief Psychotherapy Clinic in 1980, and by 1985 was ready to write my first book, *The Complex Secret of Brief Psychotherapy* (1986/1997a) for which I am best known. Essentially, I argued that the psychodynamic field could not be right to assume that everything flowed from the intrapsychic situation. The *surrounding field* of interpersonal relations has tremendous force of its own, and *beyond* that the group dynamics or systemic dynamic field of society itself obviously has tremendous coercive force which cannot be ignored. In other words, the fate of a patient is not just a matter of what he or she brings from inside, but also a matter of the people around that person, and of groups the individual belongs to, that will limit or augment his or her possibilities (Wachtel, 1993).

The Accuracy of a Novel

The trouble with introducing these forces as relevant to the story is that it can be difficult to keep the procedure of treatment simple and linear. Instead of a short story with one episode, we now have the scope of a novel of 500 pages, which portrays the character, the envelope of people around him, and the machinery of society in which all of this is embedded.

The Psychodynamic Field Bypasses Its Own Center in Dreams and Its Own Home in the Medical–Psychiatric Clinic

To make matters even worse, the novel's persuasiveness still lacks a contemplation of further forces that must be of extreme importance. What about the medical and pharmacological considerations? What about dreams? Strangely, the psychodynamic field seemed to bypass its own center in dreams and acted as if it could ignore its home in the medical–psychiatric clinic.

The Dilemma Posed: Comprehensiveness AND Portability

To make a long story of now 20 years short, I would say it has taken me this time to reply to these problems I posed at the outset. Eight books later, I have figured out the dilemma: how to reckon with all these relevant force fields and yet offer a simple and linear procedure that is easy to teach, *in other words, how to retain comprehensiveness, and retain linear simplicity.* Otherwise, you are stuck on one of the two horns of the dilemma: comprehensiveness that is not portable, or portability that is too slight in its reckoning of the relevant forces.

Winnicott: Only Transitions

It is very interesting to me that Winnicott, my favorite writer, whom I discussed in my first book, had much of what I needed to simplify the problem of comprehensiveness. For Winnicott, everything was a problem of transitions, and the key transition was to go from the rigidity of the patient's character *back* to the disturbances that terrified him and got him to stop moving. Then this first session was repeated as necessary on demand when the patient felt stuck again in his rigidity.

Motion Simplifies

In other words, the key problem is motion, which goes awry into terrible forces, medical–pharmacological, intrapsychic, interpersonal, and systemic. So, forces on these different scales do matter tremendously. But if you simplify your attention (focus) to the motion itself, you can ask what stops it, and what frees it up again.

Condensation, by Dreams and by Computer Iteration

It took me two other long studies to see this simplicity of motion on a field in which many scales of force are operating. One was the study of dreams, almost totally neglected by the brief dynamic doctors, and the other was the study of chaos theory, which is even more neglected. These two fields come to very similar conclusions. Both are capable of superimposing many different scales, as in a dream image, which is like a series of photographic negatives from many different periods of the patient's life piled on top of one another. The resulting condensation has the patient's whole history in it, and his impending problems coming at him. Chaos theory condenses in a similar way, by countless *iterations* of very simple mathematical formulae by computer, which results in drawings of the trajectory resulting from this repetition.

Both dream condensations and computer condensations depend for their outcome on tiny differences in the first step, or item repeated. This is called "sensitive dependence on initial conditions." This turns out to be the great simplifier. If the patient can properly line up for the first step, and be oriented to the relevant forces, then beautiful new developments occur. If he or she cannot do so, then those developments will not occur.

Sensitive Dependence on Initial Conditions: The First Step (i) Is the Trajectory

Thus, the first step either leads right back into the vicious cycle, or on repetition, it leads out of it. The wisdom is in seeing this from the first step, and helping the patient to take advantage of this correct orientation.

The First Step Is an Exchange: Lévi-Strauss and Marx

Now that leads to one more long study that has helped me to appraise the first step, whether on the tennis court or in the consultation room. From the beginning of my career, I studied group dynamics. This is usually missing from the training of most psychotherapists, and yet human beings are almost totally group animals, as Aristotle (336–322 BC/1991) said a long time ago. They live or die from having a place in a group. As Lévi-Strauss (1964/1983) argued about primitive societies, and Marx (1844/1975) about modern societies, the critical matter in the quality of human life is the quality of the individual's *exchanges* with the group. Is he or she putting out a lot and getting little back, or vice versa, or is it fairly equal?

Routinely Getting Off on the Wrong Foot (i)

This social perspective allowed me to consider the exchanges of our patients in the clinic and to begin to notice that they routinely get off on the wrong foot, namely, falling into a poor exchange. This routinely leads to excessive claims on us, the doctors, to make up for them regarding how they have been cheated.

The Great Simplifier: The Terms of the Exchange (i)

Now, this is the great simplifier itself. The first step is how one readies oneself for the first exchange. This, repeated a hundred or a thousand times, is the patient's trajectory. Simply shift the terms of the first exchange, and you begin a trajectory in an opposite direction. It is like resetting the angle of the mainsail to the mast. Everything depends upon it. However, it can take a long time to see you must do it, if you have selective inattention to where you are actually going.

Security Operations Are the General Tendency

If the first step in any trajectory is the reading of the exchange, as any two dogs on our trail into the woods know, then how is it usually read? According to Sullivan (1956), it is read narrowly by human beings in terms of security. The control of one thing (i), replicated over and over again, is exchanged for cash, and cash for everything else. Thus, security becomes the increase of numbers.

The Increase Pack

Canetti (1960/1984) argued that modern increase has an ancient and primitive forerunner in what he called the Increase Pack. When there is scarcity, there is an emergency for ancient man. For example, a Plains Indian tribe dependent on the buffalo for much of its basic needs will, when the buffalo are absent, turn itself into a buffalo herd, imitating the buffalo, becoming the buffalo, until they literally show up, as if drawn by the magnetic force of the dance. The emergency heats them up tremendously. Otherwise, they live in what Lévi-Strauss called a "cold engine" (Charbonnier, 1969), in which exchange is always near the equilibrium point.

The Megamachine

Mumford (1926/1995) argued that the origin of the modern world of exchange is the megamachine of the great empire, such as the machine that built the great pyramids in Egypt. Each person becomes a cog, or machine component, regimented, as in an army, to play his or her little component part in a huge machine. In return, the individual gets security, or money. All the great empires of the ancient world relied on such megamachines to dominate their smaller neighbors, who were soon taken over by them.

The Modern Megamachine

However, it was not until 1300 (Mumford, 1926) that human beings began to disconnect the vertical dimension of salvation from the horizontal dimension of the machine, which they began with the regulation of the day by the clock (the campanile announced the new regulation, which replaced the sun as the measure of the day). Soon, human beings began to make grids of space to go with their grids of time, and their modern exploration of mechanics could become free to take off and dominate the entire world. We live in its world headquarters. Most of its business can be mapped on an x/y two-dimensional map, and its creatures move in one-dimension of increase (i), on that two-dimensional surface. This is the world empire we have of the multinational Fortune 500 companies. Their expansion accelerates every second!

The Modern Epidemic

Since all other human needs are subordinated to increase, the other needs kept in shadow build up the tension of the creature until it suddenly erupts. In 1886, Stevenson proposed *The Strange Case of Dr. Jekyll and Mr. Hyde* as the new general condition of mankind. By 1895, Breuer and Freud announced that the condition was due to the strangulation of sexuality in their *Studies on Hysteria* (1893–1895). Clearly, they were right in their five case studies, that sexuality was strangulated in the service of subordination to economic power. But Stevenson's argument is more thoroughgoing.

The Basic Assumption Work Machine

All needs are subordinated to increased activity, not just sexuality. Indeed, it has become possible to harness work to increase by fantasy. Bion (1959) argued that the three fantasies that are harnessed in the modern world to increased work are sexual, violent, and nurturing (basic assumptions of pairing, fight-flight, and dependency). A glance at any advertisement will verify this mechanism. Thus, virtually any consumer item is sold as a guarantee of sexual fulfillment, of winning contests, or of being taken care of. The part-object *becomes* the whole solution.

Man the Sacrificial Animal

Thus, man becomes a sacrificial animal to increase on a worldwide scale. Slavery in earlier empires is minor compared to the enslavement of much of the third world in the last 20 or 30 years, at a rapidly accelerating pace. The same occurs here at home where the machines are not so much the primary production of goods, but the production of counting, or bureaucracy.

Prey and Predator

The predator in control gets his prey in a trap, and devours him. Thus, all bureaucratic machines have a procedure which simply treats any object as one in a series to be put into its box. Ironically, such a controlling creature becomes a prisoner of his own procedure as it increases its numbers and time and takes him over completely in its service (Dr. Jekyll). Thus, he imagines himself to be the "controller" or predator, when, in fact, he becomes "controlled" or prey. He has sacrificed nearly everything to his dominance. One-sidedness, as Jung (1916/1953) pointed out, is the great sacrifice of modern times. Look at the cases in any textbook of psychotherapy, and you will see female subordination to caretaking, and male subordination to computers, businesses, farms (Coren, 2001, reviewed by Gustafson, 2003).

The Small World and the Great World

Ibsen (1879/1961, discussed by Lebowitz, 1990) called this the small world of security, in contrast to a great world, of sea, sky, and fire, not just earth. The true home of man is the great world, but the tragedy of modern man, and woman, is confinement to the small world.

Entertainment

Postman (1985) argued that the great world is left to others, who are the entertainers, for the vicarious participation of those confined to the small world in their daily lives. Every public function, television, movies, news, politics, sports, and so forth becomes an entertaining distraction which takes our eyes off our servitude. The Romans had circuses, at intervals, while our entertainment is, as we say, 24/7.

The Modern Citizen

So, the modern citizen, foreseen by Tolstoy (1875/1970), and Melville (1851/1956), is all control, of some procedure (W for work), and fantasy (BA for basic assumption). Thus, the lawyer sketch by Tolstoy (1875/1970, part IV, chap. 5, p. 333) epitomizes Everyman. While interviewing Karenin regarding his wish for a divorce, and acting the role of a concerned party, he is snatching moths out of the air. He is as if a man asleep in his own procedure. While doing work in his role, he is enveloped in a fantasy as a snatcher of prey (moths). Freud (1900/1975a) argued that man is asleep in his dreams in wish-fulfillment. Here is a portrait of man asleep in his daytime role, also, in a wish-fulfillment. Thus, man asleep is a one-dimensional man (Marcuse, 1964).

Circularity of Individual History

Riemann (cited in Kaku, 1994, chap. 2), Abbott (1884/1984), Carroll (1865/1985), and Saint-Exupéry (1943) all portrayed this one-dimensional man on a two-dimensional surface like a sheet of paper, which he circles endlessly without being able to see it. Only the Cheshire Cat (Carroll, 1865/1985) can see the Game of Queen's Croquet, because he has a perspective from above the plane of the croquet court. The outstanding fact of Everyman is the redundancy of his history, which is invisible to him. The explanation is simple. Everyman's history lies in the transition between two-dimensional and three-dimensional space, as between the positioning of Alice and the positioning of the Cheshire Cat.

Perspective and Its Surrender

Everyman gets to perspective, or the third dimension, in play. For example, tennis is played between driving the ball, receiving the ball, and occupying a vantage point to see oneself and see one's opponent equally, as from a point midway between them over the net. But Everyman runs back quickly to his burdens, and so he allots so little time-space to this beautiful transitional space, which Winnicott rightly called "sacred space" (1971). Thoreau argued this as the key failure of American character in *Walden* (1854/1947). He knows a little of sacred space, but arranges to miss out on it almost entirely, reserving it for when he is dead.

The Most Precious Third Dimension

The third dimension, vertical to the mundane plane of existence, is what Ibsen (1879/1961; Lebowitz, 1990) took to be his most precious dimension, depth, or height, thrilling in their reach, to the full height of divinity, and the full depth of evil. How magnificent and how terrible human beings can be.

The Fourth Dimension, of Scope

As Kaku (1994) argues in *Hyperspace* (chap. 2), an extra dimension of space is most simply generated by dragging the given space through time. Thus, a three-dimensional space that has both Flatland's plane, and the vertical of height and depth, becomes a four-dimensional space with range or scope (Abbott, 1884/1984). The cube pulled through time is a different object at one time than at another, just as we are different at one time than at another. Our range or scope has been enlarged or diminished.

The Fifth Dimension, of Return

This is a terribly important dimension to anyone who has the fourth dimension, because, this, too, in time, always has to return to the plane of the small world, and its small business. Taken in stride, it is comical, good natured, and accepting of its absurd repetition (Bergson, 1900/1980).

Five-Dimensional Space Is Religious

All of the great religious traditions of the world unfold in five-dimensional space. They regard the mundane existence as a trap, for example, as in the *Bhagavad Gita* (7.27), of craving and aversion, in two dimensions. The same is true of the circular hells of *Dante's Inferno* (Dante Alighieri, 1300/ 1994), and of attachments in the *Tao Te Ching*. They teach transcendence of Flatland, ascent of the Sacred Mountain, journeys through all the possibilities of existence, and return to participation in everyday life with detachment from its fruits.

Paradise in the World

However, the emergence of the terrible forces of the megamachine over the last 3,000 years has made the return to the world difficult to sustain. Many religious visionaries have not been able to bear it, and live apart from it. The same is true of secular versions of beatitude, especially in American literature, which tend to be placed in worlds elsewhere (Poirier, 1966/ 1985). In general, a place of paradise in the world has to be demarcated *between* raw nature and raw political power, as in a garden (L. Marx, 1964/ 2000), or in the famous bed of Odysseus and Penelope (Homer, 1996). Those in the machine are torn to pieces by the poem of force (Weil, 1937/ 1993), and those in raw nature are torn to pieces by poverty.

Intrusions into the Garden

A serenity and ease in the world has to be prepared for intrusions from the right and left. Any helping profession runs these risks continually. The intrusion from the right or external world is that persons in trouble from attempting too much always put too much into the time/space you provide for them. This is called *projective identification*, or turning passive into active, whereby they give you the very difficulty they suffer. The intrusion from the left or internal world is that they arouse identifications with their dream of themselves in your empathy for them. Thus, you take on the pain of an impossible project.

An Empty Room Has Continually to Be Cleared

This is why it is essential to reduce to a minimum what you do with any person you help. You have to start slowly, do one essential thing in the middle, and begin to end early. You can expect most of your clients to interfere with all of these measures that protect the sacred space.

A Sacred Space Is Holographic and Luminous

A space thus protected from rending forces can forego the kind of dissociation that is necessary to most people. Instead, all the opposing currents can be allowed their say, and every detail will be a microcosm of the whole integrated world. For example, see Winnicott's (1971) case of Alfred and his cough, and case of Ada, with her bow.

The Bifurcation between a Sacred Space and the Secular World

But the world is going to remain bifurcated between the great world of three, four, or five dimensions and the small world of one or two dimensions. Thus, there will be a great danger of being in a higher-dimensional space and not having an adequate base for it in the secular world, or, vice versa, having a base in the world that is merely replicative, distracted, and fantasy, and loses all meaning.

In the Box, or Out of the Box

In horizontal terms, the same is true of being in the box, of conventional thinking, which is all about control by the conscious mind, and thinking out of the box which allows the unconscious mind to have its say. The first replicates and is static and soon dead, while the second is fresh and may be readily disqualified.

Riemann's Crumpling of the Paper of Two-Dimensional Space and Its One-Dimensional Lines of Its One-Dimensional Creatures

Riemann did not accept the linear grid of Euclidean geometry, because it required tremendous complications to explain the nonlinear forces of gravity, magnetism, and electricity. Rather, he introduced higher-dimensional space, indeed, 10 dimensions, in order to make these forces simpler as *consequences* of the geometry. The bending of space, like the crumpling of paper, makes the forces tremendous in the region of the bending or crumpling. This seems to me to be also the case in terms of the forces of human interaction. The two simplest strange attractors are the group and the body. In the region of the group, there is a huge crumpling of the paper, that makes for tremendous forces between being in the box of the group, and being out of the box of the group. In the region of the body, there is another huge crumpling of the paper, which makes for tremendous forces between a person's dream of himself and the remainder of the world. He can sleep only in the region of his dream of himself.

Bateson's Law of Mapping

Bateson (1972, discussed in Gustafson, 1986/1997a) argued that a structure of n dimensions can only be mapped adequately in $(n +1)$ dimensions, because only then with this perspective standing apart from n dimensions in $(n +1)$ can the observer take in the whole structure. In terms of Riemann's crumpling of the paper, an observer would have to be out of the plane of the paper in order to see it, and would be simply baffled by the nonlinear eruptions felt in the plane of the paper itself. This is why "the laws of nature appear simple when expressed in higher-dimensional space" (Kaku, 1994, p. 37).

Aristotle's Law

Aristotle argued in his *The Art of Rhetoric* (336–322 BC/1991) that persuasion is entirely dependent upon being within the box of the premise of the group being addressed. Thus, premise means assumption and it means a place. The speaker must put himself inside the premise, show that he is not disqualified by being outside or against the premise, and then add one thing, or step to the usual argument. In other words, we will not listen to you unless you are one of us, and not against us, and unless you take only one step beyond our usual thinking.

The Schools of Psychotherapy

This is why the schools of psychotherapy remain distinct entities. Each has a procedure which is useful but highly exclusionary of anyone who fails to replicate the procedure or who opposes it in any way. Thus, cognitive-behavior therapy simply teaches that the patient must be taught the opposite of what he or she is doing, so, if avoidant, the person must undergo exposure. Thus, solution-focused therapy simply teaches that the patient is already doing something different from his pathology, and that this difference must be brought out, so, if avoidant, the patient must be shown how he or she is already daring. Thus, psychodynamic therapy simply teaches that the patient is repeating something learned as a child, and that he or she will be freed of it by being shown how it fit into the past, and the past transferred into the present. Actually, all three of these theories are entirely consistent in a higher-dimensional space, which can have a perspective above the bifurcations between past and present, external and internal worlds. But such an integration is highly unlikely when there is such a huge folding of space between being an insider or an outsider to a professional group. The forces are simply too great.

The Premise of Man as Machine

An even greater force field divides an organic view of man from a machine view of man (Mumford, 1934/1963, pp. 45–51). Essentially, psychiatry as a part of medicine views man as a machine which has defects in design like any other machine such as an automobile. These defects are designed wrongly by genetics, by family training, and by society (this last is hardly mentioned). Thus, the treatments are quite like those of any automobile dealership for its wayward cars, namely, replace the defective part or at least contain its defects. Psychiatry is to make the brain run again, or function correctly, like the kidney or the lungs or some other part of the functioning body. This is called medical necessity.

The Medical Necessity of Balance

My argument is that human beings are organic rather than inorganic machines, and that they malfunction when they are one-sided, and neglect all their needs in favor of specialties that gain them an adaptation. This is our epidemic of rushed functioning. This book is a model of a counterma-chine for locating balance between functioning and being oneself, quite as argued by Winnicott (1971) in his transitional space between the claims of the world and the claims of oneself. This requires, at minimum, a perspective, in the third dimension between the two demands. It maps the possibility of individual membership, which is the only well-being which holds up in the long run.

A Perspective of 3,000 Thousand Years

I am not saying anything about a minimum perspective for balance that was not said by Homer 3,000 years ago, and by a long line of his successors in literature. Odysseus is his hero, who is loyal to his peers, but refuses to go down with them, and refinds his center in his own hall. My wife reminds me that such a practice is a long struggle, and is greatly helped by an education in traditional wisdom.

Isolated Will

I will close my theoretical scaffolding with a discussion of my last 24 hours, because it epitomizes what a practitioner will have to go through over and over again, to regain a minimal perspective. Homer would have understood this perfectly. It's the problem of hubris, or forcing things. As Allen Tate argued (1934/1999), such isolated will has become standard for us, either as scientific will, or its opposite, romantic will. How then are we to have a will for the whole situation? My last day and night will illustrate this.

A Clear Line of Inquiry

In my Brief Clinic yesterday I saw a young woman in consultation for one of the most typical problems of adolescence (Selvini-Palazzoli et al., 1989). Her mother was holding on to a relationship with a somewhat violent and sexually intrusive man at the expense of her daughter. The mother willed that the daughter just stop getting so upset about it. The daughter willed that the mother give up her allegiance to this stepfather in favor of herself. The isolated will of the status quo, and the isolated romantic will to overthrow it is an impasse, as Selvini-Palazzoli et al. (1989) showed so well. I knew this game would go on endlessly unless a perspective could be taken on the hopelessness of the game itself. I was able to help her admit that she was playing a losing game, and that forcing it in a hysterical way was only getting her farther from what she wanted, namely, to be close with her mother. Here is a nice example of a will for seeing the whole situation.

The Tennis Court

Then I went out on the court with one of my archrivals and proceeded to lose the first four games, made a nice recovery, and, at that moment, lost the last four games! Why, I asked myself, am I not keeping a clear line of inquiry on the court or a balanced perspective between my point of view and my friend's? It's very simple. I started out with my isolated will to prevail. I gave it up and got into the rhythm of playing the points. Then I got *seized* with winning again and fell back into isolated will. Hubris! Or as the *Bhagavad Gita* puts it, craving and aversion destroy a higher-dimensional space, or Great World, and throw you back into the small world like Orwell's *Animal Farm* (1946, p. 123), summarized so well in its catch phrase, "All pigs are equal, but some pigs are more equal than others."

The Pressure of Reality

I couldn't recover on the court, because, as Wallace Stevens (1942/1997) put it, "the pressure of reality" can destroy the ability to contemplate a situation. But my dream always retains its contemplation. I dreamt that I was following a protocol in which I was to dissolve a pound of my own flesh, and with this, continue successive steps in organic chemistry. An image appeared before me of a woman I had seen on the street, very austere, about 40, wearing a sweatshirt Rensselaer Polytechnic Institute (RPI) sweatshirt. I was acting like her, forcing my will. Of course, the allusion is also to Shylock and Antonio in *The Merchant of Venice* (Shakespeare, 1600/1969a), in a deadlock between conventional and romantic will.

The Infinitesimal Step

This lurching back and forth between isolated will and its impasses (from having only one or two dimensions) and will for the whole situation (having three, four, or five dimensions) will continue to be difficult for me and for everyone hoping to get back and forth between the Great World and the small world. One change in step and you are back in rhythm, one change in step and you are out of rhythm, forcing things.

A Metaphor of the Globe Theatre 2004

Peter Hoey (personal communication) measures this predicament beautifully as follows. If you are standing on the Equator, one step to the north (i) pulls you into counterclockwise rotation, while one step to the south (i') pulls you into clockwise rotation (like the water going down your sink). These are called the Coriolis forces. So it goes with conventional isolated will vs. romantic will. Both lose balance in a single step. So the problem of retaining will for the whole situation is to stay on the Equator, and see the whole Game, and its theater of the whole world at the present moment.

Where We Put Our Eyes

Where we step follows from where we put our eyes. Dante (1300/1994) understood this as a matter of life and death. His guide, Virgil, continually warns him not to look too long at hellish circulation. It either draws you down with it, or into trying to oppose it. Both steps (i and i') are useless, and dangerous to the helper, and to the patient. So what are we to do? I simply ask if the patient wants to ask anything of me? If she does, then we can quickly find out how things go the way they go, and how they go a different way. I have to see it first and then I can help her see it. I am back into transitional space or I remain in static space. I have to be *equally* ready, to have a will for the whole situation, not the isolated will which is our undoing.

The Grace of God

This takes a certain grace, and not in the trivial sense of social grace, but in the sense of the grace of God. For humanity spends most of its time and space on business nowadays, as Thoreau (1854/1947) saw in 1854. And that is a low business, by and large. And that is also a very static and redundant business. It can be hard to remember that such a nearly inorganic rigidity can dance. By the grace of God, we all can dance, and alas we mostly forget it. If you take a close look at any emergent flower you will see a dance of higher dimensions, in the relations of the stamen and pistil, stem and leaves, and the whole taken together. But who takes the time Thoreau did with this? In this sense, man has forgone much of his own organic quality, which is truly a gift from God, of the Creation itself. As Simone Weil (1937/1993) put it, gravity has taken over in its terrible weightiness, and grace is then lost.

> Take heed therefore how ye hear: for whosoever hath, to him shall be given; and whosoever hath not, from him shall be taken away even that which he thinketh he hath (Luke 8:18).

Downward Going Men

Yes, but how are we to endure patients going nowhere? Cheerfully? And not be dragged down? This is surely a secret, because my most competent friends in the profession ask me how to do this. They are dragged down regularly. I am dragged down less often, but it happens to me too. Essentially, I throw us off the descending slope to ruin, for lack of having enough, onto the opposite slope of having enough to develop. I have reset the sensitive dependence on initial conditions. Of course, some will come up with nothing *if for now*, while some may let me into what Stevenson (1892) saw:

> His life from without may seem but a rude mound of mud; there will be some golden chamber at the heart of it, in which he dwells delighted (p. 216).

This gives the responsibility back to the patient for what is necessary to get out of final despair. I leave it to him, and not to me, and thus I am cheerful.

The Great World   The Small World

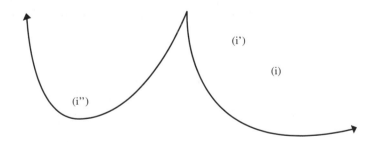

Fig. 18.1 The bifurcation between great and small worlds.

Individuation: A Theoretical Problem Not Quite Solved by Jung, Balint, and Winnicott

At last I want to take up the most important theoretical problem for those who can save themselves from the downward going path. Jung (1916/1953) called it individuation. He argued that it is defeated by one of two lines of force: either by putting on the mask, or persona, to fit into the group, or by getting carried away in identification with a god. The first is static, and the second is electrically charged.

The general tendency of Jung, Balint, and Winnicott, and analysts in general, is to emphasize the movement away from the group. Thus, in Balint's (1968) new beginning, the patient is able to turn her back completely from the group to allow beautiful new motions. In Winnicott's (1971) transitional space, Winnicott and his patient reach across from the static persona and its conventional drawings, to deeper longings which had been cut off by dissociation.

In this motion into the opposing current, they follow all of the prophets of Western culture. When the Temple is corrupted, the back door out of it is the reply, in the Exodus from Egypt about 1300 BC (McNeill, 1963), in the flight of Jesus into the Wilderness, in the theses of Luther against the Catholic Church in 1500 AD, and in Freud's invention of free association around 1900 to get rid of the yoke of an excessive burden of civilization.

A single detail sometimes will signal the turn into a new world. Thoreau's last and rediscovered manuscript is entirely clear about this emergence of large things from small things, or what he calls the dispersion of seeds (2000, pp. 241–271). Here is a particularly beautiful passage:

> [T]he restless pine seeds go dashing over it (the snow) like an Esquimaux sledge with an invisible team until, losing their wings or meeting some insuperable obstacle, they lie down once and for all, per chance to rise up pines. Nature has her annual sledding to do, as well as we. In a region of snow and ice like ours, this tree can be gradually spread thus from one side of the continent to the other (2000, p. 265).

In Winnicott's (1971) case of Ada, this detail was a bow that kept appearing in her drawings along a line roughly between the right and left halves of her pictures. As Winnicott writes: "It is for this detail that the reader has been invited to follow the development of the process in the child who has used the opportunity for contact with myself" (p. 232). Winnicott untied the bow, which held the curtain of dissociation in place.

A similar detail is discussed in chapter 14 of this book by the patient discussed as the Case of the Sacrificed Daughter. The detail was of a pattern of cracks on the hood of a car in a dream, marking the place where she had been murdered under the hood. The beautiful turn is this. From the standpoint of the headlights, where she is an object, the pattern refers to her death at age 4 and in 4 certain days of her marriage, but from the standpoint of where she sits as a passenger, or subject, the pattern is a Chinese symbol of strength, and disclosed her tremendous ability to fight back, and not die after all.

Thus, she performs a kind of *musical inversion* on the theme of her death, which, in this turn of a single detail, becomes the theme of her rebirth. This, I think, is a very beautiful moment, which shows in infinitesimal form what a profound change in trajectory is all about in a single step.

Yet it is not a complete account. A new beginning like this always has to be defended from fresh attacks when the patient turns back to the group. Jung, Balint, and Winnicott never did discuss this. Jung himself moved to Upper Lake Zurich to stay out of harm's way.

I'll relate a dream of my own, which also shows in a single detail what is the difficulty to be handled in returning to the group. I dreamt I was riding in a bus or trolley with all of my possessions, when suddenly, the driver announced the ride was over, and the trolley bus was heading back to its yard. From this beautiful bridge we had been curving upon to the left, he suddenly swerved it violently to the right. I woke in a panic, thinking I could never get my possessions off of this trolley bus in the few seconds he would give us to clear out. I woke shortly after midnight in this nightmare on a Sunday night leading into the work week of Monday. I am never awoken like this in my first dream period.

There is a great deal I could say about this dream, but I want to confine myself to its motion, which suddenly swerves to the right. That, indeed, is a line of force I am always having to be ready for. That is the terror of the group, to call a halt to any of its (collection) routes and send the vehicle back to the (grave)yard. My dream calls attention to my being lulled by the beautiful curve of the bridge to the left. I am needing to wake up and heed what is always coming from the group.

Sherwood Anderson (1921/1985) poses this same violent shift in his story, "I Want to Know Why," where a boy is lulled into the beauty of a horse and his trainer, and suddenly, the trainer is off with the other men at a whorehouse.

Bion (1959) mapped it out. The one-sidedness of the group is a step into a kind of pseudosalvation (James, 1903/2003; Thurber, 1942/1986), as if it will be saved by a kind of dependency, or a kind of fight, or a kind of sexual pairing. Thus, our central character in this book, Dr. Jekyll, is a prisoner of dependency in his patients which leads gradually into his emptiness. Suddenly, then, Mr. Hyde bursts out the back gate in the fight–flight mode which runs over anything in its path. Thus, the daily step (i) on the trajectory to emptiness is basic assumption dependency, and the compensatory fantasy (i') is basic assumption fight–flight. Their alternation is his total destruction.

Few can turn their backs on the group to be reborn and turn back to the group and be ready for its inherent violence. This is what individuation takes, as in Shakespeare's *Tempest* (1612/1969c), where Prospero makes his own garden in the wilderness, and is ready for the assault of his fellow men. Indeed, he arranges it.

The Complex Secret

I always turn to the last page of a book to see where the author got to, after I read the first page, for this is his entire trajectory from the first step. This will measure his range.

Once you understand the geometry of the force field, or, as Riemann put it on June 10, 1854, "On the Hypotheses Which Lie at the Foundation of Geometry" (cited in Kaku, 1994, p. 30), in terms of the motion of man, then you reckon any misery as a positioning in the wrong region of exchange, and look for a single step out of it, into a better region of exchange. Thrashing, willing, and forcing make things worse. A quiet contemplation of the step that brought you into a bad region, and the step that will get you out, is far preferable. Thus, Kutuzov, in *War and Peace* (Tolstoy, 1869/1966) is not so foolish as to try to will opposition to Napoleon's advance toward Moscow because winter is coming on. He simply goes to his tent, and contemplates the winter that will rise up in several months and bury his overwhelming opponent.

Almost always, mankind is caught up in the kind of momentum Napoleon had with his army, rushing to the horizon as Brooks (2004) put it. Thus, the present empire takes over the world, it seems, irresistibly, with outsourcing to millions of virtual slaves just since the mid-1980s. Millions of Jekylls fill every need, while millions of Hydes are at least going to feel like ripping out in violence.

When you are caught up in this global tide yourself, you are surely miserable, and much more violent than you can comprehend. Your plight seems overwhelming. But the bifurcation of forces is such that the back door is but a step away, as for Kutuzov into his tent. Just so long as you can take the return step, to see what foolishness the generals are up to next! How to turn your back on the group, and turn back to the group, stepping from one trajectory to another, or one world to another. That is the complex secret (Gustafson, 1986/1997a), and yet, because of the geometry of the force field, but a step away.

Ibsen on the Contrary

Or is the complex secret something discovered by Ibsen?

> There is nothing more to it, really, than placing a blank short perspective next to an infinitely lengthened one, and making a counterpoint of the two (Adams, 1966, p. 351).

The Inner and Outer Surfaces of the Brain

Pies (2004), developing Mesulam (2000), argues that almost all of the problems of psychiatry are about lack of a "mediating entity" between the inner and outer surfaces of the brain. The inner surface or limbic area connects with the hypothalamus and from there to the entire interior milieu, whereas the outer surface or cortex connects via all of the sensory systems with the surrounding or external milieu. The paralimbic region between them is the region of mediating entities between inner and outer worlds (Mesulam, 2000, p. 8, Figure 1–6).

Pies assembles a short history of these mediating entities or thirds that cross this polarity, from Plato to Freud. This is the transitional region (Winnicott, 1971) where the dramas of human beings are enacted. As I have just argued, the fundamental problem for us is being caught between our own needs and those of the group. If the group rules, the tendency is self-sacrifice. If the individual rules, the tendency is to be cast out of the group. As E. F. Schumacher (1977) put it, this is the great divergent problem of human life. The inner world and the outer world diverge from each other. The entire difficulty of individuation is to find a way between these two horns of the dilemma of how to be an individual member (Gustafson, 1995a, 1995b, 1997, 1999, 2000), and not to be reduced to an individual singleton who is cast out, and not to be reduced to a member who is swallowed up by the group. The brain is selected by how it is used, literally as Edelman (1985) shows with his theory of Neural Darwinism. Thus, it will have more or less of the mediating entities, depending on whether they are discovered and put to work.

The Dream as a Single Image

I have given a full amplitude of examples in this book of the dream as such a mediating entity, starting from my first case of the Potlatch Grandma, and concluding with my last case of the Sacrificed Daughter. Recall the Grandma walking upstairs right into the path of a tornado, and the daughter having her head crunched under the hood of the family car. The single image shows the body in its collision course with the social body.

In retrospect, we have been talking about nothing else but finding the steps that balance the claims of my body with those of the social body I must fit into. I would be moving into my next book if I went further with this thought, that the dream instrument can mediate in a single image the entire struggle between the demand from within and the demand from without.

It is not only the dream instrument that can do this, but also a single line in a poem, or a paragraph in a work of prose. As Auerbach (1946/1968) demonstrates, a paragraph from Homer about the scar of Odysseus, or a paragraph from Virginia Woolf about the darning of a brown sock, shows how the representation of reality can be made in such a condensed form. Auerbach constructs the entire history of Western literature from such a series of paragraphs, a set of variations in the balance between the force from within and the force from without. I leave all of this to my next book, *The Dream as a Single Image*.

References

Abbott, E. A. (1984). *Flatland*. New York: Penguin. (Original work published 1884)

Adams, R. M. (1966). Ibsen on the contrary. In A. Caputi (Ed.), *Modern drama* (pp. 344–353). New York: Norton.

American Psychiatric Association. (1994). *Diagnostic and statistical manual of mental disorders* (4th ed.). Washington, DC: Author.

Anderson, S. (1986). I want to know why. In R. V. Cassill (Ed.), *The Norton anthology of short fiction* (pp. 1–8). New York: Norton. (Original work published 1921).

Anthony, E. J. (1976). Between yes and no: The potentially neutral area where the adolescent and his therapist can meet. *Adolescent Psychiatry, 4,* 323–344.

Aristotle (1991). *The art of the rhetoric.* London: Penguin. (Original work published 336–322 BC).

Asch, S. E. (1955). Opinions and social pressure. *Scientific American, 193,* 31–35.

Auerbach, E. (1968). *Mimesis. The representation of reality in Western literature* (W. R. Trask, Trans.). Princeton, NJ: Princeton University Press. (Original work published 1946).

Balint, E., & Norell, J. S. (1973). *Six minutes for the patient.* London: Tavistock Press.

Balint, M. (1952). New beginning and paranoid and depressive syndromes. *International Journal of Psychoanalysis, 33,* 214.

Balint, M. (1968). *The basic fault, therapeutic aspects of regression.* London: Tavistock.

Balzac, H. (1946). *Pere Goriot.* New York: Modern Library. (Original work published 1835).

Bateson, G. (1971). The cybernetics of "self": A theory of alcoholism. *Psychiatry, 34,* 1–17.

Bateson, G. (1972). *Steps toward an ecology of mind.* New York: Ballantine.

Belkin, L. (2004). Office messes. *New York Times Magazine,* July 18, 24–55.

Bergson, H. (1980). Laughter. In W. Sypher (Ed.), *Comedy* (pp. 59–190). Baltimore: Johns Hopkins University Press. (Original work published 1900)

Berlinski, D. (1995). *A tour of the calculus.* New York: Vintage Books.

Bhagavad Gita (1994). (W. J. Johnson, Trans.) Oxford: Oxford University Press.

Bibring, E. (1953). The mechanism of depression. In P. Greenacre (Ed.), *Affective disorders, Psychoanalytic contributions to their study* (pp. 13–48). New York: International Universities Press.

Binder, J. L. (2004). *Key competencies in brief dynamic psychotherapy.* New York: Guilford.

Binswanger, L. (1967). Extravagance. In J. Needleman (Ed.), *Being-in-the-world, Selected papers of Ludwig Binswanger.* New York: Harper & Row. (Original work published 1963)

Bion, W. R. (1959). *Experiences in groups.* New York: Basic.

Bion, W. R. (1967). Differentiation of the psychotic from the non-psychotic personalities. In W. R. Bion, *Second thoughts* (pp. 43–64). London: Heinemann.

Bion, W. R. (1970). The container and the contained. In *Attention and Interpretation* (pp. 72–82). London: Tavistock.

Birkerts, S. (1999). Against the current. In S. Birkerts (Ed.), *Readings* (pp. 111–121). St. Paul, MN: Graywolf Press.

Borges, J. L. (1979). The Congress. *The Book of Sand* (pp. 15–34). Harmondsworth, UK: Penguin.

Brenman, M. (1952). On teasing and being teased: And the problem of moral masochism. *The Psychoanalytic Study of the Child, 7,* 264–285.

Breuer, J., & Freud, S. (1975). Studies on hysteria. In *The standard edition of the complete psychological works of Sigmund Freud* (Vol. 2). London: Hogarth. (Original work published 1893–1895).

Brooks, D. (2004). *On paradise drive.* New York: Simon & Schuster.

Burckhardt, T. (1996). *Chartres and the birth of the cathedral.* (W. Stoddard, Trans.). Bloomington, IN: World Wisdom. (Original work published 1962).

Calvino, I. (1972). *Invisible cities* (W. Weaver, Trans.). New York: Harcourt, Brace Jovanovich.

Campbell, J. (1949). *The hero with a thousand faces.* Princeton, NJ: Princeton University Press.

Canetti, E. (1984). *Crowds and power* (C. Stewart, Trans.). New York: Farrar, Straus & Giroux. (Original work published 1960).

Carroll, L. (1985). *Alice in wonderland.* New York: Henry Holt. (Original work published 1865).

Charbonnier, G. (1969). *Conversations with Claude Lévi-Strauss* (J. & N. Weightman, Trans.). London: Jonathan Cape. (original work published 1959).

Colinvaux, P. (1983). Human history: A consequence of plastic niche but fixed breeding strategy. In J. B. Calhoun (Ed.), *Environment and population* (pp. 1–4). New York: Praeger.

Connell, E. (1986). The corset. In R. V. Cassill (Ed.), *The Norton anthology of short fiction* (pp. 235–239). New York: W. W. Norton. (Original work published 1965).

Conrad, J. (1992). The heart of darkness. In *The complete short fiction of Joseph Conrad* (Vol. 3, pp. 1–86). Hopewell, NJ: Ecco. (Original work published 1902).

Conrad, J. (1966). Youth. In *Great short works of Joseph Conrad* (pp. 179–207). New York: Harper & Row. (Original work published 1898).

Coomaraswamy, A. K. (Ed. R. P, Coomaraswamy). (1997). *The door in the sky.* Princeton, NJ: Princeton University Press.

Coren, A. (2001). *Short-term psychotherapy, a psychodynamic approach.* Basingstoke, UK: Palgrave.

Dante Alighieri (1994). *The Inferno of Dante* (R. Pinsky, Trans.). New York: Farrar, Straus & Giroux. (Original work published 1300).

Dicks, H. V. (1967). *Marital tensions.* London: Routledge & Kegan Paul.

Donovan, J. M. (2003). *Short-term object relations couples therapy.* New York & Hove, UK: Brunner-Routledge.

Edelman, G. M. (1985). Neural Darwinism: Population thinking and higher brain function. In M. Shafto (Ed.), *How we know* (pp. 1–30). San Francisco, Harper & Row.

Eliade, M. (1954). *The myth of the eternal return* (W. Trask, Trans.). Princeton, NJ: Princeton University Press. (Original work published 1949).

Engel, G. L. (1980). The clinical application of the biopsychosocial model. *American Journal of Psychiatry, 137,* 535–544.

Erikson, E. H. (1950). *Childhood and society.* New York: Norton.

Erikson, E. H. (1958). *Young man Luther.* New York: Norton.

Freccero, J. (1994). Preface to *The Inferno of Dante* (R. Pinsky, Trans) (pp. xi–xix). New York: Farrar, Strauss & Giroux.

Freire, P. (1970). *The pedagogy of the oppressed.* New York: Herder & Herder.

Freud, A. (1966). *The ego and the mechanisms of defense.* New York: International Universities Press. (Original work published 1936).

Freud, S. (1975a). The interpretation of dreams. In *The standard edition of the complete psychological works of Sigmund Freud* (Vol. 4). London: Hogarth. (Original work published 1900).

Freud, S. (1975b). Notes upon a case of obsessional neurosis. In *The standard edition of the complete psychological works of Sigmund Freud* (Vol., pp. 151–244). London: Hogarth. (Original work published 1909).

Freud, S. (1975c). Contributions to the psychology of love, I & II. In *The standard edition of the complete psychological works of Sigmund Freud* (Vol. 11, pp. 163–190). London: Hogarth. (Original works published 1910 and 1912).

Freud, S. (1975d). Totem and taboo. In *The standard edition of the complete psychological works of Sigmund Freud* (Vol. 13, pp. 1–161). London: Hogarth. (Original work published 1913).

Freud, S. (1975e).Remembering, repeating and working-through. In *The standard edition of the complete psychological works of Sigmund Freud* (Vol. 12, pp. 145–156). London: Hogarth Press. (Original work published 1914).

Freud, S. (1975f). Repression. In *The standard edition of the complete psychological works of Sigmund Freud* (Vol. 14, pp. 141–158). London: Hogarth. (Original work published 1915)

Freud, S. (1975g). Mourning and melancholia. In *The standard edition of the complete psychological works of Sigmund Freud* (Vol. 14, pp. 237–258). London: Hogarth. (Original work published 1917).

Freud, S. (1975h). From the history of an infantile neurosis. In *The standard edition of the complete psychological works of Sigmund Freud* (Vol. 17, pp. 1–122). London: Hogarth. (Original work published 1918).

Freud, S. (1975i). Beyond the pleasure principle. In *The standard edition of the complete psychological works of Sigmund Freud* (Vol.18, pp. 1–64). London: Hogarth. (Original work published 1920).

Freud, S. (1975j). Group psychology and the analysis of the ego. In *The standard edition of the complete psychological works of Sigmund Freud* (Vol. 18, pp. 65–143). London: Hogarth. (Original work published 1921).

Frost, R. (1969). The road not taken. In *The poetry of Robert Frost.* (pp. 1 and 5) New York: Henry Holt. (Original work published 1916).

Fussell, P. (1983). *Class.* New York: Ballantine.

Gabbard, G. O. (1994). *Psychodynamic psychiatry in clinical practice.* Washington, DC: American Psychiatric Press.

Genova, P. (2004). The sheet bend: A homily for new psychiatrists. *Psychiatric Times,* August, pp. 80–81.

Gilligan, C. (1990). Joining the resistance: Psychology, politics, girls and women. *Michigan Quarterly Review, 29*(4), 501–536.

Gleick, J. (1988). *Chaos.* London: Heinemann.

Goldfried, M. R. (2003). Integrating integratively oriented brief psychotherapy. *Journal of Psychotherapy Integration, 14,* 93–105.

Greenberger, D., & Padesky, C. A. (1995). *Mind over mood.* New York: Guilford.

Gustafson, J. P. (1967). *Hallucinoia.*Unpublished doctoral dissertation. Harvard Medical School.

Gustafson, J. P. (unpublished). The ecology of OCD.

Gustafson, J. P. (1987). Finding and going forward: The two great challenges of long-term psychotherapy. Myerson Lecture, Tufts University, School of Medicine, April 10, 1987.

Gustafson, J. P. (1992). *Self-delight in a harsh world.* New York: Norton.

Gustafson, J. P. (1995a). *Brief versus long psychotherapy.* Northvale, NJ: Jason Aronson.

Gustafson, J. P. (1995b). *The dilemmas of brief psychotherapy.* New York: Plenum.

Gustafson, J. P. (1997a). *The complex secret of brief psychotherapy.* Northvale, NJ: Jason Aronson. (Original work published 1986).

Gustafson, J. P. (1997b). *The new interpretation of dreams.* Madison, WI: Author.

Gustafson, J. P. (1999). *The common dynamics of psychiatry.* Madison, WI: Author.

Gustafson, J. P. (2000). *The practical use of dreams and the human comedy.* Madison, WI: Author.

Gustafson, J. P. (2003). [Review of the book *Short-term psychotherapy, a psychodynamic approach* by A. Coren]. *Psychodynamic Practice, 9,* 583–587.

Gustafson, J. P., & Cooper, L. W. (1990). *The modern contest. A systemic guide to the pattern that connects individual psychotherapy, family therapy, group work, teaching, organizational life and large-scale social problems.* New York: Norton.

Gustafson, J., & Meyer, M. (2004). A non-linear model of dynamics: A case of panic. *Psychodynamic Practice, 10*(4), 479–489.

Hardy, T. (2003). On the western circuit. (K. Wilson, K. Brady, Eds.), *The fiddler on the roof and other stories.* (Original work published 1891) (pp. 166–190). London: Penguin.

Havens, L. (1965). The anatomy of a suicide. *New England Journal of Medicine, 276,* 401–406.

Havens, L. (1967). Recognition of suicidal risks through the psychological examination. *New England Journal of Medicine, 276,* 210–215.

Havens, L. (1993). *Participant observation.* Northvale, New Jersey: Aronson (Original work published in 1976).

Havens, L. (2000). Treating psychoses. In A. N. Sabo & L. Havens (Eds.), *The real world guide to psychotherapy practice.* Chapter 6 (pp. 149–162). Cambridge, MA: Harvard University Press.

Henry, J. (1973). Sham. In J. Henry (Ed.), *Sham, vulnerability and other forms of self-destruction* (pp. 120–127). New York: Random House.

Hibbard, P. (1994). Pioneers in obstetrics and gynecology. *The Diplomate, 1,* 309–311.

Homer (1990). *The iliad* (R. Fagles, Trans.). New York: Penguin.

Homer (1996). *The odyssey* (R. Fagles, Trans.). New York: Penguin.

Hoyt, M. F., Rosenbaum, R., & Talmon, M. (1992). Planned single-session psychotherapy. In S. H. Budman, M. F. Hoyt, & S. Friedman (Eds.), *The First Session in Brief Therapy* (pp. 59–86). New York: Guilford.

Hoyt, M. F. (1995). Single-session solutions. In M. F. Hoyt, *Brief Therapy and Managed Care: Readings for Contemporary Practice* (pp. 141–162). San Francisco: Jossey-Bass.

Hoyt, M. F. (2000). *Some stories are better than others: Doing what works in brief therapy and managed care.* Philadelphia: Brunner/Mazel.

Hughes, T. (1968). *The iron man.* London: Faber & Faber.

Hughes, T. (1988). The thought fox. In R. Ellmann & R. O'Clair (Eds.), *The Norton anthology of modern poetry* (p. 1396). New York: Norton. (Original work published 1957).

Ibsen, H. (1961). *A doll's house.* In H. Ibsen, *Seven famous plays* (pp. 13–95). (W. Archer, Ed.). London: Duckworth. (Original work published 1879).

Jacobson, E. (1953). Contribution to the metapsychology of cyclothymic depression. In P. Greenacre (Ed.), *Affective disorders, psychoanalytic contributions to their study* (pp. 49–83). New York: International Universities Press.

James, H. (2003). The beast in the jungle. In (C. Wegelin & H. B. Wonham, Eds.), *Tales of Henry James, 2nd edition* (pp. 303–340). New York: Norton. (Original work published 1903).

James, W. (1958). *The varieties of religious experience.* New York: Mentor. (Original work published 1904).

Jones, E. (1951). The God complex: The belief that one is God, and the resulting character traits. In E. Jones (Ed.), *Essays in applied psychoanalysis* (pp. 244–265). New York: International Universities Press. (Original work published 1923).

Jung, C. G. (1953). The relations between the ego and the unconscious. In C. G. Jung (Ed.), *Two essays on analytical psychology* (2nd ed.). Princeton, NJ: Princeton University Press. (Original work published 1916).

Jung, C. G. (1971). The difference between Eastern and Western thinking. In J. Campbell (Ed.), *The portable Jung.* New York: Penguin. (Original work published 1939).

Jung, C. G. (1974a). Individual symbolism in relation to alchemy. In C. G. Jung (Ed.), *Dreams.* Princeton, NJ: Princeton University Press. (Original work published 1944).

Jung, C. G. (1974b). *Dreams.* Princeton, NJ: Princeton University Press.

Jung, C. G. (1989). *Memories, dreams and reflections.* New York: Vantage Press. (Original work published in 1961).

Kafka, F. (1971). The judgment. In N. N. Glatzer (Ed.), *Franz Kafka. The complete stories* (pp. 77–88). New York: Schocken Books. (Original work published 1913).

Kaku, M. (1994). *Hyperspace.* New York: Oxford University Press.

Kernberg, O. F., Selzer, M. A., Koenigsberg, H. W., Carr, A. C., & Appelbaum, A. H. (1988). *Psychodynamic psychotherapy of borderline patients.* New York: Basic Books.

Koranyi, E. K. (1979). Morbidity and rate of undiagnosed physical illnesses in a psychiatric clinic population. *Archives of General Psychiatry, 36,* 414–419.

Lebowitz, N. (1990). *Ibsen and the great world.* Baton Rouge, LA: State University Press.

Legge, J. (1962). *The texts of Taoism.* New York: Dover. (Original work published 1891).

Levenson, H. (2003). Time-limited dynamic psychotherapy: An integrationist perspective. *Journal of Psychotherapy Integration, 13,* 300–333.

Lévi-Strauss, C. (1983). *The raw and the cooked. Mythologiques* (Vol. 1). (J. & N. Weightman, Trans.). Chicago: University of Chicago Press. (Original work published 1964).

Linehan, M. (1993). *Cognitive behavioral treatment of borderline personality disorder.* New York: Guilford.

Malan, D. H. (1976). *The frontier of brief psychotherapy.* New York: Plenum.

Malan, D. H. (1979). *Individual psychotherapy and the science of psychodynamics.* London: Butterworths.

Malan, D. H., Heath, E. S., Bacal, H. A., & Balfour, F. H. G. (1975). Psychodynamic changes in untreated neurotic patients. II. Apparently genuine improvements. *Archives of General Psychiatry, 32,* 110–126.

Mann, J. (1973). *Time-limited psychotherapy.* Cambridge, MA: Harvard University Press.

Marcuse, H. (1964). *One-dimensional man.* Boston: Beacon Press.

Marks, I. (1987). *Fears, phobias, and rituals, the nature of anxiety and panic disorders.* New York: Oxford University Press.

Marx, K. (1975). Economic and philosophic manuscripts. In, *Early writings* (pp. 279–400). New York: Vintage. (Original work published 1844).

Marx, L. (2000). *The machine in the garden.* New York: Oxford University Press. (Original work published 1964).

McCullogh, L., & Winston, A. (1991). The Beth Israel psychotherapy research program. In L. Beutler & M. Crago (Eds.), *Psychotherapy research: An international review of programmatic studies* (pp. 15–23). Washington, DC: American Psychological Association.

McNeill, W. H. (1963). *The rise of the west.* Chicago: University of Chicago Press.

Melville, H. (1956). *Moby-Dick, or the whale.* Boston: Houghton-Mifflin. (Original work published 1851).

Melville, H. (1986). *Bartleby the scrivener.* In R. V. Cassill (Ed.), *The Norton anthology of short fiction* (3rd ed.) (pp. 1031–1062). New York: Norton. (Original work published 1853).

Merton, T. (1965). *The way of Chuang Tzu.* New York: New Directions.

Mesulam, M. M. (2000). *Principles of behavioral and cognitive neurology* (2nd ed.). New York: Oxford University Press.

Milgram, S. (1973). Behavioral study of obedience. In W. G. Bennis (Ed.), *Interpersonal dynamics* (pp. 60–72). Homewood, IL: Dorsey Press. (Original work published in 1963).

Miller, A. (1949). *Death of a salesman.* New York: Penguin.

Mumford, L. (1926). *The golden day.* New York: Boni & Liveright.

Mumford, L. (1963). *Technics and civilization.* New York: Harcourt, Brace & World. (Original work published 1934).

Mumford, L. (1995). The first megamachine. In *The Lewis Mumford reader.* Athens, GA: University of Georgia Press. (Original work published 1966).

Orwell, G. (1946). *Animal farm.* New York: Harcourt, Brace & World.

Pallis, M. (1960). *The way and the mountain.* London: Peter Owen.

Percy, W. (1975). *The message in the bottle.* New York: Farrar, Straus, & Giroux.

Pies, R. (2004). Do we have Hegel on the brain? *Psychiatric Times,* August, pp. 75, 78.

Pies, R., & Gustafson, J. P. (2004). Exchange of letters. *Psychiatric Times,* August 2004, p. 14.

Poirier, R. (1985). *A world elsewhere.* Madison: University of Wisconsin Press. (Original work published 1966).

Popper, K. R. (1965). *The logic of scientific discovery.* New York: Harper & Row. (Original work published 1934).

Postman, N. (1985). *Amusing ourselves to death.* London: Methuen.

Prochaska, J. O., DiClemente, C. C., & Norcross, J. C. (1992). In search of how people change: Application to addictive behaviors. *American Psychologist, 47,* 1102–1114.

Prochaska, J. O., & Norcross, J. (2001). Stages of change. *Psychotherapy, 38,* 443–448.

Reich, W. (1931). Character formation and the phobias of childhood. *International Journal of Psychoanalysis, 12,* 219.

Reich, W. (1949). *Character analysis.* New York: Farrar, Straus, & Giroux. (Original work published 1933).

Rose, P. (1984). *Parallel lives. Five Victorian marriages.* New York: Vintage.

Rushdie, S. (1994). The courter. In *East, West stories* (pp. 173–211). New York: Pantheon.

Saint-Exupéry, A. (1943). *The little prince* (K. Woods, Trans.). New York: Harcourt, Brace, & World.

Sartre, J. (1989). *No exit.* New York: Random House. (Original work published 1943).

Sashin, J. I., & Callahan, J. (1990). A model of affect using dynamical systems. *Annual of Psychoanalysis, 18,* 213–231.

Schumacher, E. F. (1977). *A guide for the perplexed.* New York: Harper & Row.

Selvini-Palazzoli, M. (1980). Why a long interval between sessions? The therapeutic control of the family-therapist suprasystem. In (M. Andolfi and I. Zwerling, eds.) *Dimensions of family therapy* (pp. 161–169). New York: Guilford.

Selvini-Palazzoli, M., Cirillo, S., Selvini, M., & Sorrentino, A. M. (1989). *Family games, general models of psychotic process in the family.* New York: Norton.

Shakespeare, W. (1969a). *The Merchant of Venice.* In A. Harbage (Ed.), *William Shakespeare: The complete works.* Baltimore: Penguin books. (Original work published 1600).

Shakespeare, W. (1969b). *Hamlet.* In A. Harbage (Ed.), *William Shakespeare: The complete works.* Baltimore: Penguin Books. (Original work published 1604).

Shakespeare, W. (1969c). *The tempest.* In *William Shakespeare: The complete works.* Baltimore: Penguin. (Original work published 1612).

Stevens, W. (1997). The noble rider and the sound of words. In *Wallace Stevens, Collected poetry and prose.* New York: The Library of America. (Original published 1942).

Stevenson, R. L. (1892). The lantern-bearers. In *Across the plains* (pp. 206–228). London: Chatto & Windus.

Stevenson, R. L. (1985). *The strange case of Dr. Jekyll and Mr. Hyde.* New York: Puffin Books. (Original work published 1886).

Sullivan, H. S. (1954). *The psychiatric interview.* New York: Norton.

Sullivan, H. S. (1956). *Clinical studies in psychiatry.* New York: Norton.

Suzuki, D. T. (1970). *Zen and Japanese culture.* Princeton, NJ: Princeton University Press. (Original work published 1939).

Swenson, R. A. (2003). *A minute of margin: Restoring balance to overloaded lives.* Colorado Springs, CO: NavPress.

Swenson, R. A. (Unpublished). Overcoming overload: balance or burnout. Lecture handout, Nov. 7, 2003. University of Wisconsin.

Talmon, M. (1990). *Single session therapy: Maximizing the effects of the first (and often only) therapeutic encounter.* San Francisco: Jossey-Bass.

Tao Te Ching (1988). (S. Mitchell, Trans.) New York: Harper and Row.

Tate, A. (1999). Three types of poetry. In *Essays of four decades* (pp. 173–195). Wilmington, DE: ISI Books. (Original work published 1934).

Terkel, S. (1972). *Working.* New York: Avon.

Thoreau, H. D. (1947). Walden. In *The portable Thoreau* (pp. 258–572). New York: Viking. (Original work published 1854).

Thoreau, H. D. (2000). *Wild fruits.* New York: Norton.

Thurber, J. (1986). The secret life of Walter Mitty. In R. V. Cassill (Ed.), *The Norton Anthology of Short Fiction* (pp. 1404–1408). New York: Norton. (Original work published 1942).

Tolstoy, L. (1966). *War and peace.* New York: Norton. (Original work published 1869).

Tolstoy, L. (1970). *Anna Karenina.* New York: Norton. (Original work published 1875).

Tolstoy, L. (1986). The death of Ivan Illych. In R. V. Cassill (Ed.), *The Norton anthology of short fiction* (pp. 1409–1455). New York: Norton. (Original work published 1886).

Turquet, P. M. (1975). Threats to identity in the large group. In L. Kreeger (Ed.), *The large group, dynamics and therapy* (pp. 87–144). London: Constable.

Twain, M. (1962). *Huckleberry Finn.* New York: Collier. (Original work published 1885).

Twain, M. (1980). *Roughing it.* New York: Penguin. (Original work published 1872).

Vaillant, L. M. (1994). The next step in short-term dynamic psychotherapy: A clarification of objectives and techniques in an anxiety-regulating model. *Psychotherapy, 31,* 642–654.

Voltaire (1949). *Candide.* In *The portable Voltaire* (pp. 229–238). New York: Viking (orig. pub. 1759).

Vonnegut, K. (1969). *Slaughterhouse-five.* New York: Random House.

Wachtel, P. L. (1993). *Therapeutic communication.* New York: Guilford.

Weber, M. (1958). *The Protestant ethic and the spirit of capitalism* (T. Parsons, Trans.). New York: Scribner. (Original work published 1904).

Weekley, E. (1967). *An etymological dictionary of modern English.* New York: Dover.

Weil, S. (1993). The poem of force. (R. Ringler, Trans.). In R. Ringler (Ed.), *Dilemmas of war and peace: A source book* (pp. 104–112). London: Routledge. (Original work published 1937).

Weiss, J., & Sampson, H. (1986). *The psychoanalytic process.* New York: Guilford.

Werner, E. E. (1989). Children of the garden island. *Scientific American,* 106–111.

Werner, E. E., & Smith, R. S. (1992). *Overcoming the odds: High-risk children from birth to adulthood.* Ithaca, NY: Cornell University Press.

Werner, E. E., & Smith, R. S. (1998). *Vulnerable but invincible: A longitudinal study of resilient children and youth.* New York: Adams, Bannister, & Cox.

White, M. (1989). Family therapy and schizophrenia: addressing the in-the-corner life style. In M. White (Ed.), *Selected papers.* Adelaide, Australia: Dulwich Centre.

White, M., & Epston, D. (1990). *Narrative means to therapeutic ends.* New York: Norton.

Winnicot, D. W. (1957). *The ordinary devoted mother and her baby. Nine broadcast talks.* (Original work published in 1949). *Reprinted in The child and the family.* London: Tavistock.

Winnicott, D. W. (1958). Hate in the counter-transference. In *Through pediatrics to psychoanalysis* (pp. 194–203). New York: Basic. (Original work published 1947).

Winnicott, D. W. (1965). The use of the term therapeutic consultation. Seminar outline. Unpublished manuscript.

Winnicott, D. W. (1971). *Therapeutic consultations in child psychiatry.* (pp. 73–103). New York: Basic.

Index